Scotti

STO

TR

Scottish
STORY
TRAILS

A LITERARY
LANDSCAPE

William Steven

NWP

First published in October 2017 by

Neil Wilson Publishing Ltd
www.nwp.co.uk

The author asserts his moral right under the Design, Patents and Copyright
Act 1988, as amended, to be identified as the author of the work.

Cover design and illustrations © James Hutcheson, 2017

ISBN: 978-1-906000-84-4
Ebook ISBN: 978-1-906000-85-1

Printed and bound in the EU.

CONTENTS

ACKNOWLEDGEMENTS

THE AUTHOR GRATEFULLY acknowledges permissions granted to reproduce extracts from the following published material.

The Crow Road by Iain Banks © Little, Brown Book Group and Mic Cheetham Agency and reproduced by kind permission of The Estate of Iain Banks. *Lanark* by Alasdair Gray © Canongate Books. *Highland River, Morning Tide* and *Off in a Boat* by Neil M Gunn © Dairmid Gunn on behalf of The Estate of Neil M. Gunn. *The Hanging Garden* by Ian Rankin © The Orion Publishing Group, Curtis Brown Group Ltd and by permission of St Martin's Press. All rights reserved. *The Prime of Miss Jean Brodie* by Muriel Spark © Penguin Books and *Curriculum Vitae* by Muriel Spark © Carcanet Press and with permission of the David Higham Agency. *Trainspotting* by Irvine Welsh © Random House Group. The picture of Rowena Farre on page 58 is courtesy of Little Toller Books.

Every reasonable effort has been made to trace any unacknowledged copyright holders of other material.

PREFACE

THIS UNIQUE GUIDE will assist readers who are curious about the lives and works of some of the great Scottish novelists and storytellers. It describes places associated with the authors themselves and with the settings of one of their major works. These cover the length and breadth of Scotland from the Borders to the northern Highlands and the Hebrides while also including some works which are set in England. *Scottish Storytrails* includes writers currently at the peak of their careers and world-renowned figures from the past, all of them native Scottish writers or writers with Scottish ancestry.

Scottish Storytrails provides enjoyment simply for the armchair enthusiast, while also creating opportunities for visits and excursions to the locations described. For each author there is a biography which includes descriptions of places associated with the writer's life. A Storytrail follows with a list of the main characters in the publication featured and an account of the narrative and its settings. Finally there is some practical information on the locations with listings of tourist information centres (TICs), museums and other places offering further information connected with the author.

William Steven, 2017

1

Iain Banks

IAIN MENZIES BANKS (1954-2013) was born in Dunfermline in Fife, his father an Admiralty officer in the nearby Rosyth Naval Dockyard and his mother a former professional ice skater. Banks was educated in North Queensferry and at Gourock where the family moved when he was age nine, his father working at Greenock where he became a First Officer. Banks attended Greenock High School and Stirling University, where he studied English Literature, Philosophy and Psychology.

Banks loved growing up in North Queensferry, where a centuries-old ferry used to cross to South Queensferry and Edinburgh, situated on a neck of land with water on three sides and linked to Inverkeithing. His bedroom window looked directly on to the famous railway bridge, which filled fully half the view.

As a child his playground included old gun placements, anti-aircraft gun batteries protecting the bridge, with tunnels and bunkers and former barracks at Port Lane. The Ferry Hills above included a small loch and island to explore. There were trees and rocks to climb and he was nearly killed when exploring a railway cutting that forms a quarter-mile-long canyon. At age seven or eight, while climbing the west side of the cutting with friends, Banks pulled at a loose boulder almost at the top and fell 50 feet but was caught by a whin bush.

He loved going down to the railway station and climbing the steps of the footbridge to wait for trains to pass underneath and being enveloped in the fog of smoke from them. He said, 'I think I fell in love with that feeling of wild abandonment, that noise, that smell. That sense of power and raw, released energy – those of you who've read my book *The Bridge* might recognise this description'. His boyhood obsession with dangerous climbs lasted into adulthood. In London, drunk, he climbed a section of the Grand Union Canal east of the Angel and in the summer of 1981 on the south side of Adelaide Road jumped off a ten-foot-high parapet with a railway on the other side. In later years he went from one wrought-iron balcony to another on the fourth floor of the Metropole Hotel in Brighton during a World Science Fiction Convention.

Banks moved back to his childhood home in 1991 on the edge of North Queensferry, a large terracotta house with three garages, next to a whitewashed cottage which he bought for his parents. Out of the kitchen window, beyond the bird table, the Forth Bridge loomed. He claimed to spend nine months of the year enjoying himself and three months writing.

He had an enthusiasm for motor cars, but in 2007 sold his Porsches, becoming more environmentally aware and thereafter drove a hybrid Lexus and a motorcycle, later a Mini Cooper and a Toyota Yaris.

There were also striking views from his next childhood home, from around age 10, in Gourock, high above Cardwell Bay, looking towards the mountains of Ben Lomond, the Cobbler and the Highlands while below, at that time, the abundant river traffic in the Clyde estuary was coming to the end of a golden age. Banks worked on the fine Gourock Pier around half-a-mile away, from which ferries and steamers left for the islands and peninsulas including the beautiful Kyles of Bute, which Banks considered one of the great sights. For two summers, when at university in the early 1970s, Banks moored ropes and hoisted gangways. Love of the islands led to him spending a week or so most years with his wife on Barra in the Outer Hebrides taking a ferry from Oban where he liked to stay at the Caledonian Hotel with its magnificent view of the harbour.

Gourock High School was a junior high school designed for younger teenagers, followed by attendance at Greenock High School from age 15 where Banks wrote stories for the school magazine. He said that at this time half his reading was of science fiction and his first attempt at extended fiction was at age 16, in pencil and longhand on his father's Admiralty logbooks. While at Stirling University from 1972-5, Banks walked all over the surrounding area, towards Alloa and Stirling, from the Gartmore Dam to the east and Doune Castle to the west. He appeared as an extra in the 1975 film of *Monty Python and the Holy Grail* at nearby Sheriffmuir.

After graduating in the late 1970s, Banks was employed by British Steel as a non-destructive testing technician (trainee) on the Dornoch Firth, north of Inverness. He stayed at Portmahomack on the Black Isle and worked at a North Sea production platform at Nigg a few miles away, his job being to check steel girders. He admits this was simply a source of income while he wrote. Here he would walk along the coast which provided atmosphere for the landscape of *The Wasp Factory*.

Banks then worked for a time for the American company IBM at Greenock before going to London in December 1979 where he worked as a clerk and a costs' draughtsman in a law office for four years. He stayed for a few months in a friend's flat in Belsize Road, then took a flat in Islington Park Street. His first date with Ann, his future wife, was in April 1980 when they drank Theakston's Old Peculier beer at the Sun in Lamb's Conduit Street.

A publisher who imagined him as a cross between Rob Roy and Rasputin before meeting him showed interest in Banks's first manuscript, resulting in the publication of *The Wasp Factory* in 1984. After marriage and two to three years in London, residing on Graham Road, he and his wife moved to Faversham in Kent in 1983, near her parents in Canterbury and Banks began to write full-time.

Banks admitted to years of experimenting with drugs and alcohol to stimulate writing, coming to the conclusion that they do not stimulate creativity but produce dross. However, he did drink 80 bottles of malt whisky as part of his research for *Raw Spirit* (2003), subtitled *The Search for the Perfect Dram*, describing a pleasant romp visiting distilleries in Islay and Campbeltown, Skye, the Orkneys, the northern and central Highlands, the Lowlands and dense-with-distilleries Speyside. His local pub in North Queensferry was the Albert Hotel, known as 'the Ferry', with its fine view of the Forth Bridge. A regular drunken exploit involved a tradition of drinking Blue Moon cocktails in the Café Royal bar in Edinburgh's West Register Street. He used to visit Cadenhead's whisky shop on the Royal Mile from his flat in South Bridge after he returned to Scotland in 1988. He ran for the rectorship of Edinburgh University on a 'Drunken Bastard' ticket, coming fifth behind a stuffed toy and in 2007 won a contest for writers on the BBC's intellectual quiz show Mastermind.

Works written as Iain Banks include *Walking on Glass* (1985), *The Bridge* (1986), which he considered his best book, *Espedair Street* (1987), *Canal Dreams* (1989), *The Crow Road* (1991), *Complicity* (1993), *Whit* (1995), *A Song of Stone* (1997), *The Business* (1999), *Dead Air* (2002), *The Steep Approach to Garbadale* (2007), *Transition* (2009), *Stonemouth* (2012) and *The Quarry* (2013).

His science fiction, written under the name Iain M. Banks (the least original nom de plume ever, he said), is mostly set in a universe inhabited by a multi-species civilisation called the Culture, a federation of human and post-human planets beset by assorted threats to humanity. He originally saw himself as a science fiction writer, attempting at least three such novels before *The Wasp Factory*. In 2009 he and Anne divorced but not before they had cut up their passports in protest at the military invasion of Iraq and posted the pieces to Downing Street. He regularly spoke at science fiction conventions and it was at one of these that he met his last partner, Adele Hartley, founding director of the Edinburgh Dead by Dawn horror film festival, who became his wife on 29 March 2013. Banks had asked her to 'do me the honour of becoming my widow', having been diagnosed with terminal cancer some months before. He died on 9 June, just three weeks after finishing his final novel, *The Quarry*.

STORYTRAIL: *The Crow Road*

THE MAIN CHARACTERS
Prentice McHoan, an undergraduate student.
Kenneth McHoan, Prentice's father, schoolmaster and children's
  writer.
Uncle Rory, a travel writer, who is reported missing.
Uncle Hamish, manager of a glass works.
Fergus Urvill of Urvill, a wealthy castle owner.
Fiona Urvill, wife of Fergus and aunt to Prentice.
Lewis McHoan, brother to Prentice and stand-up comic.
Verity, niece to Fergus and Fiona, friend of Prentice, later
  marrying Lewis.
Ashley Watt, girlfriend of Prentice.
Janice Rae, former girlfriend of uncle Rory.

The novel is largely set in Argyllshire and Glasgow as Prentice
McHoan, an indifferent student at Glasgow University, struggles
to find his identity against a background of family stresses and
secrets across the generations. The main narrative is told in the
first person along with secondary narratives in the third person
by an imaginary observer or other principal characters.

Uncle Rory, a travel writer, is missing: he may be 'away the
crow road' (slang for dead) but a manuscript also exists for a
work of his titled *The Crow Road*. The real Crow Road begins at
a junction with the A814 Dumbarton Road in Partick, west of
Glasgow city centre. Heading north to Anniesland Cross it crosses Great Western Road and ends at the Forth and Clyde canal.
Great Western Road becomes the A82 and leads west to Loch
Lomond-side and then by the A83 at Tarbet over the Rest-and-
Be-Thankful into Argyllshire. The great sea loch of Loch Fyne
borders the long tapering Kintyre peninsula, with its Mull at the
south end and in the middle the Kilmartin area, rich in prehistoric cairns, standing stones and stone circles, including Dunadd,
the ancient hill fortress of the first Scottish kings, capital of the
Celtic kingdom of Dalriada from AD 498 to 843. Dunadd is
'where the footprint is', where a new king had solemnly to place
his foot and Lewis and his fiancée Verity, look at the spot through

binoculars. (The Horseshoe Inn at Bridgend in Kilmichael Glassary displays pictures of local sites.)

Banks combines real and invented locations in the novel, the landscape of hills and lochs but adds unfamiliar features. The principal setting is the area of Argyll between the Sound of Jura (uncle Rory has a puzzle for the children: what is the sound you cannot hear?) and Loch Fyne with the imaginary town of Gallanach supposedly on Inner Loch Crinan. The town is placed in sparsely populated Knapdale but resembles the county town of Oban further north, a deep-water port with easy access to the Atlantic Ocean, with, in the novel, the neighbouring island of Jura. (There is a real Gallanach Castle about three-and-a-half miles south-west of Oban).

Gallanach, where the Watt family reside, has a glassworks factory owned by Fergus Urvill of Urvill, who is uncle through marriage to Prentice's aunt Fiona. There are also pubs, hotels, a council estate, derelict docks and the great Ballast Mound. Prentice walks along Gallanach esplanade, with its Victorian pier, Steam Packet Hotel and villas. There is a ceilidh wedding in the hotel. He stands at the former Slate Mine wharf to the north-west of Gallanach, where the Kilmartin Burn flows into Gallanach Bay and the deeper waters of Inner Loch Crinan. He walks along to the railway pier and harbour on Hogmanay and sits on the quayside drinking whisky and hearing jigs being played at the hotel. There are yachts moored and a ferry to Mull, just as there are at Oban. Tourists crowd the pier. Verity and Lewis go to the real Columba Hotel in Oban for the start of their honeymoon.

Prentice's atheistic father, Kenneth, after drinking in the Steam Packet and engaging in a heated discussion about religion, climbs the church wall and tower; there is a lightning flash, the lightning conductor collapses on to him and he falls on to the stones below.

Gaineamh Castle sits on the northern flanks of Cnoc na Moine, south of the real ancient Celtic fort of Dunadd, which rises sharply out of the flat land off the A816 north of the Crinan Canal. Restored by Fergus Urvill, it has become a family home, and even has a rooftop observatory. The castle is a little north-west of Dunamuck farm, about a mile from the junction of the A816 and the B841 to Crinan, with views towards Gallanach, 'which spreads round the deep waters of Inner Loch Crinan'.

In a flashback, at the end of the Second World War, Kenneth, his sister and others are playing hide and seek, exploring the ruined castle at Gallanach, set on a rock above a stream flowing into the River Add and down to Gallanach. The action then flashes forward to Fergus showing off wine racks in his castle cellar. Later Prentice is on the castle battlements with Lewis and Verity and here the novel ends when a bottle of malt whisky will be consumed.

Lochgair, where the McHoan family live, is a real place on the A83 on the shores of Loch Fyne in an inlet some seven miles before Lochgilphead. Achnaba is a hamlet halfway to Lochgilphead. Kenneth, Rory and his girlfriend Janice have lunch in the Achnaba Hotel near which Fergus crashes his Aston Martin into trees after a dinner party with friends, killing Fiona.

> She was thrown against one side of the seat as Fergus powered the Aston round the right-hander that took the road out of the forest, down, into and through the little village of Furnace.

The railway running down Loch Fyne through Lochgair and on to Gallanach is imaginary. The train north from Lochgair we are told goes:

> ... north along the lower loch, crossed the narrows at Minard, and stopped at Garbhallt, Strachur, Lochgoilhead and Portincaple Junction, where it joined the West Highland line and took the north shore of the Clyde towards Glasgow.

Glasgow to Lochgair 'is a hundred and thirty-five kilometres by road; less as the crow flies, or as the missile cruises,' an allusion to the American naval presence in nearby Holy Loch.

Verity, who was conceived under the famous ancient yew at Fortingall in Perthshire, was born in a howling gale beside Loch

Awe. The Glasgow to Kintyre route is traversed a number of times in the story. 'Kamikazi deer' are observed on Glen Croe, between the Rest-and-be-Thankful and Ardgartan at the head of Loch Long. Darren Watt is killed on his motorbike driving to Glasgow 'overtaking a truck on the long straight at the start of Glen Kinglas; a car pulled out onto it from the Cowal Road'. Prentice in a car behind Lewis and Verity 'on the fast dual carriageway between Dumbarton and Alexandria' opens his uncle's Crow Road folder en route back to Gallanach for Christmas and Hogmanay. Prentice rides in Verity's open-top car to Gallanach and then the Kyles of Bute viewpoint.

Kenneth McHoan makes up stories to entertain his children and their friends, often told in the open countryside above Lochgair sitting beside the old broch (a primitive circular dwelling) looking towards Loch Fyne, with yachts heading up towards the railway bridge at Minard point and Inveraray.

The black comedy which opens the story sets some of the tone: 'It was the day my grandmother exploded.' A heart pacemaker had not been removed from the corpse.

> I sat in the crematorium, listening to my uncle Hamish quietly snoring in harmony to Bach's Mass in B Minor, and I reflected that it always seemed to be death that drew me back to Gallanach.

His grandmother's hair 'was very white against the rich summer green of the Argyllshire hills'. The view from the crematorium was 'towards the town and the ocean. In the distance, through the haze, North Jura was dark pastel'. Prentice notices the train and the 'few lights of Lochgair village', the river Loran with its cataract and spray: 'the river surged round the piers of the viaduct that carried the railway on towards Lochgilphead and Gallanach' which is 'only eight miles away over the hills' and 'two stops on the train'. Loch Glashan in the hills above Lochgair is a reservoir for a small power station in the village. Prentice goes up the hill to meditate when he is sure of Fergus's guilt in the part he played in his aunt's death.

Rory's body, tied to his motorbike, is eventually recovered by divers in a loch near Gallanach. He had been working on the manuscript of *The Crow Road* before he borrowed his flatmate's motorbike and disappeared. Strathclyde Police had been advised that a drug ring was using Loch Coille Bhar, off the B8025 just south of Crinan, as a hiding place for cocaine. Their searches unwittingly uncover Rory's corpse.

Fergus Urvill commits suicide in his Cessna aircraft out over the Atlantic beyond the Butt of Lewis. He drives north from Gaineamh Castle through Oban to the Connel airstrip. He is spotted by British army radar on St Kilda in a restricted area and an RAF Nimrod tries to intercept him. Prentice drives up to the Butt of Lewis to throw a paperweight symbolically into the sea, driving by the A82 to Inverness and Ullapool then taking the ferry to arrive at the Royal Hotel in Stornoway. The next morning, at the nearest spot on land to the site of Fergus's death:

> I stood in a strong wind and light drizzle, wrapped in my
> dad's old coat, near the lighthouse at the Butt of Lewis ...

and throws the paperweight

> ... with all my might out to sea.

Fergus's memorial service takes place at the Church of Scotland in Shore Street in Gallanach.

★ ★ ★

The other main story setting is Glasgow where Prentice is an undergraduate student, living in a flat in Grant Street near St George's Cross. Later he rents a large townhouse flat in Park Terrace beside Kelvingrove Park with the museum, art gallery and university close by.

Back in Glasgow after the funeral Prentice and his flatmate Gavin are in a pub in Byres Road listening to Lewis doing a stand-up comedy act. Prentice is greeted by uncle Rory's former girlfriend Janice, his 'Aunty Janice', in Byres Road outside the imaginary Randan's. They turn into Ruthven Street, her car being parked in Athole Gardens and go to her flat in Crow Road near Jordanhill where he is given a folder with Rory's notes for his book. He leaves this on a train to Glasgow along with information about his uncle Rory that leads eventually to the solution of the mystery of his disappearance.

Prentice later walks from the Crow Road flat back to Park Terrace, although he says he is staying in Lauderdale Gardens in Hyndland. On a stationary train on a line parallel to Crow Road, waiting for signals to change outside Jordanhill station, Prentice looks up at the rear of the neighbouring flats fronting Crow Road, trying to work out which was Janice's. Later he also waits on a train by waste ground in Springburn heading into Glasgow Queen Street.

When he returns from Lewis to Glasgow Prentice goes with Ashley Watt from the house in Park Terrace via Woodlands Road to the Anarkali restaurant. A real Anarkali Asian restaurant is on Victoria Road south of the city centre. He vomits into a litter bin attached to a crowded bus shelter on St George's Road near Charing Cross. They walk back to the flat and, after making love, he watches her leave from the drawing-room window.

TOURIST INFORMATION AND VISITOR ATTRACTIONS

Edinburgh and Lothians Tourist Board
    3 Princes Street, Edinburgh EH2 2QP
    Tel: 0845 225 5121
VisitScotland Glasgow iCentre
    Gallery of Modern Art, Royal Exchange Square, Glasgow G1 3AH
Heart of Argyll Tourism Alliance
    Colchester Square, Lochgilphead PA31 8LH
    Tel: 07919 360485
VisitScotland Inveraray iCentre
    Front Street, Inveraray PA32 8UY
    Tel: 01499 302063
VisitScotland Oban iCentre
    Columba Buildings, 3 North Pier, Oban PA34 5QD
    Tel: 01631 563122

2

James M Barrie

JAMES MATTHEW BARRIE (1860-1937) was born in Kirriemuir, a small town at the foot of glens Clova and Prosen, on the A926 and A928, 12 miles north of Dundee. Barrie was the ninth child of David Barrie, a weaver and later a clerk in the mills and Margaret Ogilvy, a stonemason's daughter. The buildings in Kirriemuir are mainly of red sandstone with narrow closes, twisting wynds and steep braes and a statue of Peter Pan sits in the town square, a smaller version of the one in Hyde Park. There is even a Hook's Hotel.

James went to the Free Church school in the town, then for two or three years to Glasgow Academy, where his brother Alexander taught mathematics. Barrie returned for a short time to Forfar Academy, followed by a private school in a Lanarkshire manse. For the next five years he attended Dumfries Academy, where Alexander was then working, followed by Edinburgh University.

The famous Peter Pan story originates in Barrie's childhood and in the shared washhouse behind his birthplace at No 9 Brechin Road where the upper floors are furnished as they were in his childhood. No 11 provides an exhibition space and tea-room. The little National Trust for Scotland museum in the house where Barrie spent his first eight years contains some of his manuscripts, letters, pictures of stage productions, clothes and other memorabilia, including the original Peter Pan costume from the 1904 play and a wooden settle from his London house. A tiny solid box with padlock which contained his possessions for the move to London is on display as is his huge London desk. There is a rare first edition of the Peter Pan novel dedicated to the five sons of the Llewelyn Davies family whom Barrie declared were his muses. There is a display of the Peter Pan characters and you can enter the washhouse where Barrie held his first performances. He said this was his model for 'the little house the Lost Boys built in the Never Land for Wendy'. Here he played with a friend's toy theatre and acted impromptu dramas.

He loved stories of desert islands, notably RM Ballantyne's *The Coral Island*. There is a Pirates' Workshop (an education room) for children who are invited to look out for the crocodile in the garden where there is a Peter Pan statue, a willow topiary crocodile and children's play area.

In 1870 the family moved to Forfar when his father became clerk in a linen factory at a time when handlooms were being replaced by power looms. He returned to Kirriemuir two years later as chief clerk when the new Gairie Linen Works was built at the foot of Bellies Brae beside the Gairie Burn. The family home was a new pink-red sandstone, end-terraced villa called Strathview at No 1 Forfar Road, at the junction of the Forfar and Glamis roads, the A926 and A928, and situated opposite the white cottage which is the 'House on the Brae' in *A Window in Thrums*. As he rounded the top of Bellies Brae he might have seen his mother at the drawing room window watching local folk pass by. Here Barrie decided to be an author and wrote at least two novels in the garret.

At age five Barrie went to the Hanky School in nearby Bank Street then to South Free Church School at Southmuir on the hill beyond the burn and gasworks on the other side of town. The Auld Licht Kirk in Bank Street which his mother attended was demolished in 1893 and the Evangelical Free Church built on the site. After marriage his mother attended the Free Church in Southmuir, on the site of the present St Andrew's Church, on the left on Glamis Road. Caddam Wood in Kinnordy Estate, a mile out of town, was a childhood haunt where tinker-gypsies camped annually.

David, an elder brother idolised by their mother, died at age 13 in a skating accident after hitting his head on ice. It has been controversially suggested that the friend who was involved in the accident was Barrie himself. His mother retreated to a darkened bedroom in shock and grief for months and Barrie found himself trying to compete for his mother's love, later acknowledging the figure of a lost boy in his work.

Barrie's grave in Kirriemuir, on the west side of the graveyard near the manse, is on Cemetery Hill, signposted along Brechin Road, past the Bowling Club and on the left up Cemetery Road, 300 feet above the town. Following Barrie's instruction that there should be 'no embellishment of any kind' his name appears after those of his parents, sisters and brother on the plain granite gravestone.

Above the town on top of Kirriemuir Hill is the cricket field where Barrie and others played enthusiastically. It is sited by the Standing Stone with panoramic views towards the Angus glens, Strathmore and the Sidlaw hills. Housed in a turret room in the cricket pavilion is the camera obscura which he gifted to the town in 1929 when he was made its only Freeman. A play park on a Neverland theme was created on Kirriemuir Hill in 2010 to mark the 150th anniversary of Barrie's birth.

Barrie's brother Alexander (Alick), having gained First Class Honours in Classics at Aberdeen University, became a teacher at a school in Bothwell in Lanarkshire and then in 1867 became Classics master at Glasgow Academy. In 1868 Barrie moved to Glasgow and became a pupil at the school on the corner of Great Western Road beside the River Kelvin, living in Burnbank Terrace nearby.

In 1872 Alick became schools inspector in Dumfries and Barrie then attended Dumfries Academy. His first home in Dumfries was with his brother and sister Mary in Irving Street, opposite the Reformed Presbyterian Church. Dumfries Academy was in a single building in Academy Street, overlooking Irving Street, although it was rebuilt in the 1890s. Between 1875 and 1878 the Barries lived at No 6 Victoria Terrace, overlooking the goods yards of the railway station and a plaque marks the spot. Dumfries Museum, in the Observatory, has some of his manuscripts.

In Irving Street to the rear of the school, where it meets George Street, is the garden of Moat Brae House, a handsome Greek Revival two-storey red sandstone villa. Here there is another plaque, where the boy Barrie is said to have first imagined Peter and Wendy. School friends Stuart and Harold (Hal) Gordon, sons of Henry Gordon, a prominent solicitor and Sheriff Clerk, lived in Moat Brae and the boys played in the gardens which extended down to the River Nith. Barrie maintained that playing there inspired *Peter Pan*. They acted out fantasies of shipwrecks, desert islands and adventure on the high seas in the manner of Ballantyne's novel. Barrie wrote of how 'When the shades of night began to fall, certain young mathematicians changed their skins, crept up walls and down trees, and became pirates in a sort of odyssey that was afterwards to become the play of Peter Pan. Our escapades in a certain Dumfries garden which is enchanted land to me was certainly the genesis of that nefarious work.' The Peter Pan Moat Brae Trust has raised funds to renovate the property and has plans for its development as a visitor attraction and centre for children's literature opening in 2018.

The Dumfries Amateur Dramatic Society, of which Barrie was founder and secretary, performed at the Assembly Rooms in George Street in 1878 and Barrie wrote his first play *Bandelero the Bandit* for it. Encouraged by his head teacher to attend, Barrie saw many performances at the Theatre Royal in Shakespeare Street, built in 1790, which he considered his favourite theatre. His preferred seat was at the end of the front row by the pit where he could see what performers were doing in the wings. The theatre, which is run by volunteers, was threatened with closure, but funding has ensured that it will continue with facilities improved.

In 1878 Barrie left Dumfries for Edinburgh University. As a student he lodged initially in a top flat at No 14 Cumberland Street, then at No 20 Shandwick Place, then after graduation at No 3 Great King Street from 1879-82, at the west corner of Drummond Place, off Dublin Street in the New Town, where there is a plaque. In his second year at Edinburgh he persuaded the editor of the *Edinburgh Courant* to let him review plays, leading to 82 articles over four years. Then followed two years in Nottingham as a leader writer for the *Nottingham Journal* where he wrote two columns at least each day, work also reflected in *When a Man's Single* (1888).

On visits to Kirriemuir he began writing stories about his home town, fictionalised as Thrums, for *Cornhill Magazine* and *St James's Gazette*. On such occasions he fished, took long walks into the glens and wrote in the study at Strathview. *Auld Licht Idylls* and its companion piece *A Window in Thrums* mixed personal observation with memories, especially from his mother of the early 1800s. The articles and works were well received, with their combination of sentiment and realism. Others followed on a regular basis: *Margaret Ogilvie* (1896) is a tribute to his mother, while *Sentimental Tommy* (1896) and *Tommy and Grizel* (1900) anticipated *Peter Pan or The Boy Who Wouldn't Grow Up* (1904). Popular novels and plays included *The Little Minister* (1891) based on an Angus setting, *Ibsen's Ghost* (1891), *Quality Street* (1890), *The Admirable Crichton* (1902), *What Every Woman Knows* (1906), *Dear Brutus* (1917), *Mary Rose* (1920) and many others. While primarily a dramatist for adults Barrie's most memorable contribution to the theatre was to be a play ostensibly for children.

In 1885 he went to London and took lodgings in Guildford Street near the British Museum, convenient for its great reading room and in the next four years he produced huge amounts of material, including some 800 journalistic articles. Barrie attended Lord's cricket ground and went on to found a cricket club, forming the idea while walking around the Surrey village of Shere near Guildford. He persuaded assorted actors and writers to participate for fun, but nevertheless in earnest, as the Allahakbarries, a play on the Arabic with a pun intended on the final syllables.

In 1892 his play *Walker, London* opened in London with the pretty little actress Mary Ansell in a leading role. Barrie felt comfortable with her being shorter than him and the relationship resulted in marriage at Strathview in July 1894 by his uncle the Revd David Ogilvy. Childless, the couple acquired an enormous St Bernard dog, bigger than either of them, which they had seen in Switzerland on their honeymoon. They named him Porthos after the dog in George du Maurier's novel *Peter Ibbetson*. The Barries stayed in various lodgings; from 1895-1901 they occupied a first-floor apartment at No 133 Gloucester Road in South Kensington, where Barrie's study was above the front door. Here he wrote *Sentimental Tommy* and *Margaret Ogilvy*, both reflecting life in Kirriemuir.

Daily routine for Barrie in the late 1890s included a short walk across Kensington Gore with Porthos into Kensington Gardens, formerly the private gardens of Kensington Palace. Its 275 acres had been laid out in the early 18th century adjoining Hyde Park, at that time less cultivated (apart from the Broad Walk and Round Pond) with sheep grazing in the long grass and wildfowl on the Serpentine island. The love of dogs was to outlast his marriage. Nana, the Newfoundland dog of the famous story, may be based upon Porthos or his successor, the Newfoundland Luath.

In Kensington Gardens began Barrie's romance with other people's children from well-to-do families; infants in massive prams wheeled by nannies in starched uniforms. There was much informal play with the dog and later the children, blending fantasy and reality, which all stimulated his work.

The Llewelyn Davies family lived at No 31 Kensington Park Gardens in Notting Hill. George, four years old and the younger Jack, with their nannie Mary Hodgson, played games with Barrie and his dog in the gardens. Barrie became obsessed and the boys were a rapt audience for his stories. He eventually met their adorable mother Sylvia, daughter of the famous writer Gerald du Maurier, at a dinner party and subsequently her husband Arthur, although relations with him were not so agreeable. However, Barrie became a close friend of the family, holidaying with them and fulfilling fantasies in someone with no children of his own. By the time of the publication of *Peter Pan* the bohemian family included five sons.

Barrie's 1902 novel *The Little White Bird*, uses the fantasy of the childless writer and a dead child and became so popular that he was accosted by mothers and sons in the gardens. Peter Pan, the boy fairy, appears for the first time in this story. The narrator is clearly based on Barrie who tells the little boy David, based on George Llewelyn Davies, that children were once birds in Kensington Gardens. 'Nothing that happens after we are twelve matters very much', claimed Barrie. (In October of 1903 he was given the unusual honour of a key to the gardens so that he could visit them when locked up.)

Mary, Barrie's wife, had been searching for a house in the country as a holiday retreat and in 1900 found Black Lake Cottage, almost 40 miles from London in Surrey with a large overgrown garden and a lake in a clearing along a dirt track. Here Barrie wrote part of *Peter Pan* in the pine forest behind his country home. Porthos is buried here. For six weeks in the summer of 1901 the Llewelyn Davies boys (the family took a cottage at Tilford nearby) and Barrie acted out adventures in the manner of *The Coral Island*. There was a make-believe lagoon, with the boys shipwrecked and marooned, Barrie as the pirate, making them walk the plank with Porthos acting the part of a tiger and with Redskins present.

In 1902 the Barries moved from Gloucester Road to a small Regency house on Leinster Terrace, backing on to Lancaster Gate, called Leinster Corner by Mary, adjacent to Bayswater Road on the northern edge of Kensington Gardens. George Llewelyn Davies's private school was nearby in Orme Square. The property included a stable at the bottom of the garden which became a garage with a study in the hayloft. Here, between 1902 and 1909, Barrie wrote part of *Peter Pan* and *What Every Woman Knows* and walked Luath in the gardens. *Tommy and Grizel* was written partly on a shady bench by the Round Pond.

In late October 1904 rehearsals were underway for the theatrical production of *Peter Pan*, an amalgam of play, ballet and pantomime, at the Duke of York's Theatre, backed by his friend, the American Charles Frohman. Costumes were based on the clothes of the Llewelyn Davies boys and the first performance took place on 27 December. Gerald du Maurier doubled as Mr Darling and Captain Hook, a tradition in the theatre which continues to the present day and Hilda Trevelyan was Wendy, the name being Barrie's invention, based upon 'friendy-wendy'. Barrie had befriended the six-year-old Margaret Henley who could not pronounce her r's, calling Barrie her 'fwendy'. She died young and is commemorated in the character.

In 1929 Barrie donated all royalties from the play to the Great Ormond Street Hospital for Sick Children, a practice still continued by special legislation although the copyright ran out in

1987. The novelistic version *Peter and Wendy* is closest to the play as acted on the stage for so many years. The work has often been simplified, yet the original is sophisticated, not whimsical as is popularly assumed and with a profound awareness of darkness as Barrie appealed to both adults and children.

The growing Llewelyn Davies family eventually moved from No 23 to No 31 Kensington Park Gardens and then to Berkhamsted in Berkshire, 25 miles away, where they lived in Egerton House. With their father's death in 1907 they returned to London and a house at No 23 Camden Hill Square, near their old home and Barrie's Leinster Corner. He remained Uncle Jim to them and assisted in the purchase of their house. On Sylvia's death in 1910 she bequeathed it to him as a home for the five boys with Barrie as guardian.

In 1909 Barrie refused a knighthood but accepted the honour in 1913. Meanwhile the sculptor George Frampton was commissioned to make a statue of Peter Pan to be installed in Kensington Gardens, modelled on Michael Llewelyn Davies in a fighting pose, holding a stick and wearing a romantic Peter Pan costume. The finished work was secretly installed overnight, under Barrie's instruction and at his expense, for May morning 1912, near the Long Water and Westbourne Gate entrance, so that it would seem to children to have appeared 'as if by magic'. Peter stands on a pixilated plinth, hidden in an alcove of foliage, so that he is encountered all of a sudden, a monument to the passing of childhood in the manchild as assorted fairies, mice, squirrels, birds and rabbits frolic around the base. Barrie reputedly was dissatisfied with the statue 'because it doesn't show the devil in Peter'.

Barrie sued Mary for divorce in 1909 on the grounds of infidelity and afterwards moved to Adelphi, an area between the Strand and the River Thames, built by the Adam brothers in 1768, but now partly demolished. It lies east of Charing Cross station and just up from Somerset House. There were warehouses below and four elegant streets above with views over Embankment Gardens and the River Thames. Robert Street has a plaque for No 1-3 Adelphi Terrace where Barrie occupied the top-floor flat with its angled windows from 1911 until his death.

St George's Church in Aubrey Walk on Campden Hill has become known as the Peter Pan church, appearing in the original poster for the play in 1904 with its spire on the right as Peter and Wendy set off for the magical adventurous land. Great Ormond Street Hospital for Sick Children was founded in 1851 and has a Peter Pan Surgery Ward, a Barrie wing and Peter Pan Cafeterias for outpatients with characters represented on the walls. A Tinkerbell Play Area includes a waiting room and play facilities. The Hospital Museum contains original editions of *Peter Pan* and other memorabilia and the Chapel of St Christopher has a plaque. A Peter Pan statue was erected at the entrance in 2000, picturing him as the impish boy who blows fairy dust over the Darling children to enable them to fly.

Barrie had supported the hospital since the early 1900s and was asked to join a committee in 1928 to assist expansion. He declined but shortly after assigned the *Peter Pan* rights to the hospital. The premises of the hospital archives across the street at No 55 Great Ormond Street have a small Peter Pan Gallery displaying Barrie photographs and other items, including original stage production materials. An annual competition for children aged 6–16 invites them to make children smile through writing, art or photography.

George Llewelyn Davies was killed in the First World War and in 1921 brother Michael, a poor swimmer, was drowned in the River Cherwell while an undergraduate at Oxford. Their deaths grieved Barrie greatly. It has been claimed that obsessive behaviour on Barrie's part was a factor in two of these premature deaths. Barrie said that Peter was an amalgamation of the Llewelyn Davies boys: 'By rubbing the five of you violently together, as savages with two sticks to produce a flame, I made the spark of you that is Peter Pan.' Mrs Darling was a blend of Sylvia Llewelyn Davies and Barrie's mother.

In April 1960 Peter Llewelyn Davies, one of the five boys and by then a 63-year-old publisher who hated being labelled as the inspiration for Peter, left the Royal Court Hotel, crossed Sloane Square to the tube station and threw himself under an oncoming train.

At the Bayswater Road end of Kensington Gardens, at the top of Broad Walk, a children's playground has been erected on a Peter Pan theme in memory of Princess Diana. Here there is a full-scale pirate ship with mermaid cove, tepee and tree house.

A Peter Pan swim in the Serpentine Lake in Hyde Park takes place annually on 25 December when dozens vie for a Peter Pan Cup, first presented by the author. A Peter Pan Treasure Hunt takes place annually in July in Kensington Gardens. Hunters explore Neverland to find treasure and other articles, the proceeds going to a theatre appeal for paediatric medicine.

The Duke of York's Theatre is in St Martin's Lane in London, where the play was first performed and where centenary celebrations took place in December 2004.

At Thorpeness, on the B1353, two miles north of Aldeburgh in Suffolk, a mock medieval village with a mere and islands named after the Peter Pan characters was built for a friend of Barrie.

A Peter Pan statue by Alex Proudfoot sits in the grounds of Mearnskirk Hospital in East Renfrewshire, south of Glasgow, a leading hospital for tubercular children after it opened in 1930. A bronze plaque showing Wendy and John flying after Peter into his fantasy world which formerly adorned the statue is now mounted beside the front door of the nearby Hazeldene nursery school.

STORYTRAIL: *Peter Pan*

THE MAIN CHARACTERS
Wendy, John and Michael, the Darling children.
Mary and George Darling, the children's parents.
Nana, a Newfoundland dog and nurse to the children.
Peter Pan, a motherless figure.
Tinker Bell, a fairy assistant to Peter Pan.
The Lost Boys and the Redskin tribe, residents of Neverland.
Captain Hook, pirate chief.
Tiger Lily, Redskin princess.
Mr Smee, Hook's bo'sun.

The Darling family actually reside in Bloomsbury, the area to the north of Covent Garden, rather than Kensington, adjacent to the gardens and from there they soar into the night sky over the London rooftops with Peter Pan to the magical Never Never Land where children have adventures involving pirates, croco-diles, mermaids and fairy dust. The associations with Kensington Gardens are nevertheless clear. Mr Wilkinson, head of the boys' private school in nearby Orme Street, was said to be a model for Captain Hook. In an early version Hook is disguised as a school-master who almost catches Peter but is himself caught by the crocodile. The Mermaid Lagoon was added later.

The weeping beech that Peter sleeps in is still to be found in the flower walk as well as the statue on the shore of the Long Water, where he lands after his voyage in the bird's nest. The island in the Serpentine was Peter's original home, the nest built by birds and used as a boat to sail over to Kensington Gardens every night and play with the fairies. When they had a ball he would sit on a big toadstool and play the pipes for their dance.

As the fairy stories told to the Llewelyn Davies boys moved on to play activity based upon 'wrecked islands', the setting of Black Lake to the north of the road between Farnham and Tilford in Surrey where the family joined Barrie at the end of July in 1901, is crucial. Barrie's Black Lake Cottage was on the far side of the road. The pine woods and shallow lake here are the real setting for Never Never Land with its Mermaid Lagoon. Here the boys and man-boy Barrie built a hut in the woods and foiled the Pirate Captain Swarthy, predecessor to Hook, and were repeatedly wrecked and rescued, experienced narrow escapes and displayed valour, sometimes with the help of Peter Pan, who is older but not grown up, and of course the presence of Porthos. There is no actual island on the lake on which to be stranded but any part of the woods became Never Never Land and a punt became a longboat or pirate ship in the games. One draft of the story was entitled *The Boy Castaways of Black Lake*.

TOURIST INFORMATION
AND VISITOR ATTRACTIONS

Angus Folk Museum
    Kirkwynd, Glamis DD8 1RT
    Tel: 01307 840288
Angus Weavers Ltd
    Dun East Lodge, Montrose DD10 9LQ
    Tel: 01674 810255
Barrie's Birthplace Museum
    9 Brechin Road, Kirriemuir DD8 4BX
    Tel: [seasonal] 01575 572646
Camera Obscura
    Kirrie Hill, Kirriemuir DD8 4PT
    Tel: [seasonal] 07938986968
Kirriemuir TIC
    Cumberland Close, Kirriemuir DD8 4EF
    Tel: [seasonal] 01575 574097
VisitScotland Angus & Dundee
    Discovery Point, Discovery Quay, Dundee DD1 4XA
    Tel: 01382 527527
VisitScotland Dundee iCentre
    16 City Square, Dundee DD1 3BG
    Tel: 01382 527527
Dumfries Museum
    The Observatory, Rotchell Road, Dumfries DG2 7SW
    Tel: 01387 253374
Peter Pan Moat Brae Trust
    92 Irish Street, Dumfries DG1 2PF
    Tel: 01387 255549
The Theatre Royal
    58-70 Shakespeare Street, Dumfries DG1 2JH
    Tel: 01387 25420
VisitScotland Dumfries iCentre
    64 Whitesands, Dumfries DG1 2RS
    Tel: 01387 253862
Edinburgh and Lothians Tourist Board
    3 Princes Street, Edinburgh EH2 2QP
    Tel: 0845 225 5121
The Edinburgh Book Lovers' Tour
    Tel: 07770 163641
The Scottish Literary Tour Trust
    34 North Castle Street, Edinburgh EH2 3BN
    Tel: 0800 169 7410/0131 226 6665

City of London Information Centre
St Paul's Churchyard, London EC4M 8BX
Tel: 020 7332 3456
Duke of York's Theatre
85 St Martin's Lane, London WC2N 4BG
Tel: 0870 060 6623
Great Ormond Street Hospital Children's Charity
40 Bernard Street, London WC1N 1LE
Tel: 020 3841 3841
Peter Pan Treasure Hunt
Tel: 0871 230 5574
Guildford TIC
155 High Street, Guildford GU1 3AJ
Tel: 01483 444333

3

John Buchan

JOHN BUCHAN (1875-1940) was born in Perth, the eldest of six children of Revd John Buchan, a Free Church of Scotland minister, and Helen Masterton, daughter of a sheep farmer at Broughton in the Scottish Borders where Buchan's father had himself been eldest son of the Free Church minister.

The manse in York Place is now divided into two and occupied by offices and a bronze plaque appears on the right hand side of the door at No 20. In 1875 they moved to the West Church, since demolished, at Pathhead, between Kirkcaldy and Dysart in Fife, where they stayed for 12 years and had another four children. The manse, Inglewood in Smeaton Road, has been demolished.

Buchan attended a dame school and the local Board School, afterwards walking three miles daily to the Burgh School in Kirkcaldy, then at the junction of Hill Street and Kirk Wynd, followed by the High School of Kirkcaldy. One window of the manse looked across the garden and a field to the Firth of Forth and Inchkeith lighthouse and at the harbour below Buchan loved to listen to a retired sea captain. The bay beyond Ravenscraig Castle was part of the North Sea and the boy loved the caves and pools. Here he 'lit a fire of driftwood, and made believe that I was a smuggler or a Jacobite new landed from France'.

Queen Mary Avenue, in the Crosshill area, two miles from the centre of Glasgow, near Queen's Park and Victoria Road, where the children enjoyed visiting the shops, is a quiet road shaded with trees and grey sandstone houses in large gardens. Here was Revd Buchan's manse, Florence Villa, at No 34, after he moved charges from Kirkcaldy. In 1888 he was called to John Knox

Church in Rose Street in Gorbals to the south of the River Clyde, an area at one time fashionable but eventually famous for its squalid tenements.

Buchan walked the two miles daily to Hutchesons' Grammar School in Crown Street in Gorbals, founded in 1650 by two brothers, but since demolished with the school moving to Crossmyloof in 1959. Revd Buchan spent 22 years in the Gorbals church until his retirement and the family of six children spent many of their Sundays there. In 1943 the church was united with Gorbals Church and in 1958 the building sold and a few years later destroyed by fire. Buchan took a Sunday school class of troublesome boys whom he nevertheless liked and who were the inspiration for the Gorbals Die-Hards of the trilogy which begins with *Huntingtower*.

For two months in the summer the children escaped industrial Glasgow to stay in a pastoral landscape with the Masterton grandparents, sheep farmers at Broughton Green. The farm is a tall white building with a steep roof, a former inn, on the west side of the A701 Edinburgh to Carlisle road at the north end of Broughton village, 'at the mouth of a shallow glen bounded by high green hills'. Family members still occupy the house. The former farm buildings are across the road. Here the children delighted in helping on the farm and exploring the countryside, rivers and hills, the ruined kirk, the trout pool, mill dam, water meadow, fishing and meeting shepherds, attending at sheep-shearing time and the dispatch of livestock to market.

Like the hero of the early novel *John Burnet of Barns* Buchan could say that 'by the time I had come to 16 years I had swum in every pool in the Tweed for miles up and down, climbed every hill, fished in every burn.' One special place was a beech tree close to a deep pool, a favourite spot for make-believe games. Another was a hollow in a nearby hill which the children believed was the entrance to King Arthur's sleeping place. They became steeped in local legends, fairy lore and Jacobite tales, much of it from their father who was a gifted storyteller.

Beyond Broughton Green, which is no longer a farmhouse, is Broughton Place, approached by an avenue of trees and home of John Murray of Broughton, secretary to Prince Charles during the 1745 rebellion. At his grandmother's death in 1901 Buchan said: 'Since ever I was a very little boy I have liked Broughton better than any other place in the world.' His little sister Violet, who died at age five, is buried in the old kirk grave-yard above the village.

Relatives in Peebles were not far away. Bank House, where there is a plaque, at the west end of Peebles High Street, was Buchan's paternal grandfather's home and uncle Walter followed his father as lawyer and banker and was town clerk. An aunt also lived there, a Buchan home until Walter's death in 1954. An exhibition entitled The John Buchan Story is housed in The Chambers Institution in Peebles High Street. This replaces an exhibition housed in the former Broughton Free Church, where the name 'Hannay' appears inscribed on a stained-glass window, gifted by WH Hannay of Parkside, to the left of the pulpit direct-ly opposite where young Buchan sat.

Summer holidays after the First World War were spent in the Scottish Borders and Highlands. In 1919 Buchan rented Gala Lodge, a Victorian villa at Calzeat at the south end of Broughton village, owned by his aunt Agnes Robb, above the road on the side of a hill looking over the wide glen to the heather and screes of Ratchel Hill. If there were admirers calling and he wished pri-vacy he retreated out the back of the house to the hills by the Hill O' Men which rose abruptly behind the steep garden.

In 2003 a John Buchan Way was opened, eight-and-a-half miles of waymarked hill tracks between Peebles and Broughton, following countryside close to Buchan's heart, beginning beside the farm at Broughton and ascending the Broughton Heights, then crossing the B712 and the River Tweed at Stobo and on into Peebles at the bridge near Bank House. Scottish Borders Council Ranger Service provides an escorted trip along the Way.

Buchan went to Glasgow University in 1892, a Victorian Gothic edifice overlooking Kelvingrove Park. Meanwhile holi-days were still largely spent at Broughton and Peebles, although he holidayed in Kinghorn in Fife in 1895, the year of his first novel *Sir Quixote of the Moors*, a historical romance describing the adventures of a French gentleman and includes a ride taken from Galloway to Leith.

In October 1895 Buchan proceeded to Oxford University, staying in room 7 on No 1 stair in the Old Quad of Brasenose College, founded in 1509, in his time a small college of about a hundred undergraduates. In his fourth year, from October 1898, he stayed at No 41 High Street. He continued to publish articles and pursue his enthusiasm for walking and climbing holidays. In 1896 he undertook various tours in Galloway and in 1897 he was in the Highlands by way of Glen Orchy, the Black Mount, Kingshouse Inn, Rannoch Moor, Buachaille Etive Mor in Glencoe and thence to Ballachulish and Appin, landscape associated with the plot of Robert Louis Stevenson's *Kidnapped*.

His first book of essays, *Scholar-Gipsies*, published in 1896, was dedicated to the memory of his grandfather John Masterton of Broughton Green and inspired by Peeblesshire. The romantic adventure *John Burnet of Barns* appeared in 1898 with a 17th-century setting in the upper Tweed and the Low Countries. In 1899 *Grey Weather Moorland Tales of My Own People* appeared, recalling the shepherds, drovers, fishermen, tinkers and poachers with whom he had been familiar since boyhood. Broughton is the Woodilee of *Witch Wood* which is set during the Civil War of 1644-6 and considered by Buchan to be his finest novel. At the foot of the loan between Broughton and Skirling, near the churchyard and the ruined kirk, was an eerie place with ancient twisted trees and a cluster of stones which had once been the manse. The young minister, Revd David Semphill, arrives in the parish and struggles to assert the Christian gospel in a place where there is pagan worship, a coven of witches and strange happenings in the old sinister wood of Caledon.

After being called to the Bar, Buchan resided at No 4 Brick Court in the Temple area of London, then in December 1900 moved to No 3 Temple Gardens overlooking the River Thames. From September 1901 two years were spent in South Africa where the landscape, he thought, was not unlike that of Scotland. He met Susan Grosvenor, of a titled family and cousin to the Duke of Westminster, at No 30 Upper Grosvenor Street in Mayfair in London and they were married in 1907 at St George's, Hanover Square.

From 1907-29 Buchan was a partner and literary adviser to the Edinburgh printer and publisher Thomas Nelson & Sons and after marrying the Buchans stayed at Abden House, a Gothic villa now in the grounds of Edinburgh University's Pollock Halls of Residence off the Dalkeith Road, with a view of Arthur's Seat. The printing works, since demolished, was at Parkside on Dalkeith Road. Thomas Nelson was an old Oxford friend to whom he dedicated *The Thirty-nine Steps*. The Buchans also stayed for a time with friends at No 6 Heriot Row.

Returning to London before the outbreak of the First World War their first home was at No 40 Hyde Park Square, then from 1911 at No 13 Bryanston Street near Marble Arch (now a block of flats) and in 1913 at No 76 Portland Place, a spacious house near Regent's Park with large rooms in grand Adam style, since occupied by the Institute of Physics. Buchan was living here when he wrote *The Thirty-nine Steps* whose hero lives beside Portland Place in a first-floor flat, where he finds a body and escapes dressed as a milkman.

In 1912 he developed a duodenal ulcer which bothered him for the rest of his life and in the summer of 1914 he convalesced at St Cuby's, a house on Cliff Promenade at North Foreland, Broadstairs, which belonged to his wife's cousin and her husband. Close by steps led down to a private beach and a small cove. Here he took his mind off his illness by completing *The Thirty-nine Steps* which so caught the mood of spy fever at the time with 25,000 copies sold between publication in October 1915 and the end of the year. The family were later to maintain that the figure 39 was chosen simply for imaginative reasons.

During the First World War he was correspondent on the Western Front for *The Times* in 1915 and became Director of Information from 1917-8. During this time he published Nelson's *History of the War* (1915-9). From 1919 he worked for Reuters news agency and from 1927-35 he was MP for the Scottish Universities.

As an undergraduate Buchan loved the Oxfordshire countryside with its gently rolling hills and rich agricultural land and he explored Oxfordshire, the Chilterns, Cotswolds and Berkshire Downs on foot, bicycle and horseback. Four years of war left him 'with an intense craving for a country life' and so, early in 1920, the Buchans settled in The Manor, a house with 20 acres of land at Elsfield, four miles north-east of Oxford. The front door of the house, of 17th-century Cotswold stone with some Victorian additions, opened from the village street and a secluded rose garden and lawns sloped down to water-meadows by the River Cherwell with a vista across 30 miles of woods and fields to the ridges above Stow-in-the-Wold. The garden had a pond, a stream, outhouses for children to play in and a 12th-century barn which became a performance space with a stage. This was their home for the next 34 years. Weekends were spent shooting, fishing, canoeing and horse riding and enjoying the pretty garden. In the library upstairs he wrote many of the stories which came to him while walking, riding, fishing and journeying on trains. Senior members of the university and undergraduates would visit Elsfield on foot, by car or bicycle.

Buchan became Baron Tweedsmuir of Elsfield in 1935, the year he also became Governor General of Canada. The title recalls the two places for which Buchan had particular affection, the Oxfordshire village and a hamlet south of Broughton in the upper Tweed valley close to the high moor north of the Devil's Beeftub above Moffat, where the sources of the rivers Annan, Tweed and Clyde rise.

His early fiction is in the tradition of Scott and Stevenson and includes *John Burnet of Barnes* (1898). Later historical novels include *The Path of the King* (1921), *Midwinter* (1923) and *Witch Wood* (1927). Non-fiction works include biographies of Montrose and Sir Walter Scott, but especially he is remembered for his adventure stories, famous for their derring-do, intrigue and description of landscape, beginning with *Prester John* (1910), which has an African setting and heroes, including Richard Hannay, who are successful figures of the Empire. The best known is *The Thirty-nine Steps* (1914), followed by *Greenmantle* (1915), *Mr Standfast* (1916) and *John Macnab* (1918). He published a thriller a year between 1922 and 1936. His final work was *Sick Heart River* (1941) and is set in Canada.

Although a barrister with a distinguished career in public life, reflected in his autobiography *Memory-Hold-the-Door* (1940), Buchan was proud to be a countryman and fisherman. He produced hundreds of articles and thousands of letters, over a hundred books, including 30 novels, seven collections of short stories, 66 works of non-fiction, poetry, 26 pamphlets and 63 contributions to other books.

Buchan's ashes are buried in the St Thomas of Canterbury churchyard in Elsfield and The Manor was sold in 1954.

STORYTRAIL: *The Thirty-Nine Steps*

THE MAIN CHARACTERS
Richard Hannay, retired mining engineer.
Franklin P Scudder, American neighbour of Hannay.
Characters whom Hannay encounters in south-west Scotland:
the literary innkeeper, political candidate, spectacled roadman and bald archaeologist.
Sir Walter Bullivant, Permanent Secretary at the Foreign Office.

The novel, with its gang of anarchists trying to destroy world peace, dramatically caught the pre-war public mood as the plot turns on unmasking unscrupulous dangerous foreigners. Hannay is hunted by both spies and the police from London to the Scottish moors until he unravels the secret coded message about the 39 steps. The veneer of civilisation is removed and courage and responsibility are needed to do one's duty, qualities in Hannay which appear again in five successive novels.

Richard Hannay, a 37-year-old mining engineer who has spent many years in Rhodesia, is returning to his London flat off Portland Place having dined at the ornate Café Royal at No 68 Regent Street. His American neighbour, Franklin P Scudder, claims there is a conspiracy to destabilise the international situation and murder the Greek premier on a forthcoming visit to London. Scudder asks for Hannay's help but is quickly murdered. Hannay finds his notebooks with a cryptic message about 39 steps. Hannay is now a suspect and on the run to protect information and save the country from the Germans.

Hannay flees by train to south-west Scotland, to Dumfries, Galloway and Tweeddale that Buchan knew intimately, areas of moorland, rivers and hills. There are both real places and imaginary landmarks in the description. Hannay is 'on the central boss of a huge upland plateau', in fact the Galloway moors where he could see for miles but also be seen. He is spotted by an aeroplane and is pursued over hills, burns and glens.

The evidence suggests that Hannay alights from the train first at Mossdale on the disused Dumfries to Newton Stewart railway, between Kirkcudbright and New Galloway. The Glasgow and South Western Railway from Carlisle to Portpatrick, known as 'the Port Road' or 'the Paddy Line', was opened in 1862, but closed by the government's adviser Dr Richard Beeching in 1965. This route was lengthy and sinuous as it took in outlying communities with branches to Kirkcudbright and Wigtown, Garlieston and Whithorn.

From Castle Douglas the line went north, parallel to the A713, to the eastern shores of Loch Ken. The first station was at Crossmichael, the track then passing along the side of the loch to another small station at Parton. At the narrowest part of the loch the line crossed it on a viaduct built in 1860 on three stone piers, the three arches still standing, visible from the A713 or, picturesquely, across fields from a minor road on the west side of the loch. It is said that Buchan borrowed the hero's name from the owner of the land around the viaduct, Robert Hannay. Next the line plunges into woods and alongside the Black Water of Dee. The surviving track-bed then curves round to Mossdale, the site of New Galloway station. From the road bridge there is a good view of the former yard and surviving platform, now part of a garden in the old station house.

West of here the track followed wild and otherwise inaccessible moorland and forest visible from the bridge. The surviving track now forms a long distance farm access path for several miles to Loch Skerrow, over what were bare hills but since massively afforested.

There is a Buchan Hill, Buchan Burn and Buchan Woods in the Glen Trool Forest a little further north, a coincidence of names which would have amused the author. Mossdale is off the

A762, five miles south of New Galloway and a little over a mile from the Loch Ken viaduct. Hannay 'got out ... and emerged on a white road that straggled over the brown moor.' He heads north-west towards Cairnsmore or the Black Craig of Dee, then south-east and back towards the railway and the old halt at Loch Skerrow, where the platform remains and 'to increase the desolation the waves of a tarn lapped on their grey granite beach half a mile away.'

He catches another train here back to Mossdale, taking a ticket for Dumfries, then goes south-east beside the River Dee. He gets off at an unscheduled stop beyond Mossdale, 'at the end of a culvert which spanned a brawling porter-coloured river', assumed to be the Loch Ken viaduct, then east to the B794 and north to the A712. He heads left for a mile, over the Urr Water, then north on a minor road towards the A702. Near the bridge over the Fell Burn at Waterhead an isolated dwelling on the edge of the moor may be the model for the Literary Innkeeper's house, about two-and-a-half miles before the A702.

Hannay tricks his pursuers and goes off in their car to the A702 and north-east towards Thornhill, through Moniaive and Penpont, which is probably the 'long straggling village' with a post office. The castle he mentions is surely Drumlanrig, two miles to the north. After Penpont the river is the Nith just before Thornhill, north of which he follows the valley of the Penpont Burn to Auchenbainzie, crossing the Nith at Eliock Wood. Then he goes by the A76 to Mennock and east on the B797, known as the 'corkscrew road', by the Mennock pass and the Lowther Hills (the railway mentioned is from Glasgow to London at Elvanfoot).

Hannay crashes the car in an area where the M74 now passes. The political meeting would be at Lockerbie. He is now around the upper River Tweed and heading towards Buchan's ancestral home at Broughton. Above Tweedhopefoot and beside the A701 Edinburgh to Moffat road is the site of the meeting with the Spectacled Roadman, who lives at Blackhopefoot (Smidhopefoot), where a burn joins the River Tweed. With Jopley's car Hannay heads towards Tweedsmuir and the Stanhope valley, some five miles further on to the right, then to a remote homestead around Dollar Law to the east. He 'spent the night on a shelf of the hillside' at the head of Stanhope Glen.

At Manorhead at the foot of Dollar Law he escapes the trap using explosives. From here he can glimpse the sea, the Solway Firth. He joins cattle drovers heading south, on tracks east of the A701, past Ericstane Hill, across the River Annan and down the valley to a 'humble Moffat Public House', probably the Black Bull Hotel. He then walks two miles to catch the 'night express for the south at Beattock.'

He travels to Attinswell, probably based on Kintbury near Newbury on the River Kennet, in Berkshire, which Buchan had fished. Sir Walter Bullivant's home may be modelled on the former Donnington Priory where Buchan had stayed. Hannay then goes to London and finally Broadstairs in Kent, thinly disguised as Bradgate (an amalgamation of Margate and Broadstairs), where villas near North Foreland had a staircase down to the beach and where the spies plan their escape. At Kingsgate, a village three miles east of Margate to the north of North Foreland there are steps from the castle to the beach at Kingsgate Gap which locals claim to be the original of the steps.

Local tradition in Fife maintains that the steps on the west side of Ravenscraig Castle, leading down to the beach at Pathhead, provided the idea for the famous steps.

TOURIST INFORMATION AND VISITOR ATTRACTIONS

VisitScotland Fife iSign
  War Memorial Gardens, Kirkcaldy KY1 1YG
  Tel: 01592 583206
VisitScotland Perth iCentre
  45 High Street, Perth PH1 5TJ
  Tel: 01738 450600
VisitScotland Peebles iCentre
  23 High Street, Peebles EH45 8AG
  Tel: 01721 728095
The John Buchan Story
  The Chambers Institution, High Street, Peebles EH45 8AG
  Tel: [seasonal] 01721 720123

Scottish Borders Council Ranger Service
   Tel: 01835 830 281
VisitScotland Castle Douglas iCentre
   Market Hill Car Park, Castle Douglas, DG7 1AE
   Tel: 01556 502611
VisitScotland Dumfries iCentre
   64 Whitesands, Dumfries DG1 2RS
   Tel: 01387 253862
VisitScotland Glasgow iCentre
   Gallery of Modern Art, Royal Exchange Square, Glasgow G1 3AH
Moffat TIC
   9 The High Street, Moffat DG10 9HF
   Tel: 01683 221210
City of London Information Centre
   St Paul's Churchyard, London EC4M 8BX
   Tel: 020 7332 3456
Margate Visitor Information Centre
   Stone Pier, Margate CT9 1JD
   Tel: 01843 577577
Brasenose College Oxford
   Radcliffe Square, Oxford OX1 4AJ
   Tel: 01865 277823
Oxford TIC
   15-16 Broad Street, Oxford OX1 3AS
   Tel: 01865 686430

4

Arthur Conan Doyle

ARTHUR CONAN DOYLE (1859-1930) was born at No 11 Picardy Place, Edinburgh, son of Charles Altamount Doyle, a surveyor and Mary Foley. The property was a three-storey building named after a 17th-century settlement of French silk weavers, demolished in the 1960s to make way for a roundabout, where York Place meets Broughton Street on the edge of the New Town.

In 1969 a statue of Sherlock Holmes clutching his pipe was erected near the site and there is a Conan Doyle pub across the road with memorabilia. His father, Irish Catholic in origin, was an assistant surveyor to Her Majesty's Clerk of Works and did drawings for a fountain in the forecourt of the Palace of Holyroodhouse. He supplemented his income by painting and illustrating and was an able caricaturist. Two of his paintings are in the Edinburgh City Art Centre's collection. His work appeared in London magazines, a children's book called *Our Trip to Blunderland* and he provided initial drawings of Sherlock Holmes. His alcoholism and probable epilepsy led to premature retirement, eventual institutionalisation and later dementia in a series of sanatoria. He died at the Crichton Royal Asylum in Dumfries. His wife Mary Foley was granddaughter of his land-lady and Arthur Conan Doyle was her third child and first son.

As his father's condition deteriorated the family moved to Tower Bank House, since demolished, at Portobello, on the coast east of Edinburgh, where rents were lower. At age five Doyle was sent to stay with his mother's friend Miss Burton, a relative of John Hill Burton, the Historiographer Royal of Scotland, who resided at Liberton Bank House in the village of Liberton, about three miles south-east of the city centre, now a suburb. The house was beside the Braid Burn at the north end of Gilmerton Road, near the present Cameron Toll shopping centre and here Doyle enjoyed a rural idyll. Saved from demolition, Liberton Bank House has been restored for use as a school for children with special needs and occasional community events. The garden has a small auditorium, plaques and stone slabs inscribed with literary references to celebrate the spot where the young Doyle first wrote stories. He appears to have attended Newington Academy in Salisbury Place, later the site of Longmore Hospital and returned to live with his family at No 3 Sciennes Hill Place nearer the city centre, one of several addresses they had while his mother tried to make ends meet.

Doyle's education, now paid for by wealthy uncles, continued under the Jesuits at the boarding Hodder Preparatory School from 1867 and at the neighbouring Stoneyhurst College, occupying a former Elizabethan country mansion close to the village of Hurst Green on the B6243 in the Ribble valley in Lancashire. The schools were in open countryside on the edge of the Lancashire moors and Forest of Bowland. Doyle was good at sport, becoming captain of cricket and there were long walks in the beautiful countryside. He became known as a good storyteller and on wet half-holidays he would sit on a desk with an audience of little boys around him. At Christmas in 1874 he first went to London to visit his uncle Richard, an artist, illustrator and cartoonist and spinster aunt Annette, who lived in Cambridge Terrace, near Hyde Park, but stayed at the uncle's studio at No 7 Finborough Road in West Brompton.

In the autumn of 1875 Doyle was sent for further education for a year at the Jesuits' Stella Matutina at Feldkirch in the Austrian Tyrol before returning to Edinburgh in 1876 to study medicine, eventually graduating in August 1881.

While at Edinburgh University the Doyles stayed variously at No 2 Argyle Park Terrace looking on to the Meadows, No 23 George Square, residence of Dr Bryan Charles Waller, a well-to-do doctor and published author who had taken the family under his wing. This house is now occupied by the Catholic chaplaincy and there is a plaque here. They then moved on to Howe Street in the New Town and No 15 Lonsdale Terrace, beside the Meadows, the rent being paid by Waller, from 1881-2. Doyle regularly walked between the Old College and the Surgical Hospital at the foot of Infirmary Street. The adjacent Pathology Museum in Surgeons' Hall on Nicolson Street includes a Conan Doyle exhibition and there is a plaque at the medical school.

The Sir Arthur Conan Doyle Centre at No 25 Palmerston Place in Edinburgh's West End was opened by the Edinburgh Association of Spiritualists in 2011.

From 1882 Doyle's mother lived for 30 years at Masongill Cottage off the A65 in Yorkshire on the estate of their benefactor Waller. Here Doyle enjoyed visiting the Marton Arms in neighbouring Thornton-in-Lonsdale.

While an undergraduate Doyle undertook a number of vacational jobs. From May 1878 he was variously a medical assistant in Sheffield and the Shropshire village of Ruyton-XI-Towns, off the A5 north-west of Shrewsbury. In 1879 he was with Dr Hoare at Clifton House in Aston Road in Birmingham. Doyle took a trip in 1880 as ship's doctor on an Arctic whaler, the steam-powered *Hope*, sailing out of Peterhead and the taste for adventure led to another voyage to West Africa as medical officer on board the *Mayumba* out of Liverpool, returning early in 1882 after four months at sea. He then went to London and stayed with his relatives at Cambridge Terrace and at Clifton Gardens in Maida Vale while his uncles and aunt discussed his future.

Sherlock Holmes was based upon Dr Joseph Bell, the astutely observant professor, surgeon at the Royal Infirmary and mentor of Doyle, a pioneer of forensic medicine with great deductive powers. Doyle became his out-patients' clerk and paid tribute to him in the preface to *A Study in Scarlet*: 'his strong point was diagnosis, not only of disease, but of occupation and character.' A letter from Doyle to him states: 'It is most certainly to you that I owe Sherlock Holmes' and Bell's sharp features and aquiline nose were reproduced in the character: 'He was a thin, wiry, dark man, with a high-nosed acute face, penetrating grey eyes, angular shoulders', very like the description of Holmes when he first appears in *A Study in Scarlet*. He even had a deer-stalker hat for birdwatching. Bell could diagnose before patients opened their mouths: 'He would tell them their symptoms, he would give them details of their lives, and he would hardly ever make a mistake.' Doyle noted Bell's 'eerie trick of spotting details' in strangers and likewise practised the deductive parlour trick. Bell, who called Doyle 'one of the best students I ever had', owned Mauricewood House, a grand Victorian mansion at Milton Bridge nine miles south of Edinburgh and his grave can be seen in Dean Cemetery, off Queensferry Street on the edge of the New Town.

Another model for Holmes, and later for Professor Challenger in *The Lost World*, was Sir Robert Christison, professor of medical jurisprudence and an expert on poisons. He carried out a specific experiment in Edinburgh which was later conducted by Holmes at the beginning of *A Study in Scarlet*. Holmes's companion Dr Watson may have been based on Dr Patrick Heron Watson, a colleague of Bell and President of the Royal College of Surgeons who had served in the Crimea, rather than Afghanistan.

Doyle was offered a job with Dr Budd, a fellow Edinburgh graduate, who lived in well-to-do Elliott Terrace at The Hoe in Plymouth, his surgery being at No 1 Durnford Street in Stonehouse, the part of town where Doyle lodged. However, Doyle stayed only a month or two with the charlatan Budd. In September 1882 Doyle took a steamer to Portsmouth, landing at Clarence Pier, intending to set up practice in Southsea, a residential suburb, but he had very little capital. He resided at No 1 Bush Villas in Elm Grove, next to the Bush Hotel and St Paul's Baptist Church, in a property which was bombed in 1941. There is a plaque on the side of Bush House in Elm Grove. Here he had a housekeeper who may have been a model for Mrs Hudson of 221B Baker Street and in time the practice grew a little.

Nevertheless, he would go for a stroll only at night for fear of missing patients, walking miles down to Clarence Parade, crossing Southsea Common and along the seafront to Portsdown Hill or along the shore from Clarence Pier to the spit at Eastney and the entrance to Langstone Harbour. In November 1883 he became a member of Portsmouth Literary and Scientific Society and his social life developed. Dr Watson of the Holmes stories may be based partly on Dr James Watson, a friend and President of the Society.

In August 1885 Doyle married Louisa Hawkins, nicknamed Touie, sister of a former patient, at the 13th-century parish church of St Oswald's in the hamlet of Thornton-in-Lonsdale. At Southsea his interest in spiritualism began. Séances were held at Bush Villas and in 1893 he joined the Society for Psychical Research a month after his father's death. At Portsmouth he also started to study ophthalmology at the Portsmouth Eye Hospital, which had been founded three years before and in 1889 went to Vienna to study ophthalmology.

Also while at Southsea the character of Sherlock Holmes was conceived and first appeared in the novel *A Study in Scarlet*. Other novels written at Portsmouth include the Holmesian *The Sign of Four*, *Micah Clark* and *The White Company*, the latter a historical romance and his own favourite, with a 14th-century setting inspired by visits to the New Forest.

Portsmouth City Museum & Art Gallery in Museum Road has a permanent exhibition entitled 'A Study in Sherlock', with interactive displays and 40,000 items of memorabilia, formerly the collection of the scholar Richard Lancelyn Green, with books, production posters, letters and artifacts. There are also occasional themed guided walks organised by the museum. On Victoria Road South, not far away, was the Temple of Spiritualism to which Doyle donated money after his son Arthur died of pneumonia.

In March 1891 Doyle moved to London and leased No 2 Devonshire Place, between Devonshire Street and Marylebone Road, where he advertised himself as an oculist. He later leased a consulting room and waiting room at No 2 Upper Wimpole Street, round the corner from Harley Street, with its elegant fantail window above the door where there is a plaque, but, he said, he soon found that 'they were both waiting rooms.'

He walked every day from his lodgings at No 23 Montague

Place, (where there is a plaque), off Montague Street in Bloomsbury, facing the back entrance to the British Museum, and waited from 10 am to 4 pm but as no patients appeared he wrote instead. The 'first fruits of a considerable harvest' enabled him to give up the surgery and 'to trust for ever to my power of writing'. 'A Scandal in Bohemia' and 'The Red-Headed League' were written during this period. In May 1891 Doyle was stricken with influenza at home in Montague Place and decided to abandon medicine and write full-time. On recovery in June and with financial success from publication he moved house to No 12 Tennison Road in South Norwood, a suburb on the edge of the Surrey countryside, a three-storey red brick house with 16 rooms, with a study on the ground floor to the left of the front door.

By the autumn of 1892, following the success of *The Sign of Four*, the Sherlock Holmes phenomenon was developing and letters were arriving, addressed to Holmes, and were to do so for the rest of Doyle's life. Following the publication of *A Study in Scarlet* the American Joseph Marshall Stoddart, proprietor of Philadelphia's *Lippincott's Monthly Magazine*, invited Doyle, along with Oscar Wilde, to dinner at the Langham Hotel in August 1889 to commission another Holmes story for the American market where Doyle was already successful as a result of pirate publication. The luxurious hotel, north of Oxford Circus, in Portland Place at the corner of Upper Regent Street, had been a resort of the rich and famous since 1865 and became the setting of three Holmes adventures. Subsequently taken over by the BBC, it reverted to being a hotel in 1991 and has a Conan Doyle Suite. Doyle offered Stoddart *The Sign of Four* which was published the following February and another 12 stories quickly followed, all for the *Strand Magazine*.

Doyle himself solved a mystery at the Langham Hotel. A guest vanished one night leaving behind his evening clothes which he had been wearing earlier that evening, after which neither he nor the luggage was seen again. Doyle said, accurately, that the fellow must be in Glasgow or Edinburgh and leading a restricted social life. Doyle reasoned that he must have left unseen as the foyer was full of returning theatre-goers. If he had travelled the short distance to a local station he would have been seen and so must have gone to a major terminus and only trains for Glasgow and Edinburgh left at that time of night. Without white tie and tails his social life would have been slight.

In 1893, as his wife Louise was suffering from tuberculosis, the Doyles went to Davos in Switzerland. Tired of his fictional character and at the suggestion of English clergymen who were fellow holidaymakers, Doyle disposed of Holmes and his archenemy Moriarty over the Reichenbach Falls at Meiringen, to the east of Interlaken, in 'The Final Problem'. Meiringen now has its own Sherlock Holmes Museum in the basement of the English church on Conan Doyle Place. Doing away with Holmes created uproar and letters from over 20,000 readers cancelling their subscriptions arrived at the Strand Magazine offices at No 12 Burleigh Street off the Strand. Reluctantly Doyle resumed the stories until April 1927 when 'The Adventure of Shoscombe Old Place', the last Holmes story appeared in the magazine.

In April 1893 Doyle had written: 'I am in the middle of the last Holmes story, after which the gentleman vanishes, never never to reappear. I am weary of his name.' He planned to stop the stories after the second series of six: 'I think of slaying Holmes in the sixth & winding him up for good & all. He takes my mind from better things.' Doyle casually wrote in his notebook: 'Killed Holmes' and recorded, 'If I had not killed Sherlock Holmes I verily believe that he would have killed me.' But it was not to be. There were no Holmes stories for seven or eight years, although those already published were lucrative. A stream of requests for Holmes's autograph appeared and gifts were sent of tobacco, pipe cleaners and violin strings. Doyle was forced to admit: 'You will find that Holmes was never dead, and that he is now very much alive.'

In 1897 Doyle had a new home built, partly to his own design, at Hindhead in Surrey, 50 miles south-west of London at the junction of the A287 and A3, where the microclimate was reckoned to be good for Louisa's tubercular condition. For most of 1897 he stayed at Moorlands, a boarding house in Hindhead, while his house was being built. Earlier he had stayed in rooms at No 44 Norfolk Square near Hyde Park while planning the new house. He named the new property Undershaw, a gabled red brick mansion up a long winding drive and set in four acres of wooded land near the crossroads in the centre of Hindhead. They moved into the house in late 1897. At Undershaw Doyle wrote his most famous work *The Hound of the Baskervilles* and other stories. The author's initials are monogrammed on the ground floor doors and stained-glass windows incorporate the family crest and a monograph appears on the wrought iron gate. Unfortunately the 36-room property later fell into disrepair after it ceased to be a hotel but a local trust has secured its future as a special needs school. At Hindhead he met Jean Leckie, daughter of wealthy Scots living in Blackheath, who later became his tour and lecture organiser and eventually his second wife.

Early in April 1901 Doyle and Bertram Fletcher Robinson, a journalist with the *Daily Express* whom he encountered on the boat returning from South Africa who was interested in folklore, took a short golfing holiday on the north coast of Norfolk, staying at the Royal Links Hotel in Cromer. As they played the course and later at the 19th hole, Robinson intrigued Doyle with supernatural folktales of the legendary, fierce, spectral hounds said to roam Dartmoor in his native Devon, a wild area which Doyle had already visited from Plymouth. Doyle considered writing a 'real creeper', he told his mother, not at this stage intending a Holmes story, but did mention the intended title to her before visiting Dartmoor along with Robinson at the end of the month. He told her: Robinson 'gave me the central idea and the local colour' and that 'Robinson and I are exploring the moor over our Sherlock Holmes book.'

The Links country holiday park now stands on the site of Cromer's former Royal Links Hotel. The Gothic Cromer Hall nearby, with its ivy-covered mullioned windows, may have influenced the description of Baskerville Hall and Black Shuck, a giant spirit dog, was said to frequent a track which is now Mill Lane and Sandy Lane. Hill House, the pub in Happisburgh, off the B1159 coast road 12 miles south of Cromer, was visited by Doyle and has a corner devoted to Holmes. The building is the setting for the short story 'The Adventure of the Dancing Men', set in a 'flat, green landscape' punctuated by 'enormous square-towered churches' and the cipher featured in the story appears above the door.

Doyle and Robinson took rooms at Rowe's Duchy Hotel in Princetown, the largest and highest town on the moor, near the famous prison built by French prisoners of war in Napoleonic times. The hotel had been barracks for officers and is now the premises of the National Park's Dartmoor Visitor Centre. From here and from Ipplepen, where Robinson was born, they traipsed around the moor visiting Brook Manor, Grimspound, Fox Tor Mire, a notorious bog two miles south-east of Princetown, Child's Tomb and possibly the hamlet of Merripit. Baskerville coincidentally was the name of the driver of the pony and trap who escorted them at Park Hill. They would hear tales of escaped convicts from the nearby prison.

Doyle wrote to his mother from the hotel that they had gone 14 miles that day over the moors, observing legendary settings in the great wilderness of rock and bog with its ghost hounds, headless riders and devils. It was 'very sad and wild, dotted with the dwellings of prehistoric man, strange monoliths and huts and graves.' They reached Fox Tor Mire and then turned east to Grimspound, where Holmes later hides, and then went back to the hotel, a distance of almost 21 miles. The plot idea and some local colour came from Robinson, but there is no evidence otherwise of collaboration. Doyle returned to Dartmoor for a short walking tour at the end of May, by which time nearly half of the story was already written.

Tales of spectral hounds are not specific to Dartmoor as Black Shuck testifies but a particular Dartmoor legend dating from the 17th century involved Brook Manor near Buckfastleigh on the edge of the moor, owned by the evil squire Richard Cabell who attacked his wife in a jealous rage. She fled across the moor with her faithful hound but was pursued and killed. The hound tore the husband's throat out before dying of knife wounds inflicted by the squire. The dog was said to appear to each new generation of the family. There were also the legendary fiery-eyed black Whist Hounds hunting with the Devil on his headless horse in Wistman's Woods, on the banks of the West Dart river, where they resided by day and hunted by night, devouring the souls of sinners or unbaptised babies, said Robinson, a mixture of Devil and pagan gods stalking the moors.

It has been claimed that Doyle conspired to murder Robinson, who died unexpectedly in 1907, probably of typhoid, to cover up plagiarism of ideas for the novel. Robinson was allegedly poisoned with laudanum because Doyle was having an affair with his wife Gladys, who was blackmailed into poisoning her husband through threats to expose the adultery. A local historian's proposal that Robinson's body in the graveyard at Ipplepen be exhumed for examination was rejected by the parish church committee.

Louisa died in July 1906 and is buried at Hindhead. Doyle, who had been knighted in 1902, married Jean Leckie in 1907 at St Margaret's Westminster, and they had two sons and a daughter. In order to live nearer Jean's parents, who had moved from Blackheath, and to excise the memory of Louisa, Doyle bought a cottage called Little Windlesham in Sheep Plain on the edge of the small town of Crowborough on the A26 in East Sussex. He had visited the town in late 1906, staying with the Leckie family at a house called Monkstown in nearby Lordswell Lane. Doyle extended the cottage into a large family house with 14 bedrooms and five reception rooms and renamed it Windlesham Manor. Doyle lived there until his death, although he also rented a flat near London's Victoria Station at No 15 Buckingham Palace Mansions. A large long-room known as the Billiard Room, with Jean's piano at one end, could accommodate up to 150 guests and was used as a dance floor. There was a wooden summerhouse in the rear garden where Doyle sometimes wrote, although he preferred the first-floor study of the house with its dramatic view of the Sussex Downs.

Here he wrote some Holmes stories and science fiction including *The Lost World, The Poison Belt, The Land of Mist* and *The Maracot Deep. The Poison Belt* is set in Sussex and in it he describes the view from his first-floor study across Crowborough Common towards Rotherfield. The view has since been altered by the planting of trees, but the common and golf course had lots of heather and gorse. Also at Windlesham he wrote *Sir Nigel, Round the Fire Stories, Tales of Adventure* and *Medical Life, The British Campaign in France and Flanders* and books on spiritualism.

Doyle golfed at nearby Crowborough Beacon Golf Club

where he became captain. He continued to play cricket, including playing for the MCC at Lord's against Cambridgeshire, at the age of almost 50, taking seven wickets for 51 runs. He also captained the Authors against Publishers in 1902. On one occasion, returning from the golf club, he walked home in his stockings having given his shoes to a tramp.

Doyle liked to walk around the town. A favourite was up to the Cross by way of Whitehill, down St John's Road to the mill ponds by the forest, then to Heavegate and back home across the A26. He sometimes stopped at the Red Cross Inn, now the Crowborough Cross pub.

Doyle tended to take up causes and even investigate cases and crimes and there was also his greatly increased interest in spiritualism and psychic research which dominated his later years. The family held regular séances at Windlesham in the old nursery next to the billiard room from around 1921. He held séances at Groombridge Place, a 17th-century moated manor house off the B2110 north-east of Crowborough. Doyle was fond of its Drunken Garden. It is said that he subsidised the spiritualist movement with funding of £250,000. The Psychic Bookshop at No 2 Victoria Street near Westminster Abbey in London has a museum of spirit photographs such as once entranced Doyle.

Doyle's belief in fairies and the occult, it has been suggested, was the outcome of a psychosis inherited from his father. Doyle and many others were embarrassingly deceived by the notorious case of the Cottingley fairies. Two girl cousins were playing by the beck behind the garden at No 31 Main Street in a village outside Bradford. Elsie took a photograph of Frances apparently playing with 'fairies'.

Eventually they admitted their fabrication and Doyle and others had to admit they had been deceived. He enthusiastically supported the College of Psychic Studies, housed at No 16 Queensberry Place, off Cromwell Road in south-west London, particularly after the First World War, influenced partly by a desire to communicate with his son John who was killed in action. Six days after Doyle's death 6,000 people were disappointed in attending a spiritualist memorial service at the Royal Albert Hall, hoping to feel his presence in an empty chair provided for him, although the medium in charge insisted there was indeed a 'psychic presence'. Critics have pointed out that Holmes and Watson form a duality of obsession and common sense which was characteristic of Doyle himself.

On 7 July 1930 Doyle collapsed in the hallway at Windlesham. He was propped up in a chair at his request to look out of a window at his favourite view across the Common, but he had suffered a heart attack and soon died. A funeral service took place in the rose garden, with no mourning at his request and he was buried in a grave there, with an oak grave-board, close to the little hut where he worked and where he and Jean took tea together beneath a copper beech tree.

Lady Conan Doyle lived on there until her death in 1940 when she was buried in the garden beside Doyle. On the sale of the estate in 1955 both bodies were exhumed and re-interred in the churchyard of the 13th-century Norman Church of All Saints, near the small central green at Minstead, three miles north-west of Lyndhurst, off the A337 in the New Forest and not far from his second home, Bignell House. The grave is beneath a large oak tree on the south side of the graveyard. Windlesham Manor is now a private residential care home.

Bignell House had been bought in 1925 following Jean's desire for a quaint, thatched cottage by a stream and Doyle had been fond of the area since his time at Southsea. In 1889 he stayed at Emery Down near Lyndhurst, renting a woodland cottage and grew to love the area. Bignell House was an early Georgian property with a croquet lawn on the edge of Bignell Wood at Wittensford near Minstead, one of the loveliest villages in the New Forest. From 1925 the family divided their time between Windlesham and Bignell House, but in 1929 its thatched roof caught fire. It was restored but the Doyles abandoned living there. Locals suspiciously linked this with Doyle's spiritualism and in 1960 new owners felt that they had to exorcise the spirit of Doyle.

In 1992 a plaque was unveiled by Doyle's daughter on Montargis Terrace in Crowborough and in 2001 a statue by local sculptor David Cornell was erected by the town council at Cloke's Corner, the central crossroads in the town.

The Sherlock Holmes House Museum at No 239 Baker Street in London, beyond Melcombe Street, where a plaque identifies it as Sherlock Holmes's address, reconstructs the famous sitting room at No 221B, as described in the stories, together with costumed staff, waxwork figures, reconstructed rooms, assorted possessions and a shop. There was no such number in the street at the time Doyle invented the address and the continuation of Baker Street above Marylebone Road was called Upper Baker Street. Renumbering took place in 1930. The museum building dates from 1815, a long narrow townhouse which was indeed lodgings from 1860 to 1934. It is presumed that No 221 was the number of Mrs Hudson on the ground floor who dealt with visitors. It is generally accepted that the original of the famous residence was towards the lower end of the street on the western side, now occupied by Marks and Spencer's store. This was No 21, then the private residence of a friend visited by Doyle who eventually changed the number to avoid annoyance.

A block of luxury apartments straddles the actual 221B address where the former Abbey National Building Society building once stood at No 215-229, on the corner of Melcombe Street. A window display included a statue and backdrop of various characters. Since letters for Holmes constantly arrived at that site a member of the public relations staff was given the role of Secretary to Sherlock Holmes and responded formally to correspondence. Credulous inquirers were reminded that Holmes had retired to Sussex to keep bees. Children who wrote to the address received a gift pack, badge, leather Sherlock Holmes bookmark, set of commemorative stamps and a booklet explaining the society's connection. Holmes's reconstructed sitting room from the 1951 Festival of Britain was transferred from the Abbey National building in 1957 to the Sherlock Holmes pub in Northumberland Street. No 239 now bears the number 221B and houses the museum.

A bronze statue of Holmes by John Doubleday, wearing a deerstalker at Reichenbach Falls where he fought to the death with Moriarty, sits on Marylebone Road beside the entrance to Baker Street Underground station. Inside the station familiar silhouettes on ceramic tiles greet the traveller. Further down Baker Street, on the opposite side to the museum, the Sherlock Holmes Hotel uses Holmesian themes with memorabilia in its public areas and a luxury Baskerville Suite, Reichenbach Suite, Moriarty's Restaurant and Dr Watson's Bar.

The Langham Hilton Hotel, built in heavy Italianate style in 1865, where Doyle met his American publisher, features in several of the stories and provides a sumptuous Victorian atmosphere.

The Sherlock Holmes pub in Northumberland Street, near Charing Cross, at the junction with Craven Passage, is filled with Holmesian memorabilia over two floors. Doyle's face and name are engraved on the windows and there is a plethora of playbills, together with cinema and television stills showing actors who have played Holmes and Watson with encased exhibits, including a head of the Baskerville hound, a coiled cobra recalling 'The Case of the Speckled Band', Victorian police whistles, poison bottles, magnifying glass and a picture of Mrs Hudson whose name is also enshrined above the food area. There is a bust at the window and soil from beside the Reichenbach Falls. Upstairs behind glass is a recreation of Holmes's study, originally made for an exhibition at the 1951 Festival of Britain, with book-lined walls and assorted artifacts, including Holmes's pipe, violin and deerstalker and a model of the detective. The bar serves a Sherlock Holmes Ale.

The London Walks company provides an escorted walk entitled 'In the Footsteps of Sherlock Holmes' and Scotland Yard, interestingly, has a computer nicknamed 'Holmes'.

Doyle preferred his historical, science fiction and romances, but these works have been overshadowed by the phenomenal popularity of the detective stories and the cult status of Holmes. The stories have been translated into over 50 languages and used in other media including film, radio, television, cartoons, comic strips, ballet and advertising.

STORYTRAIL: *The Hound of the Baskervilles*

THE MAIN CHARACTERS
Sherlock Holmes, the distinguished detective.
Dr Watson, his companion.
Dr James Mortimer, native of Devon.
Sir Henry Baskerville, heir to the estate of the late Sir Charles
    Baskerville.
Mr and Mrs Barrymore, servants at Baskerville Hall.
Selden, a convict escaped from Dartmoor prison.
Jack Stapleton, a naturalist.

The famous tale is set in London and Devon, the metropolitan
setting on the face of it being more safe and secure. As in so
many of the tales, at the beginning of the story Holmes and
Watson are visited in their rooms at Baker Street by someone
pleading for help, the Devonian Dr Mortimer who arrives with
a tale of mysterious events surrounding the recent death of Sir
Charles Baskerville.

Later the suavely attired Holmes and Watson stroll along
Oxford Street and Regent Street as they shadow Dr Mortimer
and Sir Charles's son, Henry. Further down Regent Street
Holmes and Watson are in turn followed by a mysterious hansom
cab containing the naturalist Stapleton wearing a false beard.

The Northumberland Hotel, where the fictional Henry
Baskerville stays after arriving in England, is at No 10
Northumberland Street, now the Sherlock Holmes pub. Here
Stapleton purloins Sir Henry's boot to let the hound get his
scent. Publicans have suggested that Holmes and Watson customarily visited the pub when going to the Turkish baths opposite.
Some claim the hotel where the detective first met Sir Henry
was based on another in the same street, the Grand, the
Metropole or Victoria. In Craven Street, which could be reached
by Craven Passage, was the site of the Craven Hotel, since
demolished, the model for the Mexborough Private Hotel. An
art gallery in Bond Street and Waterloo Station also feature in
the story. Stanford's, the noted mapsellers and travel book spe-
cialists at No 26 Cockspur Street at Charing Cross, is mentioned

in the novel, although it is now at Long Acre in Covent Garden.

The 365 square miles of the rolling granite uplands of Dartmoor with its prehistoric atmosphere had a 'grim charm' according to Doyle who emphasises the sinister bleakness and the threat of a convict escaping from the notorious prison adds to the terrors of treacherous bogs and an archetypal beast.

Doyle explored and wove local moorland landmarks and names into his narrative. Fox Tor Mire, reputedly the largest in Dartmoor, lies at the end of a country lane going south from the B3212 in the centre of Princetown. Three miles away at the end of the lane is Whiteworks, an abandoned 19th-century tin mine of the sort more commonly found in Cornwall. From here the mire stretches a mile-and-a-half to the south and half-a-mile in other directions. A 'false step yonder means death to man or beast' at the point where Seldon the convict signals across the mire from Fox Tor. (A tor is a tower-like hill with a granite top.)

Watson sees a pony sink into the mire and later it secures the murderer's fate. An unmarked footpath traverses the centre of the mire, linking isolated hillocks, as in the story, but safer is a route west to firmer ground where a medieval stone cross indicates a safer path once used by monks crossing the open moor.

Doyle combines Fox Tor Mire, where it was known that prisoners and ponies had been swallowed in the ooze, and Grimspound Bog to become his fictional Great Grimpen Mire. The neolithic Grimspound, with its circular hut foundations, cairns and tumuli, between the B3212 and Widecombe in the Moor, may be the most complete bronze age village in England, with burial chambers, stone circles and menhirs, but also mines and quarries since ancient sites, such as at Grimspound, were sometimes commandeered by tin miners.

The hamlet of Merripit near the prison provided a name for the fictional Merripit House. Bovey Tracey could have been a model for Coombe Tracey (the name combe, a valley, is ubiquitous in the West Country). The name of the convict Selden was borrowed from that of a brutal prison warder. Baskerville Hall appears to be on the site of the Whiteworks cottages facing across the mire. Princetown is moved to another location.

Holmes and Watson climb Black Tor, a tor of that name lying

a little south of Princetown and another elsewhere. High Tor and Foulmire are fictitious, although Dartmoor has a Higher Tor and Higher White Tor along with Fox Tor Mire. Bellever and Vixen Tor exist, the former not far from Princetown. Lafter Hall is fictitious, but there is a Laughter Hole Farm on Dartmoor. Yew Alley of the novel is partly inspired by the Dark Walk at Stoneyhurst College, part of the grounds in Doyle's day which was frequented by smokers and, as in the story, having a gate and a section leading to rougher ground associated with mists and the supernatural.

Watson's description of his first approach to the moors clearly reflects the route from Ashburton station into the heart of the moors, by old tin miners' roads and bridges to the old stagecoach route traversing the moor between Exeter and Plymouth. The fictitious village of Grimpen, just to the north of Baskerville Hall, recalls Postbridge on the B3212 and Holmes's hiding place clearly recalls Grimpound. Baskerville Hall is invented, but its moor-gate is typical of Dartmoor properties, an entry to the wilderness and the avenue of trees forming a tunnel, with saplings planted on top of a stone wall and left to seed.

The clinical Holmes, combatting irrational superstitions, does not appear in six chapters and then suddenly appears as the Man on the Tor. Doyle emphasises the atavistic power of the dog:

> A hound it was, an enormous coal-black hound, but not such a hound as mortal eyes have ever seen. Fire burst from its open mouth, its eyes glowed with smouldering glare, its muzzle and hackles and dewlap were outlined in flickering flame.

Yet it has been said that Holmes is the real hound of the Baskervilles, since he is, in effect, tracking the bloodhound.

TOURIST INFORMATION
AND VISITOR ATTRACTIONS

Edinburgh and Lothians Tourist Board
  3 Princes Street, Edinburgh EH2 2QP
  Tel: 0845 225 5121
Surgeons' Hall Museums
  Royal College of Surgeons, 9 Hill Square, Edinburgh EH8 9DW
  Tel: 0131 527 1711/1600
The Sir Arthur Conan Doyle Centre
  25 Palmerston Place, Edinburgh EH12 5AP
  Tel: 0131 625 0700
The Scottish Literary Tour Trust
  34 North Castle Street, Edinburgh EH2 3BN
  Tel: 0800 169 7410/0131 226 6665
The Edinburgh Book Lovers' Tour
  Tel: 07770 163641
Lewes TIC
  187 High Street, Lewes, BN7 2DE
  Tel: 01273 602000
Groombridge Place Gardens & Enchanted Forest
  Groombridge, Tunbridge Wells TN3 9QG
  Tel: 01892 861444
Ashburton TIC
  Town Hall, North Street, Ashburton TQ13 7QQ
  Tel: 01364 653426
National Park Visitor Centre
  Tavistock Road, Princetown PL20 6QF
  Tel: 01822 890414
Portsmouth TIC
  Clarence Esplanade, Southsea PO5 3NT
  Tel: 02392 826722
Portsmouth Museum TIC
  3 Museum Road, Portsmouth PO1 2LJ
  Tel: 02392 483448
Ivybridge TIC
  Watermark, Erme Court, Leonards Road, Ivybridge PL21 OSZ
  Tel: 01752 897035
Okehampton TIC
  3 West Street, Okehampton EX20 1HQ
  Tel: 01837 53020

5

Rowena Farre

THE MYSTERIOUS AND reclusive Rowena Farre (1921–79), pen name of Daphne Lois Macready, was born in London, daughter of Brigadier General John Macready and Marguerite Mary Milling. When she was aged two her father moved to Hong Kong and four years later was posted to Singapore and later India. From there Farre was sent back to England. At this stage she may have been in the care of an aunt Miriam, a Scots-born schoolteacher living and working in the Home Counties, who retired from teaching and took her niece, aged ten, to live in Sutherland in the far north of Scotland where she appears to have received no formal education.

Farre claims to have spent years thereafter wandering through Britain and studying a seal colony in Iceland. In 1942 she was a WAAF on a radar station in Pembrokeshire, followed by taking a course, which she did not complete, at a London art school and then more travelling.

At the time of publication of her bestselling *Seal Morning* (1957) she was living with gypsies and her publishers were unable to trace her to hand over royalties. Gypsy life is reflected in her second book *A Time from the World* (1962) after which she disappeared to Australia, India and elsewhere. She returned to Hong Kong and India, recounted in *The Beckoning Land* (1969), her last book. She was fascinated by eastern mysticism and sought out a guru in the Himalayas, moved into a cave nearby and set herself a strict regime of meditation and abstinence.

Her death announcement in *The Times* stated simply that she was the daughter of Brigadier General John Macready of Hythe, Kent. Her cremation was private and the brief obituary recorded that she had been estranged from her family since 1953. She had died in Canterbury and was buried in the family crypt in St Mary's Cemetery, Kensal Green, London.

The publication of *Seal Morning* took the reading world by storm with five reprints in five years and immense popularity in Europe, America and Japan. The account of a girl's childhood in a remote part of the Highlands of Scotland, with a feeling of a free childhood in a wild, beautiful place, was considered enchanting by critics and readers in general. It was admired for its honesty, sincerity and depiction of a Highland idyll and yet it has never been clear to what extent the work is fictional. Farre shunned publicity and interviews and there is no indication in her subsequent books about this period of her life, and, some evidence of inconsistencies. She concealed her real name, was secretive and a known fantasist. At boarding school she never mentioned her seven years in Sutherland. It is difficult to imagine the legal requirement of formal schooling being avoided.

The mystery of the location of the house in *Seal Morning* has continued to intrigue. A television version in 1986 transposed the work to East Anglia. Attempts to identify the spot at the time of publication were thwarted by her having disappeared to live with gypsies and no interviews took place. The croft presumably lay well inland from Brora and Helmsdale, probably between Strath Brora and Ben Armine, a wild area with few settlements. A retired gamekeeper was convinced the location was at Gobernuisgach and an estate manager thought she had spent six weeks in a tent on the Gordonbush estate beside Loch Brora. Dalbreck, a shepherd's cottage on a path to Ben Armine, has also been suggested and a ruined cottage at Cnocan in Strath Skinsdale. There is another Cnocan far up Strath Brora, beside the River Brora. It is difficult, however, to find any nearby lochan as in the story. Understandably, some say the work is largely autobiographical while others are sceptical. Lairg, which she mentions, is on the railway line, at the southern end of Loch Shin and to the north of the area she described are the B871 from Kinbrace to Bettyhill and B873 by Loch Naver.

In *The Beckoning Land* Farre recounts travels in Asia, including Mauritius, Ceylon, Hong Kong and the Himalayas and her

quest for spiritual fulfilment. She talks of childhood and self discovery as she lived with her parents in Mount Austen Barracks
in Hong Kong, her father at that time being a junior army officer. She is scathing about having parents in name only and their
lack of affection. At the conclusion she has retreated to a
Himalayan cave as a disciple of a guru.

She declared that her family originated in the Highlands of
Scotland, but in the 17th century, for unknown reasons, her half
of the clan left for Ireland, settling in the Dublin area. Her great
grandfather was William Charles Macready (1793-1873), the
noted actor-manager of the Covent Garden and Drury Lane
theatres. She notes that he overtook Edmund Kean as the most
distinguished actor of his age and toured Europe and the USA.
Farre's grandfather was the youngest son of William Macready
and became a noted London surgeon. There is evidence to suggest that she was of Romany stock and the pen-name Farre may
have been chosen because of the gypsy name Fa (sometimes
Farre). Coincidentally there is a village called Farr in north
Sutherland which was the end-point of her adolescent trek
described in *Seal Morning*.

Kirk Yetholm in the Scottish Borders, home to Scotland's
biggest gypsy population, is where the king and queen of the
gypsies lived in the Gypsy Palace (a cottage which is available to
rent). Memorabilia of them can be found in the Border Hotel
and Plough Hotel in the twin villages of Town and Kirk
Yetholm.

STORYTRAIL: *Seal Morning*

THE MAIN CHARACTERS
Rowena, the storyteller.
Miriam, aunt to Rowena.
Mr McNairn, a local shepherd.
Mr and Mrs Fraser, crofting neighbours.

Although there has always been a sense of mystery about where in the Scottish Highlands the storyteller resided, she is nevertheless quite clear: she says the mountainous Ben Armine range lies to the west, to the east are the Knockfin Heights [north-east of Kinbrace, the railway line and the A897] and Cnoc Coire na Fearna. Much of the area comprises deer forest, she says, with the rivers Black Water and Skinsdale and their tributaries. To the north lies the Borrobol Forest, through which flows the River Free and further north a series of lochs, including Loch a'Chlair and Baddanloch. She points out that 'forest' here does not mean trees but uncultivated, usually hilly or mountainous country given over to deer and other game. On the map the only names are of river, loch and hill without a clachan or township. Above and east of the croft lies Cnoc Cille Pheadair, to the west of Balnacoil and the Black Water.

Cnocan, one settlement of a number of that name, is a ruin on the River Skinsdale, with a lochan a little uphill of it and Borrobol Forest to the north-east. Loch Baddanloch is to the north, with the River Helmsdale flowing out of it and Loch-nan Clar to the west. The Black Water flows into the River Brora above Loch Brora at Balnacoil and the River Skinsdale flows into the Black Water about four miles above Balnacoil.

Farre climbs from Strath na Seilga, which is the strath of the Black Water, where Ben Armine lodge lies and climbs to Creag Mhor, to the north towards Ben Armine itself with Gorm-Loch Mor to the right. Somewhat lost, Ben the dog leads her home through mist by the River Skinsdale – she was five miles from home.

At one point she describes tinkers camping by their lochan who head for Lairg the following day. When aunt Miriam is going to visit friends in Argyll the narrator says that she drove her down to Lairg in the trap, yet the descriptions imply that the croft is nearer Rogart station. The road to Strath Brora is alongside the river and near the station.

When she is older she makes an expedition through the wilderness stretching northwards from the croft some 30 miles to the mouth of the Strathy Water. A good road crosses this country midway from Kinbrace to the Naver valley but she says that she did not wish to go as far east as Kinbrace. She explains that she followed the River Skinsdale and headed through the Borrobol Forest, then north to a road. Lochs Baddanloch, Chlair and Nan Cuinne were to her left. She crosses the road, the B871 and camps close to Loch Leum a Chlamhain [Loch Druim a' Chliabhain], Ben Griam Beg to her rear.

On the third day the land is flatter. From the northern end of Loch nam Breach she follows the Uair which runs into it and is a tributary of the Strathy Water. At the junction of the Uair and Strathy she follows a track by the Strathy Forest and by the fifth day has arrived at the mouth of the river. That evening she pitches her tent near Strathy Bay. Going north from the croft she would surely reach the B871 at Badanloch Lodge, then fork right off that road after three miles before Garvault Hotel by a track skirting the slopes of Ben Griam Mor. Her subsequent route is somewhere between the B871 through Strathnaver and the A897 through Strath Halladale.

The Strath, or valley, of Kildonan contains numerous ruined brochs, ancient beehive shaped dwellings, together with cairns and souterrains. This is part of the Flow Country, comprising flat, deep, wet, peat blanket bog, the largest such area in Europe, a desolate but evocative area. The Flow Country Visitor Centre, where maps and guides can be obtained, is in the isolated station building by the railway line at Forsinard and includes a display by the Royal Society for the Protection of Birds.

The Ferrycroft Countryside Centre in Lairg has displays related to Sutherland's landscape, wildlife and history. The Strathnaver Museum in Bettyhill in Sutherland tells the story of the Highland Clearances, crofting life and the Farr stone. The poet Rob Donn, the celebrated bard of Reay, a favourite of the crofter Mr McNairn, is buried at Balnakiel near Durness on the north coast of Sutherland.

TOURIST INFORMATION
AND VISITOR ATTRACTIONS

VisitScotland Inverness iCentre
    36 High Street, Inverness IV1 1JQ
    Tel: 01463 252401
Heritage Centre
    Coal Pit Road, Brora KW9 6LE
    Tel: [seasonal] 01408 622024
Falls of Shin Visitor Centre
    Achany Glen, Lairg IV27 4EE
    Tel: 01549 402888
Ferrycroft Visitor Centre & Information Point
    Ord Place, Lairg IV27 4TP
    Tel: [seasonal] 01549 402160
VisitScotland Durness iCentre
    Sango, Durness IV27 4PZ
    Tel no: 01971 500905
Strathnaver Museum
    Clachan, Bettyhill KW14 7SS
    Tel: [seasonal] 01641 521418

6

Lewis Grassic Gibbon

JAMES LESLIE MITCHELL (1901–35), who used the pseudonym of Lewis Grassic Gibbon, was the youngest of three sons of James McIntosh Mitchell and Lillias Grant Gibbon. He spent his first six years at a lonely croft house, now derelict, rented with three fields at Hillhead of Seggat, Auchterless, between the A947 and B992 about five miles south of Turriff in Aberdeenshire.

He was clearly a gifted child but his lack of interest in farming when local children were largely reared for farm work led to estrangement since Mitchell was quiet and bookish. It is said that his mother sheltered him in a corn stook wrapped in a plaid and he believed that the noises and smells of the land entered his subconsciousness.

Gibbon's father was not brutal but in other respects resembled John Guthrie of *Sunset Song* and Mitchell had more affection for his mother. Around Seggat, which became Segget in the novel *Cloud Howe*, were abundant primitive remains, including stone circles, tumuli and cists, which caught the boy's imagination and encouraged an interest in the growth of civilisations. He attended school briefly at Auchterless before the family spent a year in Aberdeen in 1907 and in the spring of 1908 they took a lease on the croft of Bloomfield, two miles above Arbuthnott on the B967 in the Howe of the Mearns in Kincardineshire.

The Mitchell farm was a little east of the Bervie Water which flows from the Grampian mountains to the North Sea at Inverbervie. To the north and west lay the moor and woodland of the Reisk plantation, felled during the First World War, part of the Arbuthnott Estate whose mismanagement is referred to in *Sunset Song*. It was difficult to make a living from the croft beyond mere subsistence.

The three Mitchell boys walked the two miles to the village school where Alexander Gray became schoolmaster in 1913 and recognised Gibbon's ability. Arbuthnott School, which Mitchell attended from 1908-16, is now adapted for use as holiday homes. Revd Peter Dunn, the minister of the 13th-century Arbuthnott parish church, provided him with books and was a model for Revd Gibbon in *Sunset Song*.

The Grassic Gibbon Centre, celebrating the author and the community, is by the roadside on the B967, near the church and school, midway between the A90 and the A92 and contains exhibition space, archives and photographs. The church, where Mitchell's ashes are buried in a corner of the churchyard, is signposted from the Centre. Further down the B967 on the left is the Reisk road over the hill to Gibbon's childhood home. The house of Greenden, used as a title for a short story, lies empty off to the right. Bloomfield is on the left at the roadside, Mitchell's home from 1908-17 and the model for Chris Guthrie's house in *Sunset Song*, although not identical. Fifty yards further on is Hareden, the neighbouring croft where the Middletons lived, whose daughter Rebecca became Mitchell's wife, herself quiet and withdrawn. Her father, easily recognised as a model for Long Rob of the Mill in *Sunset Song*, had little time for books.

Drumlithie is across the busy A90 in the lee of the Grampians. Barras is on the road to Kinneff, reached by turning right at a junction beyond Bloomfield. There are splendid views of the Howe of the Mearns from higher ground looking towards the sea, where there are standing stones, about a mile from the A92 en route to the Centre. A path leads to the derelict mill and Bervie water.

Mitchell's passion for the past was developed around Arbuthnott. He searched for tools and weapons of ancient peoples and noted the standing stones and perhaps a prehistoric camp, a more recent ancient chapel, castle remains and a saint's well, all within a two mile radius of Bloomfield, what he called 'the ancient library of the hills'. In an essay entitled 'The Land' in the collected work *A Scots Hairst* he saw in his imagination the arrival of the first people to Kincardineshire seven thousand years before, coming 'over Auchendreich ... through the whins and heather.'

Mitchell was not interested in becoming a schoolmaster or minister, seeing literature instead as a form of escape. If destined for farm work he would have left the local school at age 13 but spent an extra year preparing for high school. His school essays at Stonehaven reveal his precocity, the desire to turn his back on drudgery and a tendency to blame 'society' for his disaffection. He entered Mackie Academy in 1916 but was unsettled, seen as an outsider and absconded. He was accused of overt socialism and upset his family. His formal education over, he was thereafter self-educated. He became a junior reporter on the *The Press & Journal* and returned home only as a visitor and stranger.

In the autumn of 1917 he lodged at No 5 St Mary's Place in Aberdeen where there is a plaque. He was now openly socialist and in 1918 as a young reporter attended a founding meeting of the Aberdeen Soviet and was temporarily on its Council. Rebecca visited him during his eighteen months in Aberdeen.

In February 1919 he moved to Glasgow and became a reporter on the *Scottish Farmer*, lodging in Hill Street in a property which was partly a brothel where he was appalled by the squalor of the city. This was the period of Red Clydeside and Communist sympathies and he donated money to the cause, obtained by claiming false expenses which led to his dismissal.

After attempting suicide he went home but there was animosity with his family and in August 1919 he joined the Royal Army Service Corps and went to the Middle East for three years, but, like Ewan Tavendale in *Sunset Song*, Gibbon felt dehumanised by the military experience. He corresponded with Rebecca, who was now in London working in the Civil Service.

On discharge in March 1923 Mitchell moved to London. Still unsure about his vocation, he joined the Royal Air Force in August that year. Remaining impressed by ancient cultures, a supposed trip to Mexico to study Mayan civilisation during certain 'missing months' appears to have been an invention. He trained in Uxbridge and then went to RAF Kenley in Surrey. He was reunited with Rebecca in 1924. A first short story, set in Egypt, appeared in 1924, won a competition and was published.

In June 1925 Rebecca and Mitchell returned home for two weeks spent with his parents but relations were uneasy. Nevertheless there were two subsequent visits within five years. After marriage in August 1925 he bought a typewriter. Rebecca, the model for Chris Guthrie, the protagonist of *Sunset Song*, along with himself, was pregnant and soon lost her job and almost the baby also. In July 1926 he was back in London and with the RAF at Uxbridge and rented property in Angel Road in Harrow. He failed to gain publication and there were several moves including to RAF Upavon in Wiltshire, followed by two years' residence in a flat in Percy Road in Hammersmith. In 1928 a short story and a book on exploration were accepted for publication and he left the RAF in August 1929. In December 1931 he moved to Welwyn Garden City, off the A1(M) in Hertfordshire and wrote feverishly. Between 1931-4 some 15 books were the result of frenzied writing. Rhea Sylvia, a first child, was born.

Travel stimulated an interest in exploration and archaeology leading to his *Hanno, or the Future of Exploration* (1928) and a short story collection *The Calends of Cairo* (1931). His first novel was *Stained Radiance* (1930), followed by *The Thirteenth Disciple* (1931), *Spartacus* (1933) and the notable *A Scots Quair* trilogy, comprising *Sunset Song* (1932), *Cloud Howe* (1933) and *Grey Granite* (1934), collectively published in 1946 under a pseudonym based on his mother's maiden name. He also wrote a biography of the explorer Mungo Park (1934) and *The Conquest of the Maya* (1934) which appeared under his own name. *Scottish Scene* (1934) which comprises essays and short stories, written with Hugh MacDiarmid, showed cynicism on Mitchell's part for the life of the land. His writing career would last only six years, being cut short by illness.

The family stayed at Edgar's Court, then at No 107 Handside Lane, Mitchell's final home where *A Scots Quair* was commenced in the spring of 1932 and published in August. *Cloud Howe* appeared the next year. In the late summer of 1932 he went home and his mother was upset at the negative image of the community in her son's writings.

A son Daryll was born in March 1934 and Gibbon's last visit

home was in September when he visited Alexander Gray, his inspirational old teacher, retired in Echt, a village at the junction of the B9119 and B977, 12 miles west of Aberdeen and wrote the last few pages of *Grey Granite* on Barmekin Hill above the village. In December he contracted gastritis and had a perforated ulcer, leading to peritonitis and he died the following February. He was cremated at Golders Green and his ashes were placed by the wall in the far corner of Arbuthnott Kirkyard soon afterwards, the gravestone in the form of a carved open book. Rebecca was left a virtually penniless widow.

STORYTRAIL: *Sunset Song*

THE MAIN CHARACTERS
Chris Guthrie, an adolescent girl in north-east Scotland.
John and Jean Guthrie, her parents.
Chae Strachan, Long Rob of the Mill, neighbours to the
    Guthries.
Ewan Tavendale, boyfriend of Chris and later her husband.
Revd Gibbon, Revd Colquhoun, parish ministers.

The female main character of the story is a thinly disguised version of Gibbon, who unsentimentally pictures the sunset of an age where there is beauty and harshness in the land with its enclosed communities, the cycle of human life and seasons. The mismanagement that destroys it takes many forms. War denudes the land of both trees and people and the remaining parts of the trilogy move to the grey unromantic industrial cities of the Depression. (Gibbon fantasises further about uncorrupted societies in some of his short stories and science fiction.)

This first part of a trilogy reflects the life of Chris Guthrie, beginning in girlhood on her father's farm, through a first marriage, the effects of the First World War and depression in the farming community. Love and hatred for the ancestral land and the way of life, which Gibbon himself felt, are expressed in fine, lyrical prose. The story describes the life from girlhood of a crofter's daughter, first at home as a girl, then as wife of the young crofter Ewan Tavendale. The main body of the novel comprises four sections, Ploughing, Drilling, Seedtime and Harvest, representing the cycle of change in the farming year and providing metaphors for a universal pattern of change and in the life of Chris.

Events are seen as the outcome of what is sown, just as in the land, so it is in Chris at home and at school, with her growing sexual awareness and with Ewan Tavendale in marriage and pregnancy, the birth of young Ewan and the war. The whole is prefaced and followed by The Unfurrowed Field, comprising a Prelude and Epilude, reflecting the anonymous voice of the wider community and the pre-history and history of Kinraddie up to the period after the Great War.

Early in the novel Gibbon vividly describes the Guthries' winter journey, starting in Echt, then heading south over the Slug Road to the new croft, recalling the Mitchell family's own move from Aberdeenshire to Kincardineshire.

The trilogy celebrates the Mearns parishes of Arbuthnott and neighbouring Glenbervie, together with other parts of Aberdeenshire, particularly the neighbourhood of Echt. The map provided for the first edition of *Sunset Song* has the fictional village of Kinraddie straddling the Laurencekirk to Stonehaven road, the 'turnpike' north of Arbuthnott, with Kinraddie House (the Meikle House), the Mains (home farm), church, manse and Blawearie above the main road, with the Grampian Mountains as a backdrop. South of the road lie Upperhill, Cuddiestoun, Netherhill, Peesie's Knapp, the Mill, Pooty's and Bridge End, the latter beside the Denburn. Two lots of standing stones are indicated, one above Blawearie. Netherhill recalls the real Nether Craighill on the way to Bloomfield, with a Bridgend nearby. The real Arbuthnott Kirk (of St Ternan), partially of the 13th century, which Gibbon attended, has stained glass windows in the chancel, representations of Faith, Hope and Charity which are considered 'not very decent-like in a kirk' by the anonymous folk narrator. The real villages of Drumlithie and Auchenblae are north of the A90 road although Gibbon places his Auchinblae south of Kinraddie. The fictional mill town of Segget, which is reminiscent of Brechin, Gibbon places between the two villages. The city of Dundon, called Duncairn in *Grey Granite*, is on the coast north of Kinneff, near which is Todhead Point, the foghorn of which Chris hears from her window on misty nights.

Continuing on the Reisk road around two miles beyond Bloomfield and east of Nether Pitforthie farm lies the flat topped Bruxie Hill with a lochan which Gibbon transfers to a location above Blawearie. A mile south of the hill, near Cotbank of Barras, are the overgrown remains of a stone circle which he enlarges and places beside the loch.

The figure on the hillside surveying the community and meditating about the past as an outsider is based on Gibbon himself and the circle of Blawearie Loch is a constant presence in the novel. Chris retreats to the standing stones when married and expecting her first child and after a quarrel with her husband and various other occasions. At the standing stones also Chae has a vision of a primitive man fleeing the invading Romans, as simple people face imperialist assault. In the Epilude, eight years after the novel's opening, an anonymous folk narrator surveys the parish from the standing stones and notes that bigger farms have been created for commercial profit. Meanwhile there is now another stone edifice, a war memorial representing loss and the sunset of an age and epoch where a way of life with its intense relationship with the land is gone.

Chris's secondary education at Duncairn recalls Gibbon's at Stonehaven. Chris hates harshness and cruelty but there is an escape route in being clever at school and she is encouraged by her teacher to approach higher education: 'Two Chrises fought for her heart and tormented her', as she is repelled by what she knows is part of her. Inheritance after her father's death means that she could continue to pursue her education.

Chris goes with Ewan to Dunnottar Castle, on a spectacular cliff projecting on to the sea, off the A92 south of Stonehaven and the educated side of her is interested in its history, an impulse not shared by Ewan and yet she feels especially close to him by the sea. Before Ewan leaves for the army and its brutalisation they note a plaque in the castle which emphasises the abuse of ordinary folk, like himself, who may become simply a name on a war memorial. They also visit the 16th-century Edzell Castle with its beautiful gardens, off the B966 north of Brechin, on a day's outing. They clamber among the ruins and examine the crumbling carvings on the walls. Chris responds to the building intellectually, while Ewan is clearly happier on the land.

TOURIST INFORMATION
AND VISITOR ATTRACTIONS

VisitScotland Aberdeen iCentre
    23 Union Street, Aberdeen AB11 5BP
    Tel: 01224 269180
VisitScotland Stonehaven iCentre
    66 Allardice Street, Stonehaven AB39 2AA
    Tel: 01569 762806
The Grassic Gibbon Centre
    Arbuthnott, Laurencekirk AB30 1PB
    Tel: 01561 361668
Montrose Museum
    Panmure Place, Montrose DD10 8HE
    Tel: 01674 673232

7

Kenneth Grahame

KENNETH GRAHAME (1859-1932) was born at No 32 Castle Street in Edinburgh, in the elegant New Town and opposite the castle crag, in what is now the offices of a chartered surveyor, where a plaque, erected before he became known for his most famous work, reads 'Kenneth Grahame of *The Golden Age* was born here' but has recently been altered to refer to his authorship of *The Wind in the Willows*.

His father became Sheriff-Substitute of Argyll in Inveraray and so the family moved to Ardrishaig and rented Annfield Lodge, a large Victorian granite villa on the Tarbert Road, now the Allt-na-Craig guest house, some four miles south of Lochgilphead, overlooking Loch Fyne and near the yacht-filled eastern basin of the Crinan Canal. Two years spent there, mixing with fishermen, led to a love of 'messing about in boats', like his famous animal characters. This playground was the Kintyre coast and length of the canal, described as 'Britain's most beautiful short-cut', across the Kintyre peninsula from Ardrishaig which cuts a hundred miles off the dangerous passage around the Mull of Kintyre. The nine-mile canal with a picturesque towpath and 15 locks was opened in 1801, allowing vessels to reach the Hebridean fishing grounds more easily, but is now used mostly by yachtsmen heading for Scotland's west coast. It is claimed that here Grahame first made his acquaintance with the creatures and riverbanks which inspired his most famous work.

In 1863 the family moved into a new house, Tigh na Ruabh, a red sandstone building which is now the Loch Fyne Hotel on the A83 just south of Inveraray, the major township on the shores of Loch Fyne. After his mother's death in 1864 and due to his father's alcoholism the four children were sent to Granny Ingles, Bessie's mother, aged 60, who lived along with their mother's twin David who was a curate at The Mount, an old shooting lodge near Cookham Dean railway station, on the edge of the Berkshire Downs in the Thames valley between Marlow and Maidenhead. This was a beautiful old house with roses round the door, flowering creepers climbing towards tiled eaves and leaded windows with acres of terraced gardens, lily ponds and orchards; a wonderful setting for childhood games and exploration of the lanes, meadows and the River Thames nearby.

There was a large upstairs room called the Gallery which the children were allowed to commandeer and it became an imaginary city. Beyond the house, gardens and orchard was Quarry Wood, usually considered a source of inspiration for *The Wind in the Willows*, and water meadows running down to the meandering Thames with its reeds and overhanging willow trees. Grahame developed a lifetime love for the stretch of riverbank from Cookham Dean to Pangbourne. As a boy he would go on the river with his uncle David and his passion for 'messing about in boats' was much encouraged. This experience was to be reflected in two best-selling books, full of childhood reminiscence of the natural riverside world, an eternal childhood but with the loss of the father figure, *The Golden Age* and *Dream Days*, published later in the 1890s. The idyll ended after only two years around the time Grahame turned seven. In 1866 an uncle, John, who was guardian to the family pressed them to move to Fern Hill Cottage in Cranbourne, a few miles away. Here there was no great garden for make-believe.

At age nine Grahame went to the prestigious independent St Edward's School in Oxford, founded in 1863, beside the Woodstock Road between St Margaret's Road and Summertown, which Grahame considered awful. Nevertheless, he had the opportunity to roam the city of dreaming spires, the 'good grey Gothic' buildings and 'the cool, secluded reaches of the Thames ... remote and dragon-fly haunted.' He learned to canoe and later became an enthusiastic skuller. He became Head Boy at St Edward's, where there is a memorial window dedicated to him in the school chapel, captain of the rugby XV and passed the examinations for entry to Oxford University.

He was keen to study there, but his uncle John was unwilling to pay for it and so Grahame had to gain employment in the City of London. In 1876 he went to stay at his uncle Robert's house, Draycott Lodge in Fulham (since demolished) and worked in an office in Westminster. He began as a clerk in the Bank of England in Threadneedle Street in January 1879 and lodged in a flat in Bloomsbury Street, the most select district that was still within walking distance of the bank. He enjoyed Old Compton Street and Soho with its restaurants and hints of Mediterranean culture. In 1886 he occupied a top-floor flat off Chelsea Bridge Road at No 65 Chelsea Gardens, which he described as his crow's nest, with a spiral staircase in the manner of a lighthouse and here most of *The Golden Age* was written. He took great pleasure in the closeness to the Thames and would take a steamer to work from Chelsea Pier.

In 1884 Grahame visited the Lizard area of Cornwall where he loved the fishing and contact with the water generally, which renewed his childhood pleasures and he returned there several times. By 1894 he was Acting Secretary at the bank and subsequently moved from his Chelsea flat to No 5 Kensington Crescent. The bank was happy for its staff to be creative and Grahame wrote for the 18 years that he was there. In 1903 a customer fired a gun containing blanks at Grahame and then fled, but only into the Director's Library where he was locked in and eventually disarmed by the fire brigade. He claimed he was using the gun since Grahame had produced documents which were bound with black ribbon, usually a sign of impending doom.

Grahame's first published work was *By A Northern Furrow* (1888) and there were articles and stories in papers and magazines, including *Pagan Papers* (1893). Essays appeared in the periodical *The Yellow Book* and in 1895, expanding on his previous *Pagan Papers*, appeared the highly successful *The Golden Age*, 18 stories with a boy narrator concerning a fictionalised family of five orphans in a large country house enjoying closeness to nature and recalling his own experience at Cookham Dean. In 1898 at age 39 he became Secretary of the Bank of England and published *Dream Days* which concerned the same children and was also rapturously received.

A chest infection took Grahame back to Cornwall to recu-
perate and he stayed at Fowey (pronounced 'Foy') and loved it.
Here lived Sir Arthur Quiller-Couch, Oxford professor and novelist, at The Haven and they became instant friends, exploring
together the backwaters and creeks of the charming River
Fowey and estuary. Grahame seemed to be a confirmed bache-
lor but in 1899 married an admirer Elspeth Thompson, who also
hailed from Edinburgh, a bluestocking hostess for her stepfather
in Kensington. The wedding was at St Fimbarrus's Church in
Fowey and after a honeymoon at St Ives Grahame returned to
Fowey and further opportunities to mess about in boats.

The Grahames took a long lease on a house at No 16
Durham Villas in Campden Hill. Alastair, their only child, was
born in 1900, known as 'Mouse' because of his prominent ears;
he also had a congenital cataract in one eye and a bad squint in
the other. Grahame doted on the child who was spoilt and his
bad moods were suppressed by bedtime stories which started on
the night of his fourth birthday and were elaborated over three
years.

The Grahames then moved to a villa at No 16 Phillimore
Place, off Argyll Road from Kensington High Street, from 1901
until his retirement from the Bank in 1908. Here he wrote most
of *The Wind in the Willows*, published shortly after his retirement
and a plaque there acknowledges his residence.

In 1906 the family rented The Hillyers and then lived at
Mayfield, now called Herries School, in Cookham Dean, the
setting for Grahame's childhood Eden, a short distance from
Quarry Wood and the popular Winter Hill viewpoint where the
Thames can be viewed. Mouse loved Cookham Dean and here
enjoyed more bedtime stories from his father. The accounts of
Ratty, Mole, Badger and especially Toad, whose excessive behaviour was similar to Alastair's, were designed to sooth the boy. (In
Kensington Gardens where Alastair walked with his governess a
keeper had made a complaint about his kicking and slapping of
other children.)

There were further visits to Fowey for the pleasures of the sea
and river. A boat trip up the river is said to have inspired Mole's
river picnic with Rat as the animals' adventures were continued

in letters to Mouse, who was sometimes at the seaside without his parents. The first written evidence of the tales is in a letter to Alastair on holiday in Littlehampton in Sussex of 10 May 1904: 'Have you heard about the Toad?' The story continued in a series of 15 letters, preserved by his governess, between May and September 1907. The Grahames were holidaying at the Green Bank Hotel, by the harbour in Falmouth, which in its hallway displays copies of two of the letters to Alistair regarding Toad, Rat, Mole and Badger. Four months later *The Wind in the Willows* was published. Critics did not react favourably but the work sold well, with four editions in six months and has remained a bestseller.

The first edition of the work was not illustrated except for a frontispiece by Graham Robertson, a Scottish friend who was an artist and playwright, which displayed three beavers and an otter playing in a waterfall. The famous illustrations by EH Shepard in a much later edition were distinctively anthropomorphic, whereas the illustrations in the previous three editions treated the animals as puppets. The original manuscript of *The Wind in the Willows* is in the Bodleian Library in Oxford.

In 1910 the Grahames moved to Boham's, a Tudor-brick thatched farmhouse which can still be seen (although a housing estate now occupies much of its farmland) at Blewsbury, a village on the northern edge of the Berkshire Downs, a few miles south of Didcot on the A417 and 12 miles from Oxford. They stayed here for over ten years. Kenneth spent his days in solitary tramps across the Berkshire Downs. During this period Mouse was at Rugby School, followed by Eton, and then Oxford University. Tragically he suffered a breakdown in May 1920 and took his own life on the level crossing at the far side of the Port Meadow in Oxford. Elspeth subsequently sold all Mouse's clothes at a jumble sale.

The Grahames, struggling to come to terms with their loss, travelled in Italy and elsewhere in 1923 and restlessness resulted in more travel throughout much of the decade. In 1924 they bought and spent their last years at Church Cottage, close to the Thames and the main Oxford road at Pangbourne, the Berkshire village on the A329. A decorative sign at the north end of the main street acknowledges

Grahame's presence. The garden at Church Cottage, with its lovely gardens and a grassy amphitheatre may be viewed courtesy of the present owner. Here the brooding Grahame walked almost daily along his beloved Thames and around here Shepard, the celebrated illustrator, did the famous drawings which appeared in the 1930 edition of *The Wind in the Willows*. The illustrations were so successful that this stretch of river has become for many the assumed home of Mole and Rat. Shepard visited Grahame who told him of locations for the story: 'he told me of the river nearby, of the meadows where Mole broke ground that spring morning, of the banks where Rat had his house, of the pools where Otter hid, and of the Wild Wood way up on the hill above the river.' Grahame claimed the book was 'only an expression of the simplest joys of life', not an allegory.

In 1930 AA Milne memorably wrote the highly successful theatre version of the work *Toad of Toad Hall*, which has become a stage classic. Two years later Grahame died at Church Cottage and his funeral was at St James the Less in Pangbourne next door. Willows gathered from the river that morning were used as church decorations; thereafter his body was transferred to the Saint Cross Churchyard in St Cross Road at Holywell in Oxford and laid beside his son. The epitaph reads:

> To the beautiful memory of Kenneth Grahame, husband
> of Elspeth and father of Alastair, who passed the river on
> 6 July 1932 leaving childhood and literature the more
> blest for all time.

The River & Rowing Museum in Henley-on-Thames, off the A4155 near the station, has a permanent walk-through attraction, a Wind in the Willows experience, using the famous original illustrations by Shepard. You can walk along the River Bank, through the Wild Wood, into Badger's house and follow the adventures in all 12 chapters. Using theatrical and audiovisual techniques with models, lighting and sound you are delightfully transported into the world of Mole, Water Rat, Badger and Toad.

The Ditty restaurant, formerly the Ducks Ditty, in Reading Road in Pangbourne has attractive décor which reflects themes of *The Wind in the Willows*.

The Bank of England Museum, on Bartholomew Lane off Threadneedle Street in London, highlights Grahame in the Victorian-era exhibit in the Rotunda Room, including a first edition of *The Wind in the Willows*. The Bank of England is mentioned in Grahame's introduction where 'these lovely visions of childhood' are contrasted with the workaday world of the bank.

An audio-visual Wind in the Willows Attraction, using Shepard's illustrations, was based in the Peak Village outlet stores at Rowsley on the B6012, off the A6 between Bakewell and Matlock in Derbyshire, but has since closed.

STORYTRAIL: *The Wind in the Willows*

THE MAIN CHARACTERS
Mole.
Water Rat.
Mr Badger.
Toad of Toad Hall.
The Wild Wooders, predatory stoats, weasels and ferrets.

Although written for young readers and an acknowledged classic of children's literature, the story has perennially appealed to adults partly because of its fine description of natural beauty in river, wood and meadow. As timid Mole, gregarious Water Rat, Badger and Toad have their jolly adventures they are humanised as eccentric Edwardian gentlemen while the animal perspective is retained and their interaction is amusing. The egotistical Mr Toad is finely comic, with his enthusiasm for motor cars and impetuosity which lead to imprisonment and escape only to find his residence Toad Hall occupied by stoats and weasels. The usurpers are repelled with help from Toad's friends, after which he promises to turn over a new leaf. Strolling peacefully in the Wild Wood of a summer evening is resumed and Water Rat returns to 'messing about in boats'.

It has been noted that there is in the story an undercurrent of fear of social class upheaval and apprehension about the new fangled invention, the motor car. The characters yearn for the quiet life which is unchanging like the wind through the willows. Meanwhile there is a lyrical celebration of the simple joys of life in home, good food and company, the beauties of nature and a timeless pastoral landscape with hints of darkness among the dappled sunlight.

Cookham Dean, Grahame's childhood home by the Thames and where he later lived with his wife and child, has a particular claim to being a source of settings for the story. Toad, he said, was based on a local bigwig who drove his car around sounding his horn. Quarry Wood 'up the hill' to the north of Bisham Woods is considered to be the model for the Wild Wood. Grahame is known to have spent many hours walking among the ancient beech trees and on the Thames-side path.

Various old manor houses claim to be the model for Toad Hall, notably Mapledurham House, the huge mansion built in 1588 by the Blount family on the opposite bank of the Thames from Pangbourne, with parkland running down to the river. The house, four miles north-west of Reading, may be reached by the A4074 Reading to Oxford road, from Pangbourne by the ancient Whitchurch Bridge and the B4526, or by boat from Reading leaving from Caversham Promenade behind the Holiday Inn hotel.

The Thames-side Harleyford Manor, off the A4155, upstream from Marlow and on the opposite bank from Cookham Dean, built around 1755 for a Lord Mayor of London and now offices, is another possible model for Toad Hall. Nearby are Hurley weir and various islands, a setting which is very likely to be the spot where Mole and Ratty, on the river at night searching for baby Otter who has gone missing, approach a weir with islands below it and have a beautiful and mystical experience.

Fawley Court, just outside Henley, designed by Christopher Wren in 1663, with Robert Adam interiors, which can be glimpsed from the river, is another possible Toad Hall, as is Hardwick House, a gabled Tudor mansion on the Oxfordshire bank nearer Pangbourne with the tree-clad slopes behind being a possible Wild Wood.

Lullebrook Manor at Odney in Cookham is also said to be the inspiration for Toad Hall since its owner, Colonel Francis Ricardo, was the first person in the village to have a motor car, a yellow Rolls Royce.

The boathouse of Coombe End, near Goring-on-Thames in Oxfordshire, an imposing pile left to the National Trust in the 1930s but not open to the public, is reputed to be the inspiration for Ratty's home.

Historic Reading Gaol, a massive red-brick castellated building, may be a model for the prison where Toad is incarcerated. It is said to be a 'grim old castle'. The railway and canal he travelled along may be the mid-19th-century line built by Brunel, parallel to the Thames and Kennet and Avon Canal which meets the river at Reading.

Grahame's repeated visits to Cornwall, where he often rowed on the charming River Fowey, are considered to be a source of settings for his story. The 'Wayfarers All' chapter includes a description by Sea Rat of a typical 19th-century Cornish sea port, based surely on Fowey: 'the little grey sea town I know so well, that clings along one steep side of the harbour.' The description of an inlet 'like a little land-locked lake' with green turf sloping down to either edge and 'with a weir' and a 'grey-gabled mill house', may refer to the Old Sawmills at Golant, upstream from Fowey.

The Wild Wood is said to be inspired by Ethy Wood and the thickly wooded slopes of Lerryn Creek, three-and-a-half miles north-east of Fowey off the A390. Sir Arthur Quiller-Couch, the local scholar, academic, novelist and fellow sailor, who is probably caricatured as Water Rat, is commemorated in a granite memorial on Penleath Point.

TOURIST INFORMATION
AND VISITOR ATTRACTIONS

Edinburgh and Lothians Tourist Board
   3 Princes Street, Edinburgh EH2 2QP
   Tel: 0845 225 5121
Heart of Argyll Tourism Alliance
   Colchester Square, Lochgilphead PA31 8LH
   Tel: 07919 360485
VisitScotland Inveraray iCentre
   Front Street, Inveraray PA32 8UY
   Tel: 01499 302063
Allt-na-Craig Guest House
   Tarbert Road, Ardrishaig PA30 8EP
   Tel: 01546 603245
Henley-on-Thames TIC
   Market Place, Henley-on-Thames RG9 2AQ
   Tel: 01491 578034
Mapledurham House, Reading RG4 7TR
   Tel [seasonal]: 01189 723350
The River & Rowing Museum
   Mill Meadows, Henley-on-Thames RG9 1BF
   Tel: 01491 415600
Thames Rivercruise
   Pipers Island, Bridge Street, Caversham, Reading RG4 8AH
   Tel: 01189 481088
Marlow Information Centre
   55a High Street, Marlow SL7 1BA
   Tel: 01628 483597
Abingdon TIC
   Guildhall, Abbey Close, Abingdon OX14 3HL
   Tel: 01235 522711
Oxford Visitor Information Centre
   15-16 Broad Street, Oxford OX1 3AS
   Tel: 01865 686430
City of London Information Centre
   St Paul's Churchyard, London EC4M 8BX
   Tel: 020 7332 3456
Bank of England Museum
   Bartholomew Lane, London EC2R 8AH
   Tel: 020 7601 5545
Fowey TIC
   5 South Street, Fowey, Cornwall PL23 1AR
   Tel: 01726 833616

Falmouth TIC
  11 Market Strand, FalmouthTR11 3DF
  Tel: 01326 741194
The Greenbank Hotel
  Harbourside, Falmouth TR11 2SR
  Tel: 01326 312440

8

Alasdair Gray

ALASDAIR GRAY (b.1934) is the son of Alexander Gray, a First World War veteran and factory worker who operated a machine which cut cardboard boxes. His mother, Amy Fleming, was an assistant in a Glasgow clothing shop who sang in the Glasgow Orpheus Choir. Gray was brought up with a younger sister at No 11 Findhorn Street in Riddrie, off the A80 Cumbernauld Road in the east end of Glasgow. Gray says perfunctorily he was born in a good corporation flat, one floor up, where a living-room window in the gable wall faced Cumbernauld Road. When asked further about his upbringing he said simply that it was all in *Lanark* anyway.

His father was an enthusiast for the outdoors, hiking and climbing, who did voluntary secretarial work for the Scottish Youth Hostel Association but Gray, troubled by asthma and eczema in his childhood, preferred books, comics and films and made great use of Riddrie public library, a treasure house of written and graphic stimulation. Books at home had an intellectual and socialist slant, including the works of Lenin and William Blake.

During the Second World War his father helped set up hostels for munitions workers and he was assistant manager at a munitions factory for a time in Reading, then from 1941-4 manager of a Royal Ordnance Factory residential hostel at Wetherby in Yorkshire with 200 staff. Gray was evacuated with his mother and sister from 1940-6, first to a farm near Auchterarder in Perthshire, where he had his first asthma attack beside a threshing machine, referred to in 'The Oracle's Progress' section of *Lanark*, then to Stonehouse, a small mining town in

Lanarkshire, an experience he used in *1982, Janine*. Here the boy Gray was already writing, his sister a first audience and he sent material to children's magazines and radio programmes. Ruth of *Lanark* is strongly based upon his sister Mora who has said with a smile that her brother had verbal diarrhoea and was exhausting. The picture of Duncan Thaw's parents in Book One of *Lanark* does not give sufficient credit to Gray's real parents. He admits that he was describing his own upbringing until age 17 and a half but making it much more miserable. The settings of Wetherby and Auchterarder Gray transfers to the west Highlands in *Lanark*. *Old Negatives*, his first poetry book, was dedicated to his mother.

At age 11 Gray read a four-minute piece of his own composition on BBC Scotland's Children's Hour. In 1946, of her own initiative, his mother took him to a Saturday morning art class for children at Kelvingrove Museum and Art Gallery where those who attended were supposed to be referred by their schools; he then attended regularly for the next five years.

Of special significance to Gray is the novel *The Horse's Mouth* by Joyce Cary, its protagonist the mural painter Gully Jimson, with vivid description of a Creation mural in a derelict church. This was to fire Gray's imagination and he went on to imitate his hero. William Blake, poet and visionary painter, was another key influence.

During his education from 1947-52 at Whitehill Secondary School, since demolished, he was writing constantly but stricken still by the facial eczema and asthma which caused frightening breathing difficulties, panic and nightmares. With a friend George Swan, who is Coulter in *Lanark*, he walked and talked and biked, but was not sporty and preferred to talk at the literary and debating society at school. A memorable talk was on a hole at Eglinton Toll, south of the city centre, in which dwelt strange creatures. Difficulty in relating to girls was a continuing problem. His school magazine contributions showed his characteristic blend of reality and fantasy, sometimes comically violent. His English master, Arthur Meikle, encouraged and advised him, including drawing his attention to what might give offence.

In 1952 Gray went to Glasgow School of Art shortly after his mother died and specialised in design and mural painting. The second part of the Duncan Thaw story reflects friends at art school and some dealings with staff. There he filled notebooks with detail he planned to use in his 'Portrait of the Artist as a Young Glaswegian', fictionalising personal experience, emphasising Thaw's dourness and inability to attract women.

Gray knew he could not make a living from his art in Glasgow in the 1950s, when most of his fellow students became teachers. In the summer of 1954 he worked on his novel instead of seeking temporary employment. By the end of the vacation he had written what is chapter 12, 'The War Begins' and the hallucinatory episode at the end of chapter 29, 'The Way Out'. His models were Franz Kafka's *The Trial* and *The Castle* whose cities recalled 1950s Glasgow: old, industrial and grey, where the stranger finds he is in hell and the ordinary meets the supernatural in the dark world of *Lanark*.

Gray should have graduated in 1956 but spent part of several summers in hospital because of eczema and asthma and so took another year to finish his diploma, after which he gained a scholarship trip to Gibraltar.

Between 1952 and 1958 Gray frequented the downstairs smoking room in the former Brown's Tearoom on Sauchiehall Street. This was a haunt of art school students until the owners resented them gathering there as they rarely spent much money. A contemporary said that Brown's was Gray's territory, a home where he sat and worked, sketching those who came in. Thereafter, until his marriage in 1961, Gray's main social centre was a café above the nearby New Cine picture house.

While an art student, Gray completed a mural in the ground floor of a house in Belmont Crescent in Glasgow's West End, headquarters of the Scottish-USSR Friendship Society. The subject was the horror and aftermath of nuclear war, involving a crucifix and the theme of man's inhumanity to man. His mural work on the ceiling and side wall on the theme of creation at Greenhead Church of Scotland in Bridgeton in the east end of Glasgow is that which features in the 'Genesis' chapter of *Lanark*. The church was demolished not long after to make way for a new road. Another lost mural was in a synagogue in Belleisle Street near Cathcart Road in Crosshill, on the south side of the city. Only photographs remain of that work. Working without payment at Greenhead Church he believed would get him noticed. Its detail, reflecting the Seven Days of Creation with God in human form, appears in Book Two of *Lanark*.

From 1958-62 Gray worked intermittently as an art teacher, then as scene painter for Glasgow's Pavilion and Citizens' theatres and, like his protagonist in *Lanark*, painted murals in places of worship. He taught at Wellshot and Riverside Secondary Schools but was irritated by administration and child management which brought back memories of his own frustrations at school. He was unsuccessful in gaining a publisher for Book One of *Lanark* as an independent work in 1963. He completed Book Three by the mid-1970s and linked it to Book One with 'The Oracle's Prologue'. Books Two and Four were completed together, the whole being finished by the end of July 1976. After publication in 1981, following 30 years' gestation, he was able to sustain himself financially and *Lanark* had a powerful effect on the Scots literary scene. Innovatively, he designed the four books himself, a trend in his subsequent publications: artwork interacting with text, dust jacket, title page and frontispiece. His influences, he said, were Blake, Dante and Bosch.

In the summer of 1961 Gray was working at the Edinburgh Festival Fringe Cabaret Club, experience he would fictionalise in *1982, Janine*, where he tells the story of an idealistic company of left-wing actors putting on a show. Gray was employed as a singing performer and scene painter at a venue, since demolished, in the West Bow. Happy to lose his shyness in performance, Gray did cabaret turns, including 'how to build your own rhinoceros' and singing melodramatic Victorian ballads. It was during this that he met Inge Sorensen, an 18-year-old Danish student nurse whom he sketched. They married six weeks later but divorced in 1970.

The couple resided with Gray's father at Findhorn Street, but after her return from a visit to Denmark, probably already regretting the hasty marriage and sceptical about her husband's prospects, Inge threatened to leave unless new accommodation was found. They moved to No 158 Hill Street, later No 160 in

Garnethill near the School of Art, the move to the downstairs flat next door necessitated by the landlady being murdered by a lodger. The property was demolished in 1968 to make way for an approach road to the Kingston Bridge. In 1963 Inge fell pregnant and a son Andrew was born. Gray was drawing welfare benefits at this time and Inge started having affairs.

Gray's poems had appeared in magazines from the early 1960s and a short story 'The Star', based on HG Wells's 'The Crystal Egg', had been published by Collins as early as 1951. From the mid-1960s there was some success with more than 20 plays for radio, television and stage performed. *The Fall of Kelvin Walker* was an early broadcast piece. At the end of 1968 the Grays were eventually offered a council flat on the third floor at No 39 Kersland Street in the Hillhead district.

Two years later Gray left his wife and son and lodged at nearby No 6 Turnberry Road in Hyndland. In 1976, when his son went to boarding school and his wife to work in England, Gray returned to Kersland Street. In 1977 he was appointed writer-in-residence at the University of Glasgow, although the breakthrough with *Lanark* did not take place until 1981, when Stephanie Wolfe Murray, founder of the Edinburgh publisher Canongate, took notice. Later Gray became joint Professor of Creative Writing at Glasgow University with James Kelman and Tom Leonard.

Struggling financially Gray led a bohemian existence in the flat in Kersland Street, sharing with several folk, some of whom were artists, until 1989. There were further radio and television plays, but he struggled to meet deadlines and control his alcohol consumption. After the publication of *Lanark* he had a relationship with Bethsy Gray, a Danish jeweller, for some eight years. In 1991 he married bookshop assistant Morag McAlpine having met her two years before in the Ubiquitous Chip in Ashton Lane off Byres Road a few minutes walk from her flat in Marchmont Terrace. (His first wife died in 2000 and Morag was to follow in 2014.)

There are noted murals by Gray in the back stairwell of the Ubiquitous Chip dating from the late 1990s, for which he was paid in meals. There is another mural downstairs in the restaurant and nearby at Òran Mór, an entertainment and arts centre in a former church building where Byres Road meets Great Western Road. Òran Mór means 'The Great Music' or 'The Grand Melody' in Gaelic. Here Gray continues to paint a striking celestial ceiling mural, one of Glasgow's largest pieces of public art, best seen from the gallery in the upper level of the auditorium. It was commenced in October 2003, picturing a star-speckled night sky for which he admitted using *The Ladybird Book of Stars*. The work, still in progress with the help of assistants, spreads from the ceiling to the side walls of the auditorium, down a spiral staircase to the entrance porch. Gray has also written for the centre's lunchtime series of short plays known as, 'A Play, a Pie and a Pint'.

Some of Gray's paintings and drawings can be seen at the People's Palace, a social history museum on Glasgow Green. This work was commissioned in 1977 when Gray was employed for a year under a Job Creation Scheme to produce a series of snapshot portraits of contemporary Glasgow and its people, 30 in all, nine of them writers, with settings including the industrial landscape, East End streetscapes, a West End flat and a pub.

Murals of 'Jonah and the Whale' and 'Black and White Earth Mother Phantasmagoria' are to be found in a private dwelling at No 10 Kelvin Drive in Glasgow's West End and 'Falls of Clyde Landscape' at the Riverside Bar and Restaurant, formerly the Tavern, at Kirkfieldbank on the A72 near Lanark. This work is four feet high and 25-feet long and is the only real landscape painted by Gray outside Glasgow. A mural by Gray entitled 'The Book of Ruth' can be seen in Greenbank Church on the B767 Eaglesham Road in Clarkston on the south side of Glasgow. There are murals also at the Palace Rigg Nature Reserve in Cumbernauld, off the A80 north-east of Glasgow, reflecting an ecological cycle and at the Abbot House Local History Museum in Dunfermline in Fife. Here between 1994-6 he worked on 'The Thistle of Dunfermline's History', providing the 'whole history of Dunfermline' in one room, reflecting hundreds of years with over 80 portraits. Self-portrait drawings are in the Scottish National Portrait Gallery in Queen Street in Edinburgh. Rodge Glass, Gray's hero-worshipping biographer, concedes that Gray's art is not important except when accompanying his books, providing a political statement or adorning the wall of a pub.

In the 1970s he became part of an important writers' group fostered by Philip Hobsbaum of Glasgow University and continued with plays for radio and television, painting and murals. Other works followed, including the comic surrealism of *Unlikely Stories, Mostly* (1983) and *1982, Janine* (1984), the sado-masochistic musings of Jock McLeish, which Gray considered pornographic. Mischievously he included fictional poor reviews on the cover. The novel of his play *The Rise of Kelvin Walker* appeared in 1985 along with *Lean Tales*, shared with Agnes Owen and James Kelman. There was then a volume of poetry, *Old Negatives* (1989), followed by *McGrotty and Ludmilla*, a political satire set in Whitehall and *Something Leather*, both of which appeared in 1990. *Poor Things* (1992) is a pastiche of the Victorian mystery novel genre and won the Whitbread and Guardian Book Prizes.

Other works include short stories in *Ten Tales Tall & True* (1993), *A History Maker* (1994), set in the Scottish borders in the 23rd century, the romantic novel *Mavis Belfrage* (1996), *A Short Survey of Classic Scottish Writing* (2001). Polemical works include *Why Scots Should Rule Scotland* and *The Book of Prefaces* and further short stories in *The Ends of Our Tethers* (2003) and *Old Men in Love* (2007) followed. *A Life in Pictures* (2010) contains autobiography and his artwork. *Of Me & Others* (2014) is autobiographical and discursive. *A Gray Play Book* (2009) contains collected drama works. *Collected Verse* appeared in 2010 and *Every Short Story 1952-2012* in 2012.

Gray first met his biographer, the Mancunian novelist Rodge Glass, a postgraduate student at Glasgow University, when he was working as a barman in the Curlers Rest pub in Byres Road. Gray does not recall who served him a drink then, but as the friendship developed and Glass's readiness to shadow Gray and be his biographer became clear, Gray allegedly joked that Glass could be Boswell to his Dr Johnson.

With nearly 20 books since *Lanark* Gray has become a grand old man of Scottish letters, eccentric, endearing and frustrating. Around the year 2000 his eczema and asthma returned and he suffered a heart attack and stroke in 2003. Much of 2005 was spent in Gartnavel Hospital where his skin complaint was treated. In 2015 he sustained a fall outside his home leading to seven months in hospital.

STORYTRAIL: *Lanark*

THE MAIN CHARACTERS
Duncan Thaw/Lanark, the principal character/protagonist and his alter ego.
Sludden, ringleader of the café coterie, later Provost.
Gay, partner of Sludden, later a journalist.
Rima, Lanark's girlfriend, later his wife.
Alexander, their son.
Staff of the Institute: Dr Munro and Professor Ozenfant.
Marjory, a fellow art school student, girlfriend to Thaw.
Ken McAlpine and Aitken Drummond, fellow art school students.
The Thaws, Duncan's parents, and his sister Ruth.
Ritchie-Smollet, a clergyman.
Lord Monboddo, a regal figure in the Institute.
Nastler, supposed author of *Lanark*.

At a key point in the novel the artist-protagonist Duncan Thaw surveys his native city from a hilltop above Cowcaddens in the 1950s and declares to his friend McAlpine, 'Nobody imagines living here ... If a city hasn't been used by an artist not even the inhabitants live here imaginatively.' Settings, beautiful or bleak, gain an aura when celebrated by the creative artist.

The naturalistic Thaw sections of the novel and the surreal Lanark episodes picture Glasgow and Unthank and reflect Gray's vision of the Victorian city which was the second city of the British Empire, a pre-eminent centre of heavy engineering which, by the time of writing, had become typical urban sprawl with skyscrapers and urban motorway alongside factories, gasworks, clock towers, the Royal Infirmary's cupolas, the Victorian West End and second generation inner-city slums.

In Unthank, like Glasgow of the 1960s, 'old streets between towers and motor lanes had a half-erased look, and blank gables stood behind spaces cleared for car parks.' Gray sees the decline of the city, a version of Glasgow at the time of writing but more grotesque, as symbolic of the decline of the Western world. In the Glasgow of the 1980s, as it happens, after a highly successful advertising campaign, employment in the arts overtook the numbers formerly employed in the Clyde shipyards and tourism blossomed. There is a hamlet of Unthank a few miles from Stonehouse in south Lanarkshire, but the name appears elsewhere in Scotland and England.

Gray offers a nightmare with no sunlight where inhabitants disappear, just as industry has declined on the Clyde, prophetically become a wasteland city. The inner city parallels the real Glasgow, depopulated through dispersal to peripheral housing schemes, new towns and emigration, ridden with apathy and despair and oppressed by the bureaucracy of the Institute. Thaw, the protagonist of Books Two and Three, is reincarnated as a young man named Lanark living in the hellish Unthank, a victim of 'dragonhide', the scaly shell skin which is a metaphor for personal repression.

In the opening pages of Book One we learn that Thaw lives in the middle storey of a council tenement, reminiscent of Gray's Riddrie, across the canal from Blackhill, where, in a strange street, Thaw meets a junk trader with a cart and donkey. The description of streets and factories recalls Gray's childhood near Cumbernauld Road. Thaw walks along the canal path with Coulter, past an iron works on the other side. Nearby is Alexandra Park with its pagoda fountain and golf course. Thaw takes an excursion with Coulter to Cathkin Braes, a noted hilltop viewpoint south of the city, where during the annual trades holidays, the Fair, as factories shut down, a smoke-free city could be observed.

As art students Thaw and Ken sketch at Cowcaddens, to the north of Sauchiehall Street and Thaw sketches the Blackhill Locks on the Monklands canal, built by the pioneer James Watt in 1771 to transport coal, but now desolate and unused. Gray gives the scene an apocalyptic treatment, symbolising the death of heavy industry and deracination of the working class. During the lunchtime break from art school Thaw heads down from the school, on Renfrew Street, to Sauchiehall Street and sketches a tree on Sauchiehall Lane, making it skeletal and transferring it to the tenements and back greens of Riddrie.

The name of the Elite espresso coffee house, where Lanark first appears, Gray took from an ice-cream seller in Riddrie and based it on a café above the New Cine picture house on Sauchiehall Street near Charing Cross. Lanark, an artistic loner, is accosted by Sludden, the manipulative ringleader of a coterie which meets there, who declares that Rima would be a suitable partner for Thaw.

From Lanark's studio at Kelvingrove there is a view up to the fine Victorian Park Terrace. He escorts Marjory home, taking a short cut through the park by a gap in the railings, down an embankment by the fountain, pond and island bridge where an iron candelabra leans on the parapet, then by a fork where there is a monument to the distinguished Victorian writer Thomas Carlyle, over the locked gate and past the university, delivering her to the gate of her professor father's house. Thaw visits a pub off Garscube Road with art school friends and parties in an old lane off Lynedoch Street near Charing Cross.

Glasgow Necropolis, the cemetery adjacent to Glasgow Cathedral, built in 1833 and modelled on Père Lachaise cemetery in Paris, flourished for 70 years and covers 37 acres. More than 50,000 people are buried here with some magnificent tombstones and statues. There are excellent views over the city. (Guided tours are available here and Michael TRB Turnbull's *Glasgow Graveyard Guide* is an essential companion.) Here Lanark notes a glow of light especially from one memorial stone among the ring of obelisks at the hilltop before a giant mouth opens up before him.

When they leave the Institute Lanark and Rima, based upon Margaret Gray (no relation), a friend from the New Cine café, journey by the motorway and then on foot to the Necropolis: 'They looked down a slope of pinnacled monuments on to a squat black cathedral.' Lanark expects to see the dark sandstone tenements, ornate public buildings, the grid street plan and electric tram cars, but instead sees a vast motorway and tower blocks. Ritchie-Smollet leads them down 'past porticoes of mausoleums cut into the hillside.'

They cross where the tributary (the Molindinar Burn) of a river once flowed by the cathedral. They are given bedding downstairs in the cathedral from the roof of which Lanark views the city and sounds the bell after his child is born. From another parapet he hears the din from a traffic intersection and observes the Necropolis whose 'highest monuments were silhouetted against a pulsing glow in the sky.' The lamps of motorway fire engines appear round a curving bridge from the intersection and speed down the gorge between the cathedral and Necropolis.

An apocalyptic last chapter shows us 'the whole landscape tilted like a board' as subsidence and flood threaten the cathedral. Lanark heads for the Necropolis by the bridge over the tributary of the river: 'In the dim cemetery folk crouched on the grass plots or dispersed up the many little paths. From the height of the hill a loudspeaker tells people to keep clear of high monuments.' Buildings are burning, apocalyptically, in the city below and a flood flows down the valley between the Necropolis and cathedral and then recedes.

Earlier, as he goes looking for employment, Lanark passes through the nave of the cathedral and crosses the square outside to a bus stop. He reaches the city's great central square, modelled on George Square, with statues on massive Victorian pedestals and ornate stone buildings. The scene is described later by Ozenfant as, 'A city with a nineteenth-century square full of ugly statues.' One statue has a queen riding side-saddle on a rearing horse.

Thaw's mother's illness means visits to the Royal Infirmary, beside the cathedral, which becomes a model for the Institute, a hellish kind of hospital in the surreal sections of the novel. The later 'Chaos' chapter was inspired by Gray being in the old Stobhill Hospital, off the A803 Springburn Road, two miles north of the cathedral. After his mother's death the funeral purvey is held at the Grand Hotel at Charing Cross, which was removed to accommodate the urban M8 motorway. Her ashes are scattered by the shores of Loch Lomond. Later Thaw heads off to Glencoe where his father is warden in the youth hostel, but walks to Ballachulish instead and stays at a castle-like hotel. Ben Rua is imaginary.

Thaw wades into the sea, drowned literally or metaphorically, becoming immersed into a nightmarish subconscious world as the two narratives are linked, not just by plot, characterisation and theme, but by typographical contrivances.

TOURIST INFORMATION
AND VISITOR ATTRACTIONS

VisitScotland Glasgow iCentre
   Gallery of Modern Art, Royal Exchange Square, Glasgow G1 3AH
Glasgow Necropolis
   Castle Street, Glasgow G4 0QZ
   Tel: 0141 287 5108/0141 287 5064
Òran Mór
   731 Great Western Road, Glasgow G12 8QX
   Tel: 0141 357 6200
People's Palace and Winter Gardens
   Glasgow Green, Glasgow G40 1AT
   Tel: 0141 276 0788
The Glasgow School of Art
   167 Renfrew Street, Glasgow G3 6RQ
   Tel: 0141 353 4500

9

Neil Gunn

NEIL MILLER GUNN (1891-1973), the foremost writer on northern Highland life, was born in a terraced house (where there is a plaque signifying this) lying now below a flyover which traverses the strath, or river valley, of the fishing village of Dunbeath on the A9 as it hugs the coast heading north towards Wick and Thurso. A memorial statue at the harbour depicts Kenn's triumphant fight with a salmon in the novel *Highland River* (1937).

Just north of Helmsdale the A9 twists round and over ravines in dramatic loops to the Ord, or boundary, of Caithness with sea cliffs reaching a height of over 600 feet on what Gunn called the 'grey coast'. The road plunges into wooded Berriedale and six miles further north lies Dunbeath Castle on the headland to the right with the village at the mouth of its strath. Dunbeath was founded to provide work following the Clearances when a local landlord built a harbour in 1800 at the start of the herring boom; nowadays there is only a little inshore fishing for shellfish and lobster.

Caithness, 'that land of exquisite lights' according to Gunn, in the top right-hand corner of mainland Britain, forms a triangle of lowland beyond the Highlands, cut off from the south by mountains that reach the sea after Helmsdale. Two-thirds of Caithness comprise the largest peat moss in Europe, the Flow Country, edged by the mountains Morven and Scaraben which separate the county from neighbouring Sutherland. On the coast are dramatic cliffs, geos (great clefts in the cliffs), stacks (isolated pinnacles formed by erosion) and skerries (outlying islets). There are thousands of breeding seabirds and whale, dolphin and porpoise abound. The coastal plain and the area between the county towns of Wick and Thurso are arable and there are numerous small fishing harbours and ruined brochs, primitive round towers of around 50 feet in diameter, called 'Picts' houses' by the locals; they are in fact much older. As a boy Gunn felt a curiosity for those remote ancestors and felt educated by the landscape: 'the prehistoric boy in a modern strath ... the nut-cracking young savage on his river stone'.

Archaeological investigation, which continues, indicates the possibility of a lost burgh in Dunbeath concentrated on Chapel Hill where there is a cobbled section and market area on a nine-acre site with surrounding wall. There certainly were medieval trading links with the continent of Europe since fragments of German stoneware have been found. The settlement appears to have expanded in the Viking era around the 12th century, a stage on the pilgrim trail to Kirkwall in Orkney and its martyred St Magnus.

On the right off the A9 before Dunbeath lies the 'lost' village of Badbea with its isolated ruins on the bare cliff top and its monument constructed out of stones from one of the original cottages to commemorate around 80 crofters evicted during the Clearances who struggled to survive on this bleak location in the mid-19th century. It was said that both animals and children were tethered by the leg to stop them being blown off the cliffs while parents worked the land or fished.

A steep brae on the old road heads down past the fields of Dunbeath Mains to the stone bridge built by the distinguished engineer Thomas Telford in 1812 over Dunbeath Water. Just up the strath beyond the bridge is a terrace of slate-roofed, two-storey stone houses, including the one where Gunn was born. One of the oldest Scottish clans and possibly of Norse origin, the Gunns were among those affected by the 19th-century Clearances of Kildonan, inland from Helmsdale, pictured in Gunn's *Butcher's Broom* (1934). Removal to the coast coincided with the boom in herring fishing and pursuit of the 'silver darlings' and living off the land for the rest of year. In 1840, 76 boats sailed out of Dunbeath alone, at that time ten times that of Wick and at the peak in the 1860s about 150 boats sailed in the summer season: 'from that small horse shoe bay in the gaunt cliff wall of Caithness, when the fleet, all under sail, left for the fishing grounds in the afternoon or early evening!' All along the east coast of Caithness and on to Helmsdale Gunn evocatively described the sight of:

> ... the crews of hundreds upon hundreds of boats at sea on a quiet evening, after their nets had been shot, taking up, one after another, one of the Psalms of David, until it seemed the sea itself sang and the cliffs and cottages were held in wonder.

In recent times the Dunbeath quay has become largely deserted; its breakwater referred to in *Morning Tide* (1931) along with the old salmon house in the hillside. Gunn as a boy knew the 'harbour solid with boats' just around the time the herring fisheries were dying out.

Gunn's father was skipper of a fishing boat which he bought from the Duke of Sutherland and put through its paces in the bay to the cheers of locals as potrayed in *Highland River*. He lived with his first wife at Balnabruich up the Braemore road and, following her death in 1878, married Isabella Miller of Knockinnon, on the way up to Latheronwheel, her father also a crofter-fisherman. The first of nine children was born south of the village at Balcladach and as the father prospered as a skipper he built the house in the village in the late 1880s. The mother, whom Gunn describes as 'calm and wise' in *Highland River*, was keen that the seven sons should not go to sea. In any case they were born too late for the fishing boom and son James joined the civil service in London, followed by Neil in 1907. Younger brother John became a Chief Inspector of Schools.

An informative storyboard is located just north of the old bridge and downstream by the north bank is the Well Pool where Kenn, the nine-year-old hero, battles to catch the giant salmon. At the harbour a bronze memorial sculpture by Alex Manson of Halkirk pictures Kenn carrying the fish home. A 200-year-old fishcurer's store at the harbour has been refurbished and three Caithness flagstone tablets near the entrance feature past fishing scenes.

The Dunbeath Heritage Centre occupies the former primary school Gunn attended from 1896-1904, a little south of the village, signposted on the A9 and refurbished in 2001. Here there is a bust of Gunn and the Corona typewriter on which his wife Daisy transcribed his manuscripts. Art installations, photography and a unique floor-map in Gunn's former classroom, based on the winding Dunbeath Water, reflect the historical, archaeological and literary landscape, the settings of *Highland River* and *The Silver Darlings* (1941) and images and quotations from Gunn's books are much present. Local guided walks are available and there is a bookshop. Huge photographic prints represent the journey of the river from the remote Loch Braighe na h'Aibhne to the North Sea. On display also is the 1300-year-old Ballachly Stone, unearthed in 1996, and a tableau of three-dimensional figures, including a Norse invader and a herring fisher, represents key periods in local history.

The Light in the North Festival is an annual three-day arts festival which takes place in early November, centred on Gunn's writings, with a programme of talks, dramatic performances, readings, storytelling and discussions, much of it in the Heritage Centre, with ceilidhs, music, community events, tradition and fun. An afternoon of storytelling takes place at the Dunbeath salmon bothy at the harbour.

The strath, a delight for boyhood exploration and a hinterland with mystical qualities, runs by Dunbeath Water to the edge of the moor three miles upstream, lined with lichen-covered birches, hazel, rowans, alders and oaks. Here are rabbits, birds, deer, hares, grouse and berries, nuts and wildflowers. Upstream of the bridge is the Meal Mill which was in use until 1950, with a mill lade to the rear and a sluice across the river to the island. There is a car park near the mill from which it is possible to walk up the strath. Further upstream on the north bank on a mound is the ruined Chapel Hill or House of Peace, traditionally thought to be the site of a monastery. A footbridge crosses the Houstry burn, a tributary of the Dunbeath Water, with a broch, a primitive circular dwelling, the best preserved in the strath, lying on the tongue of land between the two. Another broch further upstream was in good shape when Gunn was a boy and he engaged in his own archaeological dig.

The woods open out in the gorge at the point named Soldier's Leap. Here Ian McCormack Gunn, imprisoned by the Keiths, was allowed to go free if he could jump the gorge which he did successfully. Up the hillside is the track to Tutnagail with its old whitewashed cemetery where there was a pre-Clearances community of some 400 on the bleakly majestic wide-skied moor. From here the view back towards the sea scans thousands of years of man's impact on the land, including now an offshore oilfield. In the Loedebest Wood area there is clear evidence of prehistoric antiquities, chambered burial cairns and the horned long cairn known as Carn Liath. Up the hill to the north of the cemetery a quarry dates possibly from the Neolithic period on the hill called Cnoc na Maranaich, with a standing stone on the summit, where there is alignment with the setting sun and a dip in the hills to the west on midsummer's eve. To the east lie a chambered burial cairn and south of it a well and cap-stoned burial cyst. A series of 40 photographs of Dunbeath strath appears on the award-winning Caithness community web site.

Helmsdale, where *The Silver Darlings* commences, is the first of a series of harbours which developed as fishing communities during the herring boom, with over 200 boats operating out of Helmsdale by the mid-19th century. The single-track A897 road leads west through Strath Ullie to the hamlet of Kildonan, which was decimated by the Clearances; a stone commemorates the crofters' struggle. At Helmsdale a dramatic and evocative bronze statue entitled 'The Emigrants' commissioned in 2004 depicts the plight of a family of victims with the inscription:

> To commemorate the people of the Highlands and Islands of Scotland, who, in the face of great adversity, sought freedom, hope and justice beyond these shores. They and their descendents went forth and explored continents, built great cities and gave their enterprise and culture to the world. This is their legacy. Their voices will echo for ever through the empty straths and glens of their homeland.

On the summit of Ben Bhraggie, above the small town of Golspie, sits the infamous statue of the Duke of Sutherland, instigator of the notorious Clearances in Kildonan and Strathnaver during the 19th century. Further up the coast is the ruined crofting township of Gartymore where there is a monument to the first meeting of the Highland Land League in 1881. The overgrown five-foot-high cairn is inscribed with the names of the four Sutherland men who began the crofters' fightback which resulted in the Napier Report and passing of the Crofters' Holdings (Scotland) Act in 1886 which theoretically put an end to the Highland Clearances.

The Timespan Heritage and Arts Centre in Helmsdale is a local history museum, art gallery, shop and café with a geology garden adjacent to the River Helmsdale and informative displays on the Kildonan Clearances and the later gold rush. A ten-foot-high statue entitled 'The Exiles', sculpted by Gerald Laing and unveiled in 2007 at the mouth of the Strath of Kildonan at Helmsdale, commemorates the people cleared from that area by landowners and their agents. The statue depicts a family in bronze, a kilted man looking forward and the woman looking back at the glen. Those with long memories contrast this statue with that of the former Duke of Sutherland, scourge of the northern glens, on Ben Bhraggie. An identical statue to Laing's is set on the banks of the Red River near Winnipeg, founded by those who left Sutherland in 1812. The stone foundations recall the former homes scattered through the desolate glens as a result of deliberate and voluntary clearance.

One mile north of Dunbeath at Latheronwheel is the Laidhay Croft Museum, a carefully preserved traditional croft house and at Latheron, a little further on, on the A99 to Wick and John O'Groats, just beyond the junction with the A9 which continues to Thurso, is the Clan Gunn Heritage Centre and Museum in the 18th-century Old Parish Church. Here there is a video presentation, archive and shop. Gunn's parents are buried in Latheron Parish cemetery.

From Latheron the Causewaymire road to Thurso crosses the Flow Country where the standing stones at Achavanich and the Grey Cairns of Camster on the minor road to Watten, north of

Lybster, are the kind of primitive remains which appealed so much to Gunn's imagination. The Caithness Broch Centre at Auckengill, between Wick and John O'Groats, describes the Iron Age settlements, some of which are nearby.

Wick, 18 miles north of Dunbeath, was at one time the 'herring capital of Europe', the harbour containing around a thousand herring boats in the 30-year period from 1860, when it was reckoned 12,000 or more locals relied on herring for their daily existence. In 1862 alone 1,122 boats sailed out of Wick. Summer numbers especially were swollen by fishermen and the influx of female fish workers. By the turn of the century stocks had declined and there are now only three yawls (the original herring boats) left in working order in Britain. The *Isabella Fortune*, WK499, is an original vessel lovingly restored by a small band of enthusiasts from the Wick Society, its mainsail advertising the town's Old Pulteney whisky, which describes itself fittingly as the maritime malt. A fine model of the boat by Bob Watt, a retired engineer from Wick, can be seen in the Wick Heritage Museum which has a photograph from 1865 of a thousand boats in the harbour.

The Scottish Traditional Boat Festival, one of Britain's premier sailing events, is held annually in June or July, when an impressive Moray Firth flotilla of over a hundred vessels visits ports around the firth: Portsoy, Buckie, Cromarty, Invergordon, Helmsdale, Lybster and Wick, which has its own Wick HarbourFest, together with music, crafts and a food fair. The *Isabella Fortune* appears at the festival.

The south side of Wick, known as Pulteneytown, was designed by the engineer Thomas Telford and named after Sir William Pulteney, whose name is especially associated with Bath and upper crescents in Pulteneytown are reminiscent of the English city. Construction of the self-contained fishing community began around 1811 and continued until the middle of the century as the fishing boomed. Here a migrant population followed the fishing fleet and Pulteneytown claims to be the world's first integrated industrial community with a business sector of foundries, rope works, sail-makers, chandlers, boat builders, pubs and its own police force. It was said one could walk dry-shod from one side to the other of Wick harbour (its breakwater constructed by the firm of Robert Louis Stevenson's father) across hundreds of boats. The Old Pulteney Distillery, serving an enormous population on its doorstep, used barley brought in by sea and shipped its whisky out the same way. The whisky is sold in a bottle with a bulb at the base of the neck, reminiscent of a pot still. The label pictures the traditional Wick herring drifter. In 1840 Wick had 428 native boats and 337 visiting ones for the fishing; the local minister complained that 500 gallons of whisky were being consumed in a day!

The Wick Heritage Centre, the largest museum in the North of Scotland, near the harbour in Lower Pulteneytown, contains a wonderful collection of exhibits, including an attractive set of tableaux, providing an authentic flavour of Wick during the fishing boom.

The Caithness Horizons Visitor Centre in the Town Hall in the High Street of Thurso has a huge interactive map highlighting places of interest in Caithness from prehistoric times to the present day with audio visual displays. The Waterlines Visitor Centre at the harbour in Lybster reflects the fishing and natural heritage with a boatbuilding workshop and self-operated close-circuit television for observation of seabirds. Gunn said of Caithness:

> You walk out on Caithness, and at once experience an austerity in the flat clean wind-swept land that affects the mind almost with a sense of shock. There is something more in it than contrast. It is a movement of the spirit that finds in the austerity, because strength is there also, a final serenity. I know of no other landscape in Scotland that achieves this harmony that, in the very moment of purging the mind of its dramatic grandeur, leaves it free and ennobled.

Gunn's sister Mary married a doctor named Keiller and settled in St John's Town of Dalry in Kirkcudbrightshire; Gunn went to stay with them in 1904. Here he was tutored by the headmaster of the local school and in 1907 sat the examination for the Civil

Service which he passed and he headed off to London. The autobiographical *The Atom of Delight* describes the two years in London as a clerk at the Post Office Savings Bank at Shepherd's Bush, after which he was transferred to Edinburgh where he worked with the Inland Revenue and had lodgings near the Meadows. While in Edinburgh from 1909-11 he passed the Civil Service examination, hoping to work in Customs and Excise which would take him around the Highlands. Appointment to Inverness in December 1911 was followed by years enjoying travelling and gaining an intimate knowledge of northern Scotland as an Excise Officer supervising whisky distilleries.

In 1921 Gunn was transferred to Wigan in Lancashire for a year. Here he married Jessie Dallas Frew, later known as Daisy, whom he had met in her father's jewellery shop at No 61 High Street in Dingwall, the county town of Ross-shire, where the father was provost. The following spring he was posted to Lybster, a fishing village between Dunbeath and Wick. Here they lived in a house they called Scaraben, on a corner in the main street leading to the harbour, although locals recalled them as being in a house called Yarrow. In 1923 they moved to Inverness with Gunn's appointment as Excise Officer at Glen Mhor Distillery, where he remained until resigning to write full-time.

Gunn's first home was called Moyness, a Victorian villa at No 6 Bruce Gardens, north of the River Ness and right off Tomnahurich Street. The property is now a guest house with rooms named after Gunn's novels. In 1926 after the sale of his first novel he built the bungalow Larachan in Dochfour Drive, off Bruce Gardens and the publication of *Morning Tide* paid off the building loan. From here Gunn walked to his work. The neighbouring distilleries of Glen Mhor and Glen Albyn were at the head of the Caledonian Canal on the Muirtown Basin and a favourite walk of Gunn's was down the canal from Glen Mhor. *Whisky and Scotland* (1935) provides an interesting insight into the industry at this time.

Gunn started to write in earnest around the age of 30 when stationed at Lybster and short stories were soon published. *The Grey Coast* (1936), his first novel, was fairly bleak, reflecting the economic reversal in fishing and crofting. On trips back to

Dunbeath to visit his mother from Inverness he heard stories about his father and others from a retired seaman. Gunn camped up Dunbeath Water at Achnaclyth. *The Lost Glen* (1928) and theatre scripts followed and by early 1930 short stories were collected as *Hidden Doors*, but a three-act play was not well received. *Morning Tide* was chosen for publication by The Book Society. Readers found *Sun Circle* (1933), on the Viking invasion, rather confusing. *Butcher's Broom*, about the Kildonan Clearances, appeared at a time when Gunn was becoming increasingly involved in Scottish Nationalism and a member of the National Council of the Scottish National Party. His house in Inverness became home to a northern nationalist movement.

In 1937 Gunn gave up his salary and pension rights to write full-time. Sadly, the Gunns had a stillborn child around this time. In his non-fictional *Off in a Boat* (1938), subtitled *A Hebridean Voyage*, the novelist describes how he abandoned his post as Customs and Excise Officer and the house that came with his job and bought *Thistle*, a motor cruiser which was 'a boat in doubtful condition' with 'a defective twenty-five-year-old engine.' He journeyed from Inverness to Kyle of Lochalsh, picking up the boat at Duntulm Castle and sailed round Skye, past Dunvegan Head, Loch Bracadale and Portnalong, to the Cuillins. He then continued by the Inner Hebridean islands of Canna, Rhum and Eigg to Arisaig on the mainland, round Ardnamurchan Head into the Sound of Mull to Tobermory. From there he continued to the Ross of Mull, Bull Hole near Fionnphort, Iona, past the Torran Rocks to the Firth of Lorne and Oban, then up the Great Glen through Loch Linnhe by Fort William and lochs Lochy, Oich and Ness, to arrive back in Inverness.

Fine natural description is accompanied by interesting commentary on crofting, fishing, forestry and lairdship in a work which reflected a growing understanding of the sea which he was to use in *The Silver Darlings*.

From September 1938 the Gunns rented Braefarm House, a farmhouse which was their home until 1949, on the hillside facing south below the Hills of Brae in the crofting country west of Dingwall. This was his most productive period: there were short stories, plays, essays, articles, reviews and 11 of his 20 novels, from *Wild Geese Overhead* (1939) to *The Lost Chart* (1949). The house lay three miles along the A834 road from Dingwall to Strathpeffer and half-a-mile up an unmade track with a gradual ascent through farm and croft land to the open moor and hills.

Here Gunn would write in the morning and later walk up the hill at the back, rambles which resulted in 'nature notes' he wrote for *The Scots Magazine* and published as *Highland Pack* (1949). Here is outstanding descriptive writing with a sense of wonder and delight in nature and an awareness of the rhythms of life. The farmhouse is the one in *The Shadow* (1948) and *The Key of the Chest* (1945) is set among the hill farms to the north. Gunn explains that the setting of *The Serpent* (1943) is Ross-shire but the place is 'arranged a bit', although the hill that Tom climbed is 'very like the hill and moor where Daisy and I spent wandering days when we stayed in that part of Ross-shire. I fished in the small Skiach burn while she hunted wild flowers or bathed in a pool.'

Gunn was no hermit writer: he was engaged in public life through membership of a number of boards. There was shopping once a week in Dingwall and sometimes in Inverness, fishing and curling and a jaunt to the Hebrides, Lewis, Bernera and Flannan Isles which he used in *The Silver Darlings*.

In 1950 the Gunns were obliged to leave Braefarm and went to a house called Kincraig, situated on a promontory overlooking the Cromarty Firth and Black Isle beside the busy A9 road between Dingwall and Invergordon. There was little space to walk, just a modest shore path. Here he wrote articles and short stories and *The Well at the World's End* (1951). A little to the north on the B9176 is Struie Hill and his favourite view over the Dornoch Firth, his 'well at the world's end' nearby. In 1951 he sold Kincraig and moved to the isolated Kerrow House near Cannich, off the A831, 30 miles west of Inverness on the way to Glen Affric, with a good stretch of salmon river, the Glass, just a hundred yards away to which he had fishing rights; there was also a suspension bridge across the river. From his house on the bank of the river Gunn would take an evening walk downstream or along the minor road. This was a country house surrounded by acres of woodland particularly described in *The Atom of Delight* (1956). At the same time, official work, including membership of the Crofting Commission, took Gunn all over the north and west.

Bloodhunt (1952) was an interesting thriller, atypical of his other work. There are mystical Celtic elements in *Young Art and Old Hector*, which reflects the relationship of youth and age, and in *The Green Isle of the Great Deep* (1944). In *The Serpent* and *The Drinking Well* (1946), young people go from the Highlands to the city and return to find the sources of true wisdom. *The Key of the Chest* (1945), *The Silver Bough* (1948) and *The Well at the World's End* reflect a growing interest in Zen Buddhism. The final novel *The Other Landscape* (1954) repeats earlier themes, but an indifferent critical reaction to it caused Gunn to stop writing although there were some further radio broadcasts. He published no further novels for the last 21 years of his life.

In 1960 he sold Kerrow House and bought Dalcraig, on a wooded hillock on the northern shore of the Beauly Firth on the Black Isle peninsula, about two miles west of North Kessock by the B9161, at that time served by a ferry, now by the road bridge. Here also Gunn loved to walk along the shore or uphill to the farming country and moor, west towards the mountains and east to where the firth meets the sea. A spot of personal significance was marked by a birch tree with twin trunks which Gunn and Daisy identified as themselves, at a bend in the road where there is a boathouse.

Both Gunn and Daisy were by then in poor health and Daisy died in October 1963, Gunn surviving for another ten years, but having given up writing entirely. He was interred in the cemetery above Dingwall, reached by a sharp left turn uphill on entering the town from the south.

Not far from Gunn's grave is the hill country of his former residence at Braefarm House, above which is a fine monument on a minor upper road celebrating the writer and themes in his writings. The Neil M Gunn Monument, erected by the Neil Gunn Trust in 1987, sits at a viewpoint on the Heights of Brae at a spot which Gunn regularly passed and can be reached by turning right on to Docharty Road from the Dingwall to

Strathpeffer road, then left, parallel to the main road. The monument is flanked by engraved Caithness flagstone tablets with quotations and Pictish and Celtic symbolism, including the great 'Salmon of Wisdom' and the 'Hazelnuts of Knowledge'.

An inscribed stone slab dedicated to Gunn has been laid outside the Scottish Writers' Museum off Edinburgh's Lawnmarket.

STORYTRAIL: *Highland River*
THE MAIN CHARACTERS

Kenn Sutherland, a boy growing up in the coastal northern
  Highlands.
His parents, the father a deep-sea fisherman.
Joe and Angus, Kenn's brothers.

The novel is set largely in Dunbeath Strath along the length of its river from estuary to source. The work is dedicated to Gunn's brother John and celebrates their youthful adventures illustrating different kinds of knowledge – Kenn's name is based upon the Scots word meaning to know. John becomes a scientist while the folk of the community have their own profound knowledge that derives from affinity with nature and authentic local history. The river comes to symbolise his life so that as an adult when he goes on a quest for its source, it conveys meaning which is transcendental.

The debacle between the salmon and eight-year-old Kenn begins the story and is one of the finest natural encounters in fiction. In the Well Pool, half-a-mile up from the sea and at the 'foot of a steep bank by the side the river', he spots a great salmon in the 'long dark pool'. After a magnificent struggle near the neck of the pool, Kenn drags the fish over 50 yards into the grass park and, 'From that day the river became the river of life for Kenn.'

Further downstream there is the harbour with a string of cottages and the sea and the 'wild coast of gaunt headland and echoing cliff'. A footbridge allows the fishermen to get to their cottages. On the way to school Kenn would climb on the parapet of the bridge to examine the pool below. Further upstream there is the broch on a promontory at the confluence of a tributary a mile upriver and the path up through birch wood promises 'adventures towards the source'.

Later the narrator follows his brother and friends on a rabbit-hunting expedition on the edge of a plantation of deciduous trees, taking the cart road by the birch wood that 'covered the winding slope that rose from the flat river lands'. He looks down on the river and wooded island and the sluice for diverting water to the mill lade. The church can be seen beyond the school in the middle distance. He takes in 'This bare, grim, austere Caithness, treeless, windswept, rock-bound, hammered by the sea, hammered, too, by successive races of men, broch-builders and sea rovers, Pict and Viking'. The boys stand by the Broch Pool, afraid to go up the strath because of the threat of game-keepers. An occasional winter salmon can be taken in the Intake Pool with its weir at 'the meeting of the waters' in a wooden glen with a 'quiet, lovely little valley, in its lower reach, with wild roses and hazelnuts'. Later there is a description of the broch.

They cross the footbridge over the tributary and up the strath. Further up there are the ruins of a mill and 'Ahead the sides of the strath slowly converged on a deep, rocky gorge', up to where the 'grey-green flat land had the bare loneliness of a place haunted by peewit and curlew.' There is the Achglas Pool, the Smugglers' Pool and a shallow cave which was used by whisky smugglers.

Early chapters describe the stretch from sea to broch and later the focus is on the falls and strath and then the moors with 'the long, quiet Peat Pool' and 'the source' – of the river and, symbol-ically, of life itself. There is a beautiful description of the vegeta-tion of the moor and its wild flowers where 'the shapely peak of Morven was half veiled in mist'. While the novel is dedicated to John and reflects many of his exploits, the expedition to the source of the river had actually been with his brother Alec.

The river runs through the novel with the sea, the township village at its mouth, the crofting country further up the strath and the lonely Pictish places on the moors along with the river's source. The hunt for the salmon is also the hunt for the source of life, as much for Kenn as for the salmon itself. The fish may be one for the pot in the Gunn household, a forbidden treasure, but it is also the ancient salmon of wisdom. The repeated images of the pools, from the Well Pool at the beginning through a series of others up to the final small loch, reflect spiritual progress for Kenn at each stage. The history he is taught at school does not relate to that of the folk in the strath.

TOURIST INFORMATION AND VISITOR ATTRACTIONS

VisitScotland Inverness iCentre
   36 High Street, Inverness IV1 1JQ
   Tel: 01463 252401
Strathpeffer TIC
   The Pump Room, Strathpeffer IV14 9DH
   Tel: 0845 859 1006
Timespan Heritage and Arts Centre
   Dunrobin Street, Helmsdale KW8 6JA
   Tel: [weekends only in off season] 01431 821327
Dunbeath Heritage Centre
   The Old School, Dunbeath KW6 6ED
   Tel: [seasonal] 01593 731233
Clan Gunn Museum and Heritage Centre
   Latheron KW5 6DG
   Tel: [seasonal] 01593 741700
Laidhay Croft Museum
   Dunbeath KW6 6EH
   Tel: [seasonal] 01593 731270
Waterlines Visitor Centre
   Harbour Road, Lybster KW3 6AH
   Tel: [seasonal] 01593 721520
VisitScotland Thurso iCentre
   Caithness Horizons, Town Hall, High Street, Thurso KW14 8AJ
   Tel: 01847 893155
North Coast Marine Adventures
   Longfield, Dunnet, by Thurso KW14 8YD
   Tel: 01955 611797
John O'Groats TIC
   John O'Groats, Wick KW1 4YR
   Tel: 01955 611373
Caithness Broch Centre
   Auckengill, Keiss, by Wick KW1 4XP
   Tel: [seasonal] 01955 63137

Caithness Seacoast
    South Quay, Wick KW1 5HA
    Tel: 01955 609200
Old Pulteney Distillery and Visitor Centre
    Huddart Street, Wick KW1 5BA
    Tel: 01955 602371
Wick Heritage Centre
    18-27 Bank Row, Wick KW1 5EY
    Tel: [seasonal] 01955 605393

10

James Hogg

JAMES HOGG (1770–1835), known as the Ettrick Shepherd, was second son of Robert Hogg, shepherd and tenant farmer at Ettrickhall in the Scottish Borders and Margaret Laidlaw, who had considerable knowledge of traditional ballads and folklore. Hogg was baptised on 9 December 1770 in the little church of Ettrick, idyllically set about a mile west of the B709 Selkirk to Eskdalemuir road. His father at the time was tenant farmer of the adjacent Ettrickhall. To the east of the church, on the site of the former cottage where Hogg was born, stands the Hogg monument, a neoclassical obelisk set on a plinth and erected in 1898.

Another monument to Hogg, erected in 1860 and subsequently painted over in white, sits in isolation at Cappercleuch on the Moffat to Selkirk road, overlooking the isthmus between St Mary's Loch and the Loch o' the Lowes and depicts the writer clad in shepherd's plaid with his collie dog, Hector, at his feet. On a tablet in his left hand is inscribed: 'He Taught The Wandering Winds To Sing'.

Hogg spent most of his life in Ettrick, part of the once great Ettrick Forest, a royal hunting ground. Drove roads to English markets passed through Tushielaw downstream on the Ettrick Water. The Ettrick and Yarrow Waters flow roughly parallel north–east, past Altrive and Mount Benger, the two properties where Hogg spent most of his adult life and join the River Tweed near Selkirk.

While his literacy improved Hogg also taught himself the fiddle. There was singing, dancing, drinking and a variety of sports: curling, wrestling, running, football and swimming in St Mary's Loch, together with debates and poetry competitions. Hogg was a lifelong Presbyterian and elder of the parish church and, for a time, precentor. His dog, it is said, howled along with the singing of the psalms. Meanwhile a rich folklore of brownies and bogles and sundry spirits was powerful in the local culture. His mother's treasure trove of folklore, song and story was a fine education for Hogg in itself. The maternal grandfather, William Laidlaw, a shepherd who was known as Will o' Phaup, was considered the last man in the region to speak the language of fairies and converse with them.

From Martinmas (11 November) 1786 Hogg worked at Elibank farm near Clovenfords on the River Tweed for 18 months, followed by two years spent at Willensee, a hill farm in Innerleithen parish. From 1790 Hogg spent ten years as a farm servant and shepherd at Blackhouse, a hill farm north of Ettrick and west of the Innerleithen road, owned by relatives on his mother's side, where there was a lot more contact with books and poetic composition. He became known as Jamie the poeter and Poet Laureate of the Fairies. In Edinburgh at a sheep market in the Grassmarket in 1801 he visited John Taylor's printing shop and wrote down seven poems from memory which became *Scottish Pastorals*.

In 1800 he had returned to Ettrickhouse farm to support his father for three years. In 1802 there was the famous visit of Walter Scott on a ballad hunt and the subsequent rebuke of Scott by Margaret Hogg for spoiling the traditional songs by writing them down in what became the famous ballad collection *Minstrelsy of the Scottish Border* (1802–3).

Hogg first visited the Highlands in 1791 when he went to the Trossachs as a drover. In 1800 he went to Spittal of Glenshee in Perthshire with thoughts of renting a farm there. There were subsequent jaunts to the Highlands in 1802, 1803 and 1804 later described in the *Scots Magazine*. The first was via Edinburgh, Queensferry, Kinross and Perth to Glen Garry and by Glenshee to Braemar and Tomintoul. The 1803 route was from Edinburgh to Callander, Inveraray, Fort William, Kinlochewe and Ullapool, to Lewis and Harris and back by Skye and Tobermory. The 1804 trip was via Glasgow, the Crinan Canal and Tobermory to the Outer Hebrides, returning by Fort William, Callander and Edinburgh. A plan to take over a sheep farm on the island of Harris came to nothing.

In 1805 Hogg was taken on as shepherd at the farm of Mitchellslacks in the Lowther Hills, between the A76 and A701 in Dumfriesshire and later that year he agreed to lease the farms of Locherben and Corfardin two years later. In 1807 he had had published *The Mountain Bard* and *The Shepherd's Guide*, a manual on sheep farming which gave veterinary advice. Loss of stock and finance, however, led to him abandoning the agreement and returning to Ettrick bankrupt and in disgrace in 1809.

In 1810 he began fresh attempts to sell his literary wares in Edinburgh, lodging with John Grieve, a hatter on North Bridge, who lived in Teviot Row. He also stayed in a flat on the High Street above the bookseller Peter Hill and later at Deanhaugh in Stockbridge, at that time on the outskirts of the city. In 1814 he stayed at St Ann's Street in the lee of the North Bridge and shortly afterwards at Gabriel's Road, close by at the east end of Princes Street. Later lodgings included Watson's Selkirk and Peebles Inn in Candlemaker Row in the Old Town where he usually hosted a convivial dinner on the night before departure for Ettrick. Quite often he would breakfast with Walter Scott in his house on Castle Street in the New Town. A song collection, *The Forest Minstrel*, was published in 1810 and a weekly periodical *The Spy* came into being, with poems, essays and stories by Hogg and survived for a year. The publication of *The Queen's Wake* enhanced Hogg's reputation considerably while clubbing and drinking nightly cemented another aspect of it.

In 1817 he published *Dramatic Tales* and in 1818 *The Brownie of Bodsbeck; and Other Tales*, his first extended fiction. Other fiction included *The Three Perils of Man* (1822), *The Three Perils of Woman* (1823) and his major work *The Private Memoirs and Confessions of a Justified Sinner* (1824), which made little impact upon its initial, anonymous, publication, yet is now considered a masterpiece. The first volume of his significant song collection *The Jacobite Relics of Scotland* appeared in 1819. He contributed to the famous 'Noctes Ambrosianae' symposia in *Blackwood's Edinburgh Magazine*, which commenced in 1817, the 'Noctes' articles appearing from 1822. The company met in William Ambrose's Tavern at No 1 Gabriel's Road, beside Register House, then at No 15 Picardy Place, near the junction of York Place and Leith Walk.

Early in 1815 the Duke of Buccleuch granted Hogg rent-free occupancy of Altrive Lake farm, later known as Eldinhope, south of the crossroads of the B709 road to Innerleithen and the A708 Moffat to Selkirk road. Hogg replaced the thatch-roofed clay cottage with a stone one while the old building became a stable.

The Gordon Arms, a coaching and fishing inn on Yarrow Water at that junction, was the setting of the final parting of Hogg and Sir Walter Scott in 1830 when the latter was gravely ill and heading home to Abbotsford. Hogg continued to visit Edinburgh periodically. In 1821 he ambitiously leased from the duke's uncle the large farm of Mount Benger, a short distance up the Innerleithen road and moved his own family there in 1824 so that his in-laws could occupy Altrive. However, the lease on Mount Benger was not renewed in 1830 and the Hoggs returned to Altrive. Financial difficulties continued to beset Hogg. *The Shepherd's Calendar* (1829) was a book version of articles contributed to *Blackwood's Magazine*. *Altrive Tales* (1832) was named after his dwelling house, its lease fortunately renewed around this time. *Lay Sermons* and *Familiar Anecdotes of Sir Walter Scott*, his friend and associate, appeared in 1834, the latter in America. Hogg's final publication, *Tales of the Wars of Montrose*, appeared the following year.

Hogg's enthusiasm for sport continued with him being founder and judge of the St Ronan's Border Games at Innerleithen in 1827, an annual gathering, now held in July. At the inauguration archery, rifle shooting and angling appeared along with running, leaping, throwing and wrestling and the day ended with a formal dinner at a local hotel. In 1832 Hogg fell through the ice while curling on Duddingston Loch outside Edinburgh, where the rules of the game were first devised and where there is a little curling museum. He played also on an artificial rink at Cameron's Inn in Peebles.

On 31 December 1831 Hogg arrived in London for a three-month stay, having sailed on the steamship the *Edinburgh Castle* from Leith and hoping that contacts with editors and publishers would lead to further publication. He was a great social success, and had a dinner in his honour at Freemason's Tavern in Holborn. Through overeating during this sojourn he became fat for the first time in his life. He lodged at Waterloo Place in Pall Mall with James Cochrane who, with fellow Scot John McCrone, planned to publish Hogg's *Altrive Tales* and all his fiction, but ran into financial difficulties and published the first volume only, by which time Hogg had returned home. At a dinner at the Tontine Hotel in Peebles in August 1834 Hogg stated,

> I gaed to Lunnon, and was received there as never ither man was received in this warld. I was made a member o' seven learned societies. I got free tickets sent me for a' the theatres, exhibitions, and every ither thing ... I dinna ken how many clubs I'm a member o'.

By the autumn of 1835 Hogg was frail, suffering from 'water in the chest'. Nevertheless he climbed a hill with his son to survey his beloved Ettrick, went shooting on the moors and rode to visit the Laidlaw relatives at Blackhouse. He fished the River Tweed at Innerleithen and walked to Cameron's Hotel and played bagatelle, but suffered paralysis and was transported back to Altrive where he was watched over by family and his friend since boyhood, Alexander Laidlaw of Bowerhope and Tibbie Shiel, who had been a servant in his mother's family and whose inn at the head of St Mary's Loch was well known to Hogg. He died of liver failure. Tibbie memorably said: 'Aye, Hogg was a gey sensible man, for a' the nonsense he wrat.'

Hogg's grave is in Ettrick churchyard where other family members are buried, the site surrounded by mature trees. An exhibition on Hogg, formerly housed in Aikwood Tower near Ettrickbridge, then at Bowhill House, was installed in the former Ettrick primary school, near his birthplace, in 2013.

STORYTRAIL
The Private Memoirs and Confessions of a Justified Sinner

THE MAIN CHARACTERS
George Colwan, Laird of Dalcastle.
Rabina Orde, his wife.
George Colwan, son of the Laird and Rabina.
Robert Colwan, brother of the above.
Revd Wringhim, clergyman, probably father of Robert by
    Rabina.
Arabella Logan, housekeeper to the Laird.
Gil-Martin, demon associate of Robert.
Bell Calvert, sometime prostitute and witness to the death of
    George Colwan.
The Editor, enlightened figure who pursues the story of suicide.

The imaginary Dalcastle, known also as Dalchastel and Bargrennan, probably lies in the Scottish Borders, although some suggest a location north-west of Glasgow. There are no explicit local references to the Borders in the story until Robert Colwan, demon-driven, heads from Edinburgh towards the English border and his suicide.

    Much of the action takes place in Edinburgh, beginning with the interruption of George Colwan's tennis match by his sinister brother. The game played would be real (royal) tennis, since lawn tennis had not yet been invented and there was a court at the east end of Canongate, near the Palace of Holyroodhouse, in a building which burned down in 1771. The winners of the match are to enjoy dinner and wine at the Black Bull Tavern where the company proceeds, pestered by Robert who tries to enter the tavern with them. At the instigation of the landlord he is arrested by the town guard. His father, Revd Wringhim, comes from a house at the back of the Canongate, vowing vengeance on the company at the Black Bull where a mob has gathered and a window is broken. The Black Bull, it is said, is in a small square halfway between the High Street and the Cowgate. There was a Black Bull Inn in Fleshmarket Close in the 19th century adjacent to Cockburn Street on the north side of High Street and others of the same name in the Grassmarket and Leith Street. There was also a tavern called the Bull Cellar in Bull Close, demolished in 1859 to make way for Cockburn Street. Later in the story George, leaving the Black Bull drunk and heading for a *bagnio* (brothel) on the opposite side of the street, has an encounter which leads to his murder.

The following day the tennis party is again disrupted by Robert and they switch to cricket on the links, probably at Bruntsfield, better known even then for golf. Going to the High Church of St Giles on the High Street, George is again bedevilled and again at Greyfriars Church near the Grassmarket and in the gallery of Parliament House, the theatre and kirk assembly. On another morning, bound for Arthur's Seat, the hill in Holyrood Park south-east of the Old Town, George thinks he is alone sitting on a pinnacle but is beset by Robert. A vision of a white-robed lady admonishes the latter, according to the Sinner's narrative, and glides over the rocks above St Anthony's Well and then vanishes.

Revd Wringhim is from Glasgow where Robert's upbringing presumably took place. The minister walks in the woods and fields of Finnieston to study, an area now very much in the city but then on the north bank of the River Clyde about a mile downstream. Here Robert encounters the malign influence of his alter ego, at first in the guise of a devout young man studying the Bible, later introducing himself as Gil-Martin. At the same spot Robert meets Revd Blanchard who warns him that his companion is capable of evil. The latter is enraged and proposes Blanchard's murder. Walking in Finnieston Dell in preparation for a sermon at the high church of Paisley (probably the abbey) Blanchard falls foul of his assassins who are hiding in shrubbery. The Wringhims go to Edinburgh and Gil-Martin decrees that the laird, father and son, as reprobates, should fall.

The fatal duel, witnessed by a prostitute from a north-facing window in a wynd off the High Street in Edinburgh, involves George and Robert fighting round the bleaching green beside the Nor' (north) Loch at the foot of the brothel close. In ancient times the valley between the castle ridge and the modern Princes Street was forested but flooded by King James III for defensive reasons. In 1763 the North Bridge was built to link the Old and proposed New Town and the loch subsequently drained.

Robert's final flight from Dalcastle takes him to Edinburgh, lodging at West Port, just west of the Grassmarket and the neighbouring Portsburgh. He is offered a job in a printing house, belonging to a Mr Watson, presumably James Watson, Queen's Printer in Edinburgh at the time, housed in Craig's Close on the north side of High Street. Here Robert attempts to print his 'Memoirs'.

He then heads for England, via Dalkeith, and two days later is by the River Ellan, probably Allan Water which enters the Teviot south-west of Hawick. He lodges in the village of Ancrum and then at Chesters near Jedburgh. Knowing his tormentor awaits him in Redesdale in Northumberland, Robert turns back, bypassing Hawick for Roberton, five miles west on the B711, where he spends a night in a farmhouse beside the church before finally heading to the Ettrick Forest area. The entry in his 'Memoirs' for 24 August 1712, has him at Ault-Righ, i.e. Altrive (Eltrive) farm, adjacent to Hogg's home, Altrive Lake. This property stretched towards Fall Law to the south-west.

The Blackwood's letter of 1823 notes a drover spotting the suicide's hanging body at the Hart Loup (Hart Leap), a pass linking the Yarrow and Ettrick valleys, adjacent to the farm of Eldinhope. A suicide's grave was well known in the Ettrick Forest area in Hogg's day and it is said that he and others discovered a Glengarry bonnet and other woollen cloth preserved in the moss. Fall Law, the location of the grave, is a hill north of Ettrick, now in a wooded area, and a little to the south lies Cowan's Croft, another hilltop which was at first supposed to be the location. That hill was named after a family who lived in the area in Hogg's youth, perhaps a source for the Sinner's family surname. Hogg would note the ambiguity in 'Fall Law'.

James Hogg

TOURIST INFORMATION
AND VISITOR ATTRACTIONS

The James Hogg Exhibition
   Ettrick Primary School, Ettrick Valley TD7 5JA
   Tel: [seasonal] 01750 62259
VisitScotland Hawick iCentre
   Heart of Hawick, Tower Mill, Hawick TD9 OAE
   Tel: 01450 373993
VisitScotland Jedburgh iCentre
   Murrays Green, Jedburgh TD8 6BE
   Tel: 01835 863170
VisitScotland Kelso iCentre
   Town House, The Square, Kelso TD5 7HF
   Tel: 01573 221119
VisitScotland Melrose iCentre
   Priorwsood Gardens, Abbey Street, Melrose TD6 9PZ
   Tel: [seasonal] 01896 820178
VisitScotland Peebles iCentre
   23 High Street, Peebles EH45 8AG
   Tel: 01721 728095
Edinburgh and Lothians Tourist Board
   3 Princes Street, Edinburgh EH2 2QP
   Tel: 0845 225 5121

11

Compton Mackenzie

EDWARD MONTAGUE COMPTON MACKENZIE (1883-1972), registered under his father's family name of Mackenzie, was son of Edward Compton, an actor-manager and his leading lady, the American Virginia Bateman Edward Montague.

Mackenzie was born in theatrical lodgings in Adelaide Street in West Hartlepool, an industrial town and port about 17 miles south-east of Durham, where his parents were appearing at the Gaiety Theatre. The child of touring actors, Monty, as he was known, experienced a roving existence for the first two-and-a-half years of his life, in a different town each week.

In 1886 his father bought a house in London although the Compton Comedy Company still toured. No 54 Avonmore Road, in Chiswick in West Kensington, was a three-storey red-brick house, a narrow garden at its back stretching down to a railway cutting beyond which were coal yards and warehouses. The busy Hammersmith Road was barely a hundred yards away. A nanny took the infant for a walk in Kensington Gardens every morning, his brother Frank in the pram and Monty at the side. He was clearly intelligent and an early reader by age two. At five he was sent to a kindergarten run by two spinsters, then at eight to the junior school of St Paul's and at 11 to St Paul's School itself, which moved to West Kensington in 1884 (and to Barnes in 1968).

In 1896 Virginia Compton bought a cottage in Hampshire, known as Canadian Cottage, since demolished, formerly known as Beech Farm, in Beech village just off the A339, a mile-and-a-half west of Alton. The property was used for holidays and week-ends from 1896-1900 and that part of Hampshire appeared frequently in Mackenzie's novels, both serious and comic, usually pictured as a safe haven away from slum streets. In subsequent writings the farm appears thinly disguised as Oak Farm with Alton becoming Galton.

Mackenzie went to Magdalen College Oxford in 1901. Meanwhile his religious faith and writing were developing. In the same year the London house in Avonmore Road was sold and the family moved to No 1 Nevern Square off Warwick Road. His father had prospered greatly through leases on various theatres. In the spring of 1904 Mackenzie rented a house in Burford, about 18 miles from Oxford, on the edge of the Cotswolds. The house was a small Elizabethan property named Lady Ham, with an orchard, beyond a hump-backed bridge on the bank of the River Windrush. Along with a colleague, Chris Stone, he planned the place as a retreat for writers. Meanwhile he fell for Ruth Daniel, daughter of the Bursar and Provost of Worcester College.

In London he took lodgings at No 7 Grosvenor Road, a terraced house with a view across the River Thames, at that time something of a slum area. He was now attracted to Stone's actress sister Faith, and after three weeks they were married secretly at St Saviour's Church in Pimlico and later moved to a small flat at No 127 Cheyne Walk.

Illness took Mackenzie to Cornwall in 1908 to stay with an old friend, Sandys Wason, vicar of Gunwalloe and Cury, where he was inspired to do Sunday school work, taking the children on rambles to the cliffs and beaches. He preached sermons at Polruan and later occupied a tiny four-roomed cottage with a thatched roof called Toy Cottage in Gunwalloe, then switched to the Georgian Riviere House, in the village of Phillack on the north coast, on a hill overlooking the Hayle estuary and persuaded his parents to rent it for seven years. Faith, however, was not impressed by Cornwall.

During this time Mackenzie published his first novel *The Passionate Elopement*, followed by *Carnival* and wrote part of *Sinister Street*. In 1910 he took a flat at No 27 Church Row in Hampstead for six months and, when the tenancy ran out in the spring of 1911, returned to Cornwall before being offered a share in a flat at No 45 Pall Mall. In 1912 Mackenzie took a house in London at No 6 North Street, now Lord North Street, comprising three connected Elizabethan cottages built round a courtyard and in 1914, like his hero Michael, took the decision to join the Roman Catholic Church and was received into it in 1914. He was attracted to Chrissie Humphreys, her stage name Chrissie Maud, the dancer and storyteller, whose tales of the Alhambra he used in various novels and she became the model for his leading heroines, including Jenny Pearl in the best selling *Carnival*. During the First World War Mackenzie served with British Intelligence in the Eastern Mediterranean and worked in counter espionage in Greece but was expelled from Athens in 1916 for his political views. In 1917 he founded the autonomous but short-lived Aegean Intelligence Service before being recalled to London. His time in Greece was the inspiration for *Greek Memories* and three other titles.

In 1920 he leased the Channel Island of Herm, one-and-a-half miles long with a circumference of five miles, with a Manor House at the top of the harbour road. Around this time he started to wear a Mackenzie tartan kilt. On Herm he was Lord of the Isle, but became overstretched financially and quit. He had retained the neighbouring island of Jethou and moved there in 1923, where he lived until 1930. Chrissie MacSween, a young schoolteacher from the Outer Hebridean island of Scarp, became his housekeeper companion on Jethou in 1928. Here his small house had to be enlarged to accommodate his library and some 2,000 gramophone records and papers.

He loved the vista on Jethou, looking east to Sark and west to Guernsey, but he was restless. He considered a move to Ireland, but, while in Glasgow to give a talk to the Gramophone Society, heard that Lord Leverhulme's estate in the Western Isles was to be auctioned off and made a bid for the Shiant Islands. Around this time he was developing a strong sense of identification with Scotland and in June 1926 went by Inverness to Kyle of Lochalsh, through Bonnie Prince Charlie country and by ferry to Tarbert on Harris. He also visited Inveraray to stay with the Duke of Argyll, whose castle and inhabitants Mackenzie was later to use fictionally. The Great Hall, hung with muskets, claymores, stags' heads and ancestral portraits, became the Great Hall of Glenbogle Castle in *The Monarch of the Glen*.

In the summer of 1929 he was involved in the formation of Clann Albain, an early version of the Scottish National Party and was in demand as a speaker on the subject. He also wanted to live in Scotland. Lord Lovat of Beaufort Castle near Inverness had a house called Eilean Aigas in a beautiful setting on an island in the River Beauly, off the A831 west of Inverness, where, after a narrow white bridge over rapids, the drive curved up to a mid-Victorian house, which he duly rented in December 1930, delighted to have found yet another island. The following year he became Lord Rector of Glasgow University. Dwelling on the islet of Eilean Aigas he declared was 'one of the golden ages I have enjoyed in my life.' *Water on the Brain*, his clever spy spoof, was written in a den beyond the library. Naively disclosing secret service information in his *Greek Memories*, Mackenzie was farcically tried *in camera*, found guilty and fined. Revenge took the form of satirising officialdom and the Secret Service in *Water on the Brain*. Eilean Aigas proved too costly and so he gave it up for the summer and rented a house the Outer Hebridean island of Barra. He had been there in the summer of 1929 and made a pilgrimage to Eriskay, the tiny island between Barra and South Uist where Bonnie Prince Charlie had set foot in 1745. He bought the coastguard's one-roomed hut and returned the following summer with Faith in a series of fleeting visits.

The island of Barra, nine miles long and four across, its economy dependent upon fishing and subsistence agriculture, has a strong Gaelic culture. It is the most westerly inhabited island of Great Britain with spectacular vistas. There are wonderful golden sandy beaches to the west, backed by machair, while the east coast has sheltered rocky granite coves and there is a central mountain, the 1260-ft Heaval. Mackenzie campaigned relentlessly for a circular metalled road, 14 miles long, which was laid eventually in 1939. He moved to the island in 1933, renting a cottage called No 5 Ardveenish at Northbay while planning to build a home on the island. Castlebay, the principal township, is in the south where the ferry from Oban calls and at the other end, on a square mile of cockleshell beach at Northbay, is the landing strip. Here Mackenzie lived in the cottage which he built in 1935, named Suidheachan, Gaelic for 'the sitting-down place' and which became a gathering place on Sunday evenings; there was a billiard room and his enormous library. The great and famous came here and he held court with politicians, socialites, celebrities, journalists, aspiring writers, musicians and painters. In 12 years from 1935 he wrote 23 books, numerous articles and edited the *Gramophone* periodical.

The house overlooks Traigh Mhor on the east, the cockle strand which forms the island airstrip, yet is less than 400 yards from the Atlantic beach on the west side. At this point the land narrows to a neck close to the most northerly point of the island at Eoligarry where the peninsula continues to Scurrival Point. As the ground for the house was being pegged out in April 1935 he started planning his tetralogy *The Four Winds of Love*, which he considered his best work.

In 1938 he bought Woodbine Cottage in the Vale of Health, Hampstead, near Whitestone Pond with Hampstead Heath all around it. The cottage, with a white wooden door, is the nearest on turning right at the top of the Vale of Health in the south-west corner of the Heath. Later that year he also bought a cottage in Somerset looking across to Glastonbury Tor over the Vale of Avalon. It appealed particularly to Faith, who was a keen gardener and called it Peace Close.

Following publication of *The Monarch of the Glen*, in 1938 he was asked to take over the Local Defence Volunteers on Barra, renamed soon afterwards the Home Guard. Headquarters were in Inverness and information took ten days get to the island; the inevitable shambles of exercises and manoeuvres was put to good use in his fiction. *Whisky Galore*, celebrating the real foundering of a cargo of whisky on neighbouring Eriskay, was the novel which made him rich and famous. The film by Ealing Studios involved the largest location film unit ever to leave a British studio at the time, spending two months on Barra, the crew billeted with local families, many at Northbay, six miles from the only pub at Castlebay.

The film appeared in America as *Tight Little Island*, although Mackenzie realised that an obvious alternative title would have been *Scotch on the Rocks*. *Rockets Galore*, also set on the islands and dramatising local opposition to anti-Soviet rocket ranges, followed. Mackenzie stayed on Barra until April 1944. He finished *The North Wind of Love*, disbanded the Home Guard and sold Woodbine Cottage. In November 1943 he had bought the lease on Sudbrooke Lodge in Richmond, the former home of Nell Gwyn and Judge Jeffreys. He now enjoyed the conviviality of London where he was a member of the Savile Club.

In April 1945 he moved to the Tudor Denchworth Manor near Wantage, where he stored in a tithe barn his library of 1200 books brought from Barra. In October 1945 Suidheachan was sold and, apart from a brief visit in 1948 to play Captain MacKechnie in the film of *Whisky Galore*, 32 years of island living came to an end for him. In the spring of 1953 he moved to the four-storeyed No 31 Drummond Place in Edinburgh's Georgian New Town, looking out over the gardens to the Firth of Forth. During his last decade he mostly wintered in Edinburgh and spent summer in the south of France, completing the final volumes of his autobiography.

In 1960 Faith died and in January 1962 Mackenzie married Chrissie, his companion of 35 years. After she died in 1963 her sister Lillian became his third wife in 1965. Following his death on 30 November 1972, St Andrew's Day, the plane with his body landed on the cockle beach of Traigh Mhor on Barra in a driving rainstorm. Here 82-year-old Calum Johnston, his friend since before the Second World War, waited to play a lament, piping the body to the Cille Bharra cemetery at Eoligarry. Calum collapsed and died immediately after the internment. Mackenzie is buried at the ruined church and chapel of St Barr, among friends, beneath a modest cross in the marram grass. The grave is on the hillside overlooking the jetty and within sight of Eriskay across the sound. His output was voluminous, resulting in over a hundred books of fiction, non-fiction, plays, works for children, poetry, biography, including a ten-volume autobiography, *My Life and Times (1963-71)* and several volumes on cats, having been longtime president of the Siamese Cat Club.

STORYTRAIL: *Whisky Galore*

THE MAIN CHARACTERS
Sergeant Major Fred Odd.
Peggy Macroon, an islander betrothed to Fred.
Rod McRurie, Snorvig Hotel keeper.
Dr MacLaren, the island doctor.
Paul Waggett, retired Liverpudlian stockbroker and Home Guard
   coordinator.
Father Macalister, the island priest.
Mr Brown, government agent.
Captain Buncher, captain of the SS *Cabinet Minister*.
Hugh Macroon and Jocky Stewart, islanders who come across
   sailors from the stranded cargo ship.

Mackenzie sets his comic tale on the two small Outer Hebridean
islands of Great and Little Todday, Todaidh Mor and Todaidh Beag,
based upon Barra and neighbouring Vatersay. Just west of Castlebay
the road leads to a causeway built in 1990 to Vatersay, the two islands
always having been almost connected by dunes and brilliant white
beaches. Eriskay lies across the Sound of Barra to the north. The
ferry from Oban still sails into Castlebay on Barra and Castlebay
Hotel is the model for the Snorvig Hotel of the novel. Island life in
the novel is affected by the timetable of the sea and the ferry sched-
ule and intermittent supplies from the mainland. Wartime austerity
brings the situation to crisis point with regard to whisky supplies
until a treasure trove appears in the form of the SS *Cabinet Minister*
after it runs ashore in the Sound of Todday en route to America.
Stacked with a cargo of whisky, the islanders set to retrieving it
before official salvage and customs officers.

   After two units of the Home Guard had been set up in 1940,
one in South Uist and one on Barra, Mackenzie was put in
charge of Barra. The local doctor Bartlett, a Liverpudlian who
had retired there, was full of himself, zealous in the operation of
invasion exercises and the model for the priggish and cocksure
Captain Paul Waggett of the Todday Home Guard. Dr Bartlett
wore a Royal Stewart tartan kilt yet was absurdly English, considering the islanders to be feckless and backward.

Between September 1939 and New Year 1941 the 8,000-tonne cargo ship SS *Politician* of the Harrison Line had crossed the North Atlantic from Liverpool and Manchester on 11 occasions. It was hazardous because of German U boats. In February 1941 Captain Beaconsfield Worthington was heading for Kingston in Jamaica and New Orleans with holds filled with a miscellaneous cargo of cotton, machetes, stoves, motor cycle parts, cigarettes, tobacco, soap, medicines, carpets, baths, mirrors and biscuits. In Hold Number 5 were banknotes for Jamaica valued at £3m and 22,000 cases containing 264,000 bottles of whisky for the American market. The route was via the Minch, the Inner Hebridean stretch of water between the mainland, the island of Skye and the Outer Isles, heading north and then west for safety's sake. In pitch darkness and perhaps mistaking the Sound of Eriskay, a three-quarter-mile stretch now crossed by a road, for the Sound of Barra, the boat struck a large rock and sandbank half-a-mile south-east of Calvay, just off Rosinish Point on Eriskay. The fuel tanks were fractured and the boat split in two. Local men from South Uist and Eriskay ventured to the perilous rocks of Rubha Dubh and rescued 26 sailors and took them to Eriskay.

No 5 Hold, with a customs seal on the hatch, was full of oily water. A wreck was considered a gift of God in such communities, especially during a time of great economic austery and, while word spread, at first it lay untouched. Then a few cases were taken and the hold resealed, but eventually an estimated 2,400 cases were removed by islanders, some to as far away as Mull, the mainland and neighbouring islands. Subsequent bureaucratic reaction was considered to be petulant. Customs and Excise officials appeared with police and searched crofts, but the booty had already been stashed in the hills, barns, peat stacks, hay ricks, corn stacks, hot-water bottles, under loose floorboards, behind wall panelling, sunk in creels and rabbit holes and under the soil. It was said jokingly that ploughmen thereafter placed a bottle at the end of each furrow, as a guide to keeping it straight, of course. Even the Eriskay ponies were supposedly drunk. Thirty-six islanders went to court and 19 were found guilty and imprisoned for up to two months by the sheriff at Lochmaddy on North Uist.

Occasional bottles of the whisky, nicknamed Polly bottles, which have since turned up have been sold for considerable sums, although some may be contaminated. Genuine bottles stated, 'No resale without Federal approval.' The Lochboisdale Hotel on South Uist, whose long bar has a huge photograph of the SS *Politician*, and the Creagorry Hotel on Benbecula were stocked from the boat. In the islands a toast may still be proposed: 'To the man who could not see Calvay.'

The wreck was cut in two by salvage experts and the fore part towed to the Clyde estuary for scrap while the aft end was left under the waters of Eriskay Sound. The seaweed-covered stern can be seen at low tide where it has drifted some distance north-west of Calvay Island, which can be reached on foot when the tide is out, although the wreck is deeply embedded in the sandy bottom.

The barren, hilly island of Eriskay, two-and-a-half miles by one mile, is a crofting and fishing community famous for its jerseys and the native ponies used to carry peat and seaweed. From the 607-ft high Ben Scrien there is a fine view of the whole island, Barra, South Uist, over the sea to Skye and elsewhere. A way-marked trail round the island approaches the spot off the north-east point of Calvey Island where at low tide the wreck pops its head out of the Sound. Eriskay was ironically a 'dry' island until the first pub opened in 1988, Am Politician, to the west of the island, which celebrates the connection with memorabilia and original bottles on display.

On Barra the road east from the jetty at Haun provides the nearest viewpoint for the site of the wreck, while the ferry from Lochboisdale to Castlebay passes nearby. After the release of the imprisoned islanders the episode entered Hebridean folklore with endless ceilidh stories and songs, poetry and drama perpetuated in the oral tradition by the folk of the southern isles in school halls and elsewhere.

Mackenzie's driver and mechanic on Barra, Kenny MacCormack, brought him six dozen bottles after a night's work in the hold. Mackenzie audaciously arranged the bottles along the top of his bookshelves and was soon after visited by the Scottish Secretary of State, oblivious to the significance of the display.

The proposed building of the Isle of Barra Distillery near Borve remains a work in progress, perhaps never to be realised.

On Eriskay an exhibition launched in 2009 includes reference to Mary Bowie who was cook to Mackenzie, model for Peggy Macroon who did indeed fall for an English soldier, Alan Guy.

TOURIST INFORMATION AND VISITOR ATTRACTIONS

VisitScotland Castlebay iCentre
    Main Street, Castlebay, Isle of Barra HS9 5XD
    Tel: [seasonal] 01871 810336
Am Politician
    3 Baile, Isle of Eriskay HS8 5JL
    Tel: 01878 720246
Barra Heritage & Cultural Centre
    Castlebay, Isle of Barra HS9 5XD
    Tel: [seasonal] 01871 810413
VisitScotland Stornoway iCentre
    26 Cromwell Street, Stornoway, Isle of Lewis HS1 2DD
    Tel: 01851 703088
Lochboisdale TIC
    Pier Road, Lochboisdale, Isle of South Uist HS8 5TH
    Tel: [seasonal] 01878 700286
Inveraray Castle
    Cherrypark, Inveraray PA32 8XE
    Tel: [seasonal] 01499 302203
VisitScotland Fort William iCentre
    15 High Street, Fort William PH33 6DH
    Tel: 01397 701801
VisitScotland Oban iCentre
    Columba Buildings, 3 North Pier, Oban PA34 5QD
    Tel: 01631 563122
Edinburgh and Lothians Tourist Board
    3 Princes Street, Edinburgh EH2 2QP
    Tel: 0845 225 5121
City of London Information Centre
    St Paul's Churchyard, London EC4M 8BX
    Tel: 020 7332 3456
Alton TIC
    7 Cross & Pillory Lane, Alton GU34 1HL
    Tel: 01720 268829

12

Ian Rankin

IAN RANKIN (b.1960), the UK's bestselling crime writer, was born in Seventeenth Street, Cardenden, a former mining village in Fife, son of James Rankin and his wife Isobel. Rankin grew up in a terraced council house at No 17 Craigmead Terrace in the town where there is now an Ian Rankin Court named in his honour. The area was known as Bowhill, one of four parishes which became collectively Cardenden in 1970. His father ran a grocer's shop in Lochgelly for most of his life, later taking a job in Rosyth Dockyard. Rankin's mother, from Yorkshire and employed in school kitchens, died of lung cancer when he was 18, the year Rankin started at Edinburgh University.

Rankin was educated at Denend Primary School in Cardenden, then at Auchterderran Junior High School for two years, followed by Beath High School in Cowdenbeath. He left in 1978 to study at Edinburgh University where he met his wife, Miranda (née Harvey), who was born in England and grew up in Northern Ireland.

As a student Rankin lodged in a basement flat facing Bruntsfield Links, followed by a flat in Morrison Street. He started his first Inspector Rebus story (a rebus is a picture puzzle) *Knots and Crosses* in March 1985 in the ground-floor flat he rented for two years while studying for a PhD at No 24 Arden Street in Marchmont, an area south of Edinburgh's Old Town and the Meadows. He later moved to Dalkeith Road.

After graduation Rankin went to London in 1986 and by 1990 was deputy editor of the magazine *Hi-Fi Review*, living in a flat in Tottenham in north London while his wife Miranda worked in the civil service. Restlessness made him buy an old farmhouse in the Dordogne in France in May that year, where he continued to write, with little success. Here his first son, Jack, was born in 1992 and in 1996 a second son, Kit, who has Angelman syndrome, a congenital neuro-developmental disorder. For Kit's sake the family moved back to a flat in Edinburgh where Jack started school. Eventually Rankin sold the French property to friends. He lives now with his family in a large Victorian detached house in the well-to-do Merchiston area of Edinburgh. Rankin gives his character Rebus a disabled child, a daughter who is knocked down in *The Hanging Garden*. While engaged upon postgraduate study of the novels of Muriel Spark he spent more time on creative writing, producing a long short story which became *The Flood* (1986).

He has been variously a college secretary, chicken factory worker, alcohol researcher, swineherd, grape-picker, punk musician, tax collector and assistant at the National Folktale Centre in London.

The first novel to feature Inspector Rebus of the Edinburgh police was *Knots and Crosses* (1987) which pictured a bleak, unwelcoming Edinburgh. With *Black and Blue* (1997), an award-winning Rebus story, the series became very successful. Nineteen novels involving Rebus have appeared, four involving Malcolm Fox and several novels under the pseudonym Jack Harvey. Other Rebus novels include *Hide and Seek* (1991), *Tooth and Nail* (1992), *Strip Jack* (1992), *The Black Book* (1993), *Mortal Causes* (1994), *Let It Bleed* (1995), *The Hanging Garden* (1998), *Dead Souls* (1999), *Set in Darkness* (2000), *The Falls* (2001), *Resurrection Men* (2002), *A Question of Blood* (2003), *Fleshmarket Close* (2004), *The Naming of the Dead* (2006) and *Exit Music* (2008) in which Rebus retires at age 60, although Rankin pointed out that Rebus might reappear to investigate unsolved crimes. Short stories include *A Good Hanging* (1992), *Beggars Banquet* (2002) and *The Beat Goes On* (2014). Several non-Rebus novels have appeared, including *Doors Open* (2008), a crime novel about a theft of art works in Edinburgh. *The Complaints* (2009) introduced a new younger detective Malcolm Fox, who reappeared in *The Impossible Dead* (2011). Rebus returned in *Standing in Another Man's Grave* (2012) and *Saints of the Shadow*

Bible (2013) along with Fox. *A Cool Head* (2009) is a novella and *Dark Entries* (2009) a co-written graphic novel. *Rebus's Scotland* (2005) describes the topography of the novels. *Dark Road*, Rankin's first stage play on a crime theme and co-written with Mark Thomson, was performed at the Lyceum Theatre in Edinburgh in 2013. Rankin's books have sold more than 20 million copies in around 30 languages. He has won many literary prizes, was given an OBE in 2002 and appointed Deputy Lieutenant of Edinburgh in 2007 and Fellow of the Royal Society of Edinburgh in 2015.

Rankin describes Edinburgh as 'a city of the mind, a writer's city', the life and crime of which to date he has chronicled for nearly 30 years through his maverick Detective Inspector Rebus. He says: 'anyone who has read my Inspector Rebus novels knows that Edinburgh itself is the main character in my stories ... The city has inspired my writing and reveals itself anew to me every single day.' He is struck by the split personality of the city, its 'history, museums and royalty, but at the same time there is this feeling that behind the thick walls of those Georgian townhouses there are all sorts of terrible things happening.' Add to that the contemporary problems of social deprivation and domestic abuse.

Rankin's favourite walks in Edinburgh include exploring the nooks and crannies of the wynds and vennels off the Royal Mile between the castle and Palace of Holyroodhouse and, out of town, the canal-side route to the village of Ratho and beyond to the west of the city and the Hermitage of Braid, between Braid Road and Liberton Road to the south.

The Oxford Bar at No 8 Young Street, off Charlotte Square in the New Town, provides a cross section of Edinburgh life for Rankin. He started drinking in 'the Ox' in 1984 where his flatmate was a part-time barman. In *The Hanging Garden* he says: 'A pub like the Ox was about so much more than just the hooch. It was therapy and refuge, entertainment and art.' He met policemen there and was stimulated to explore the hidden non-tourist Edinburgh. Some of his characters are based upon those he met there. The pub became a favourite also of Rebus where the name of the former proprietor John Gates is used as that of the forensic pathologist Professor Gates in the novels. Harry, the barman there, is real and became the owner. Rankin admits to having been a binge drinker.

Rankin was first winner of the city council's Edinburgh Award 2007 for raising the city's profile through his work and his handprints were engraved in Caithness stone in the quadrangle of Edinburgh City Chambers.

Rebustours, led by an actor/local historian, includes assorted locations featured in the novels. One trip leaves from the Royal Oak pub at No 1 Infirmary Street, off South Bridge, where Rebus drank in a corner and met the gangster Cafferty, and takes in the old High School, the remnants of the Flodden Wall, a housing scheme, Saint Leonard's Police Station, then goes by the Meadows, George Square, Forrest Road and Chambers Street, all settings reflected in the novels *Set in Darkness*, *Dead Souls* and *Fleshmarket Close*. Another tour leaves the Royal Oak pub for the mortuary, Cowgate, High Street, Canongate Kirk and kirkyard, the new parliament, the Regency terraces beside Calton Hill beyond the east end of Princes Street then to the Royal Mile by Fleshmarket Close. A third tour begins and ends at the Oxford Bar, heading for Stockbridge, Dean Village and the Water of Leith.

STORYTRAIL: *Set in Darkness*

THE MAIN CHARACTERS
John Rebus, detective police inspector.
Siobhan Clarke, detective constable, colleague of Rebus.
Bryce Callan, a gangster.
Big Ger Cafferty, criminal gang leader.
Barry Hulton, millionaire property developer, nephew of Callan.
Alasdair Grieve, relative of a murdered candidate for the Scottish
    parliament.
Fred Hastings, a tramp who commits suicide.

Queensberry House, an A-listed building at the foot of Canongate dating from 1667, was initially home to the dukes of Queensberry. Around 1750, when it was flatted and occupied by gentry, it was considered almost as magnificent as Holyroodhouse. Subsequently it became a hospital, barracks, a house of refuge and offices for Scottish and Newcastle Breweries until being incorporated into the new Scottish Parliament Building. When the neighbouring brewery was being demolished, the house was found to have within itself the shell of the older Hatton House and beneath the floor there were medieval closes and other structures. The new parliament building, designed by the Catalan architect Enric Miralles, opened in 1999 after archaeologists participated in the renovation of Queensberry House.

In the novel a skeleton is discovered in a sealed-off fireplace in the house during demolition - records from 1691 show that it had 52 fireplaces. Soon another body is found in the grounds, that of Roddy Grieve, a Labour candidate for the Scottish Parliament, who is from a wealthy Edinburgh family and had been receiving hate mail and death threats. DI John Rebus interviews members of the Grieve family and others, including his election agent who had had an affair with Grieve, revealed through an anonymous letter, possibly from a rival for the nomination. At the start of the story the Grieve family dine at the noted Witchery restaurant, occupying a 16th-century building with a sepulchral basement at No 352 Castlehill, the part of the Royal Mile nearest the castle. Rebus's colleague Siobhan Clarke observes a tramp committing suicide by jumping from North Bridge down on to Waverley Station platform leaving behind a bag from Jenners department store containing a building society pass-book showing £400,000 in the name of Chris Mackie. Rebus is sure there is a link between the millionaire tramp and the body in the fireplace. Someone stood to gain from Grieve's death and the decision about the parliament's location. Calton Hill, which is subject to land speculation in the novel, rises beyond the east end of Princes Street and is noted for its panoramic views.

Contractors who worked on Queensberry House 20 years before are interviewed and claim intimidation by a gangster, Bryce Callan. DC Clarke questions a 'bag-lady' about Chris Mackie, possibly a false name and discovers that he gave her a leather briefcase which she sold to a second-hand shop. The initials 'ADC' are on the case. A devotee of Rosslyn Chapel appears, claiming Mackie meant money to go to researching the Knights Templars' link with Rosslyn.

Rebus meets the criminal gang leader Big Ger Cafferty, now out of Barlinnie Prison in Glasgow, to inquire about Callan's relationship with the demolition firm. The owner's garage contains records for the period and it is discovered that Barry Hulton, a nephew of Bryce Callan, worked on the site and has gone on to be a millionaire property developer.

It is revealed that the tramp was Fred Hastings, an associate of Alasdair Grieve. Roddy Grieve was last seen in the Holyrood Tavern on the night of the murder. (This is a bare-boarded Category C-listed pub dating from 1898 at No 9A Holyrood Road near the Scottish Parliament.) Scrutiny of Hastings' files show that he, Alasdair Grieve and another (possibly Bryce Callan) had financially speculated on the proposed site of the parliament. Hulton is tailed in his Ferrari by the precocious DI Linford down to Leith, where Linford is assaulted and left unconscious outside a pub frequented by a thug seen at the time of the murder. Rebus makes his own inquiries around Leith and the suspect is picked up for questioning but brazens it out. Rebus intercepts Alasdair Grieve at Roddy's funeral and he admits to involvement with Hastings in corrupt dealings over land at Calton Hill. A hitman had been killed in a confrontation by Hastings who used the name to open a bank account with the demolisher's money. Rebus interviews a defiant councillor on his deathbed who stood to gain from Roddy Grieve's death and the decision about the parliament's location. Finally, Rebus experiences a nasty confrontation with Cafferty and his associates.

Ian Rankin

TOURIST INFORMATION
AND VISITOR ATTRACTIONS

Edinburgh & Lothian Tourist Board
   3 Princes Street, Edinburgh EH2 2QP
   Tel: 0845 225 5121
The Oxford Bar
   8 Young Street, Edinburgh EH2 4JB
   Tel: 0131 539 7119
The Edinburgh Book Lovers' Tour
   Tel: 07770 163641
Mercat Tours
   Tel: 0131 225 6591
The Real Mary King's Close Tour
   Tel: 0870 243 0160
Rebus Tours
   Tel: 0131 553 7473
The Scottish Literary Tour Trust
   34 North Castle Street, Edinburgh EH2 3BN
   Tel: 0800 169 7410/0131 226 6665
National Museum of Scotland
   Chambers Street, Edinburgh EH1 1JF
   Tel: 0131 225 7534
Scottish Parliament Building
   Horse Wynd, Edinburgh EH99 1SP
   Tel: 0131 348 5000/5200
Surgeons' Hall Museums
   Royal College of Surgeons, 9 Hill Square, Edinburgh EH8 9DW
   Tel: 0131 527 1711/1600

13

Walter Scott

SIR WALTER SCOTT (1771-1832) was born in College Wynd, Edinburgh, son of Walter Scott, a Writer to the Signet (a solicitor) and Anne Rutherford, daughter of a Professor of Medicine. College Wynd, between the Cowgate and the college buildings, has been demolished but there is a plaque marking the spot where Guthrie Street meets Chambers Street. The family later moved to No 25 George Square, the Scott family home until 1797. Scott attended The Royal High School which opened two years before Scott entered it in October 1779 and was situated at the foot of nearby Infirmary Street and at the east end of Cowgate near the present High School Yards.

He spent the summer of 1783 at his uncle's house in Kelso where Scott attended Kelso Grammar School, on the site of the nave of the Norman abbey, before matriculating at the Old College of Edinburgh University at the corner of Chambers Street and South Bridge. He was apprenticed to his father and qualified in 1792, thereafter becoming an advocate in Edinburgh from 1793-1806, Sheriff-Depute of Selkirk from 1799-1832 and a Principal Clerk to the Court of Session from 1806-30. He attended the historic Greyfriars Kirk off George IV Bridge with his family and his father is buried in the churchyard.

After marriage in 1797 to Margaret Charlotte Charpentier, a French woman from Lyon, Scott lived in the Georgian New Town at No 108 George Street, then at No 10 South Castle Street and shortly afterwards at No 39 Castle Street, the best known of his Edinburgh homes, where he lived from 1802-26 and where many of the Waverley novels were written. The site is now occupied by a legal firm and is not open to the public, but a plaque and small copy of the statue which sits under the Scott monument in Princes Street Gardens are above the door. Here Scott completed his work as Writer to the Signet in the morning and wrote his literary works for the rest of the day at the massive table in the study behind the dining room. He completed *Waverley, Guy Mannering, Quentin Durward* and *St Ronan's Well* while living there. His literary work was lucrative, but his financial affairs became perilous as partnership with a printer and bookseller led to involvement in the collapse of the publishing house of Constable. Scott had to write novels at a feverish pace to pay off a vast sum to creditors, a feat achieved honourably after his death from the proceeds of his writing.

The impressive 200-ft-high Scott Monument standing in East Princes Street Gardens, the world's largest monument to a man of letters, was the work of George Kemp and completed between 1840-44. Two hundred and eighty-seven steps lead to a neo-Gothic spire and a fine view of the castle rock, the Old Town, New Town, the Firth of Forth, Fife and the surrounding hills. Beneath, in a canopy of arches, sits a twice-life-size white Carrara marble statue of Scott in a shepherd's plaid, a book on his lap, his dog Maida at his feet with figures of 64 characters from the *Waverley* novels and Scottish history set in niches. Edinburgh is the only city in the world with a railway station (Waverley) named after a famous work of literature.

The Abbotsford Bar at No 3-5 Rose Street, built in 1902, is named after Scott's mock-baronial mansion in the Borders and the Kenilworth at No 152-4 Rose Street, its interior dating from 1899, recalls one of the novels. The upstairs rooms of the 16th-century Beehive Inn in the Grassmarket were frequented by literary figures including Scott.

At a dinner in 1827 in the Assembly Rooms, at No 54 George Street, built as a meeting place for the elite of 18th-century Edinburgh, Scott, quite late in his literary career, first publicly admitted to the rather open secret of being author of the world-famous novels. He responded to a toast to 'the author of Waverley' after seeking anonymity because of his professional connection to the law.

The National Portrait Gallery in Queen Street has fine portraits of Scott and relics and manuscripts associated with him are contained in the National Museum of Antiquities in the same building. The Museum of Edinburgh in Huntly House, the only remaining timber-fronted house in Edinburgh, dating from 1570, has an important Scott collection. The Writers' Museum in Lady Stair's House, a building dating from 1622, off the north side of the Lawnmarket in the Royal Mile, contains abundant material devoted to Scott: manuscripts, personal possessions, including his pipe, chess board, furniture, first editions and the printing press of James Ballantyne as well as a reconstruction of his drawing room at No 39 North Castle Street. A stone slab dedicated to Scott has been laid outside the Writers' Museum.

Parliament House, built from 1632-40, off the Royal Mile, housing the Court of Session and High Court of Justiciary, was especially familiar to Scott as a Clerk of the Court and there is a statue of Scott in the Great Hall. The printing works where he partnered his old school friend James Ballantyne was situated on the north side of Canongate below Calton Hill.

A literary pub tour organised by the Scottish Literary Tour Trust, referring to Scott and others, leaves from the Beehive Inn in the Grassmarket at 7.30 pm. The Edinburgh Booklovers' Tour similarly leaves from the Writers' Museum at Lady Stair's Close, beside Deacon Brodie's Tavern in the High Street. Edinburgh was the first city to be named a UNESCO City of Literature. Clermiston Tower, a simple monument among the trees off Ravelston Dykes Road to the west of the city, was built by William Macfie to mark the centenary of Scott's birth in 1871.

For the first six years of married life, from 1798–1804, Scott spent every summer in rural retreat at Lasswade Cottage, now known as Barony House, in Wadingburn Road to the west of the village of Lasswade, on the A768 nine miles south of Edinburgh. In Portobello, Edinburgh's seaside resort, Scott stayed in 1827 at No 37 Bellfield Street, between Portobello High Street and the beach, where there is also a commemorative plaque.

Scott lived at Ashiestiel House on the south bank of the River Tweed near Clovenfords, a village on the A72 three miles west of Galashiels, as Sheriff of the County of Selkirk between 1804 and 1812, when he wrote the bestselling poems *The Lay of the Last Minstrel, The Lady of the Lake, Marmion* and about a third of *Waverley*. The house, not open to the public, can best be seen across the river from the A72 between Peebles and Clovenfords. The Clovenfords Inn stands on the site of an older one where Scott stayed before gaining a home of his own in the Borders. A statue of Scott, by James Archibald, commemorating his visits stands outside the inn and the church has a memorial window to him. From here he went ballad gathering in the Yarrow and Ettrick valleys.

Abbotsford, Scott's home in the Scottish Borders from 1812 until his death and which he named after the monks of Melrose who used to ford the River Tweed near the spot, stands in a lovely wooded setting near the banks of the river, off the B6360, not far from Melrose and signposted off the A6091. He purchased the farm property, previously known as Cartley Hole, but nicknamed Clarty (dirty), in 1811 and lavishly reconstructed it in mock-baronial style between 1817 and 1824 giving it a more romantic name. 'It is a kind of conundrum castle to be sure [which] pleases a fantastic person in style and manner,' said Scott. The house contains personal memorabilia and materials of Scottish national historical interest, including Prince Charles Edward's quaich and a lock of his hair, Flora Macdonald's pocket book, Rob Roy's broadsword and dirk and Robert Burns's tumbler. The library, modelled on the famous Rosslyn Chapel, looks out on the river which runs parallel to the house beyond the terraced garden and contains 9,000 books which Scott accumulated, a bust of the author and there are portraits of him in the drawing room. The study where he wrote many of his bestselling works is largely preserved as it was when used by Scott.

With the death of his last direct descendent Abbotsford was taken over by The Abbotford Trust, leading to extensive refurbishment and a new visitor centre which opened in 2013. The area, usually described as Scott Country, comprises parts of the Border region through which the River Tweed flows and is centred on the town of Melrose.

Numerous places are famous for their associations with the novelist and poet, his ancestors and characters and plots in the stories. The beautiful ruined Melrose Abbey of the Cistercians, founded in 1136,was extensively repaired under the supervision of Scott in 1822 with support from the Duke of Buccleuch and Queensberry. To the south-east above Melrose are his beloved triple-peaked Eildon Hills and the viewpoint and panorama of the Tweed known as Scott's View. Scott declared: 'I can stand on the Eildon Hills and point out forty-three places famous in war and verse.' The horses pulling Scott's hearse paused, some say customarily, although it was accidental, at Bemersyde Hill on the B6356, at the same spot, with its vista of the meandering Tweed, on Scott's last journey to Abbotsford shortly before his death on return from Italy in 1832. This moment is recalled in a plaque south-east of Galashiels, on the way to Abbotsford, near Langlee on the Melrose road.

Near Scott's View is Smailholm Tower, which can be reached from the B6404 or B6397, a striking Border keep on an isolated hillock, dating from 1533, with magnificent views of the Cheviots, Eildons and Lammermuirs. The tower can be approached through the farmyard of Sandyknowe Farm where Scott's grandfather Robert Scott lived and the infant Scott stayed when recuperating from the poliomyelitis that was to leave him permanently lame in his right leg. The Sandyknowe Farm which he visited was a small stone cottage now built into the old farm steading a little to the west of the modern farm building. Here he was inspired by so much Borders history, lore and tales of derring- do, hearing ballads and tales at the hearthside. At age four he returned to Edinburgh where his family had moved to George Square. From 1775-6 he spent a year in Bath for its healing waters and then returned to Sandyknowe. After being called to the Bar in 1792 Scott spent his summers in the Borders, collecting ballads which eventually appeared in his famous *Minstrelsy of the Scottish Borders*.

As a boy Scott spent many summers at Kelso with his uncle Captain Robert Scott whose 30-acre estate of Rosebank was situated beside the River Tweed and which Scott inherited in 1804. The property is visible from the approach to the new Hunter Bridge. An aunt lived in the Garden House, now Waverley Lodge, at the end of Maxwell Lane facing the Abbey.

Here there is a bust of Scott on the gable wall and a statue of his dog. The adjacent gardens were on the site now of a garden centre.

In the triangular market place of Selkirk, less than four miles from Abbotsford, stands a statue of Scott by Handyside Ritchie, dating from 1839, in his robes as sheriff-depute. The Sheriff Court House, which also served as Selkirk's Town Hall, has been refurbished as a museum with audio-visual presentation reflecting Scott's life, writings and time as Sheriff. Here sit his chair and a selection of his letters. There is a Scott's Selkirk week-end every December with two days of readings, processions, dramatisations and re-enactments. The County Hotel, at No 3-5 High Street, was regularly visited by Scott and his friends. Off the A708 near Selkirk is Bowhill, the grand Border home of the Duke of Buccleuch, where proof copies of books by Scott appear alongside a splendid art collection.

Scott frequently attended the Circuit Courts at Jedburgh, some ten miles from the English border, on the A68 route from Newcastle to Edinburgh via Carter Bar. In 1793 he appeared for the first time as advocate in a criminal trial there and met William and Dorothy Wordsworth after the Judge's dinner following the court proceedings. From Jedburgh Scott made important ballad-collecting expeditions in Liddesdale.

Scott died in the dining room at Abbotsford and is buried in St Mary's aisle in the east chapel of the majestic, ruined 12th-century Dryburgh Abbey, attractively set on a horseshoe bend in the Tweed, four miles south-east of Melrose, which can be reached by the B6368 and B6356.

An official Sir Walter Scott Way is a 92-mile route across the country inspired by his novels and poems, much of it following the Tweed, between Moffat and Cockburnspath on the coast.

Tibbie Shiel's Inn is beautifully located on the isthmus between St Mary's Loch and the Loch of the Lowes, halfway between Selkirk and Moffat on the A708 and is named after Isabella (Tibbie) Shiel, who ran the inn for 54 years and which is now, regrettably, closed indefinitely. Scott often met fellow writer James Hogg, the Ettrick Shepherd, here and also William Wordsworth and others. A statue of Hogg sits across the A708 on the wooded knowe overlooking the inn.

According to tradition Scott and Hogg last met in the autumn of 1830 at the Gordon Arms Hotel, a former coaching inn further north on the A708 in the picturesque Yarrow valley, where framed fragments of some of Scott's letters adorn the walls of the bar. A devastating fire in May 2015 almost ruined the inn but it has now been restored with a more open-plan layout on the ground floor. It remains a major social hub and live music venue in the area.

A statue of Scott, by Handyside Ritchie, the first public memorial to the writer, crowns an 80-ft-high column erected in 1837 in the centre of Glasgow's George Square. An apocryphal tale claims that the sculptor placed the plaid on the wrong shoulder and killed himself out of shame on discovering his mistake. In fact Border shepherds, unlike Highlanders, wore the plaid on the right shoulder. Scott knew Glasgow well since he frequently visited on legal business, attending the old Court House in Jail Square. He liked to stay at 'a quaint hostelry', since demolished, in King Street, where he may have met prototypes for his character Bailie Nicol Jarvie. In December 1796 as a struggling young advocate he was in Glasgow for the trial of a shoemaker who had cut the throat of a friend for money and was to be hanged, an experience he used in *Rob Roy*.

Scott frequently stayed at Ross Priory, now owned by the University of Strathclyde, off the A811 on the southern shores of Loch Lomond where he wrote parts of *Rob Roy* and *The Lady of the Lake*. He also stayed at the old Kirkton manse in Aberfoyle several times between 1790 and 1809 and his poems and novels subsequently reflected the local landscape and folklore. The manse of Dr Patrick Graham, the local minister who published a book which provided Scott with source material, lay beyond the ruined walls of the Old Parish Kirk and graveyard where the road veers left past Auchenblae. Scott travelled on horseback following the journeys of his fictional characters to ascertain that factual detail was correct, journey times were feasible and terrain accurately recreated. In the 1790s Scott talked to a number of men who had met the real Rob Roy McGregor.

The Rob Roy & Trossachs Visitor Centre in Callander provides an audio-visual presentation reflecting the life, times and exploits of the Highland folk hero.

Scott stayed at the village of Gilsland, on the B6318 about five miles north-west of Haltwhistle when touring the Lake District in the summer of 1797. Here he first met the attractive young Charlotte Charpentier who was on horseback and then later that evening at a ball. Her mother had died early in the French Revolution and the daughter was under the guardianship of Lord Downshire. Scott asked her to supper and fell in love. A whirlwind courtship followed and they were married the following December at Carlisle Cathedral. The surrounding countryside subsequently provided much of the background of *Guy Mannering*.

Scott's increasing fame had rested initially on the long romantic poem *The Lay of the Last Minstrel* (1805), followed by *Marmion* (1808), an epic poem on the lamentable battle of Flodden Field in 1513 and *The Lady of the Lake* (1810), which popularised Scotland as a romantic tourist destination. But believing that he could not rival Byron as a poet Scott had turned to creating a stream of best-selling historical romances, tales of love, bravery and intrigue, on the basis of which he is considered the founder of the historical novel. His output was formidable with *Waverley* (1814), *Guy Mannering* (1815), *The Antiquary* (1816), *The Black Dwarf* (1816), *Old Mortality* (1816), *Rob Roy* (1817), *The Heart of Midlothian* (1818), *The Bride of Lammermoor* (1819), *The Legend of Montrose* (1819), *The Monastery* (1820), *The Abbot* (1820) and *The Pirate* (1821). Those with a largely English setting included *Ivanhoe* (1819), *Kenilworth* (1821), *The Fortunes of Nigel* (1822), *Quentin Durward* (1823), set in medieval France, *Redgauntlet* (1824), *Peveril of the Peak* (1823), *The Talisman* (1825) and *Woodstock* (1826). He was also a major editor and biographer of Dryden and Swift.

Scott was an inveterate verifier of factual details of people and places of which he wrote and travelled extensively for this purpose. He was responsible for the discovery of the Honours of Scotland, the coronation Regalia of the Scottish monarchs, abandoned in Edinburgh Castle since the Act of Union in 1707 and now on permanent display in the castle. He was also responsible for the restoration of Mons Meg, the great 15th-century cannon removed to London after the 1745 Jacobite Rising, which can be seen at Edinburgh Castle. He stage-managed the state visit of George IV to Edinburgh in 1822, persuading the king to wear tartan which had been banned since 1746 following the second Jacobite rebellion. By his writings and other efforts Scott did more than any other to publicise his country, its history, legends, traditions and romance. There is a monument to him in Poets' Corner in Westminster Abbey.

STORYTRAIL: *Rob Roy*

THE MAIN CHARACTERS
Francis Osbaldistone, son of a London merchant.
Sir Hildebrand Osbaldistone, country squire, uncle to Francis.
Rashleigh Osbaldistone, malevolent son of Sir Hildebrand,
    involved in Jacobite intrigue.
Diana Vernon, niece to Sir Hildebrand, with whom Francis falls
    in love.
Rob Roy MacGregor, a historical character, outlaw.
Bailie Nicol Jarvie, a Glasgow burgess who accompanies Francis
    to the Highlands.

Prior to the Jacobite rising of 1715, Francis Osbaldistone is sent by his merchant father in London to the north of England estate in the Cheviot hills of his uncle whose sons include Rashleigh, a scheming, embezzling Jacobite and a daughter Diana Vernon, with whom Francis falls in love. Rashleigh tries to destroy Francis and his father but is prevented by Diana and by the famous Scottish Highlander Rob Roy, member of a proscribed clan, who has turned to outlawry because of injustice and misfortune, yet is capable of decency and generosity.

The long preamble at Osbaldistone Hall, set in a valley of the Cheviots, with lengthy descriptions of the décor of the library and layout of gardens, reflects Scott's preoccupations at the time as Abbotsford was slowly reaching completion. He was himself becoming the country squire, inaugurating annual festivals like the Abbotsford Hunt and so a hunt is carefully described in one chapter of the novel, but emphasising the coarseness of Sir Hildebrand's sons in their love of hunting, fishing and shooting.

Scott visited Northumberland frequently, staying on one occasion 'in a farmer's house, about six miles from Wooler [on the A697], in the very centre of the Cheviot Hills, in one of the wildest and most romantic situations which your imagination ... ever suggested.' This may be his setting for Osbaldistone Hall or a location in upper Coquetdale near Rothbury, off the B6341 and B6344. Eventually Francis meets Mr Campbell, 'a Scotch gentleman', an alias of Rob Roy, at the Black Bear Inn in Darlington. He is a master of disguise, frequently appearing on the fringes of the action while keeping Frank under constant view.

Much of the novel's action is set in the vividly evoked preindustrial Glasgow. In 1717, when Andrew relates, it had a population of around 13,000. Francis is to contact merchants in Glasgow's Gallowgate and Andrew Fairservice, who escorts him from the north of England, enlightens him about Glasgow. They travel by smugglers' routes to the valley of the River Clyde and to the city where trade with the West Indies and American colonies has resulted in great prosperity. They note the fine main streets: 'The principal street was broad and important, decorated with public buildings ... built of stone' which gave them 'an imposing air of dignity and grandeur, of which most English towns are in some measure deprived.'

Bailie Nicol Jarvie, the merchant, lives there and declares: 'I can win my crowns, and keep my crowns, and count my crowns, wi' ony body in the Saut-Market, or it may be in the Gallowgate.' The lower town, below the cathedral, comprised stretches of today's High Street, Trongate, Gallowgate and Saltmarket, the four streets which had formed Glasgow Cross from the late 12th century. From here there was a track north to the Cathedral and south to the crossing of the River Clyde, where an eight-arched stone bridge was built around 1345, although a ford at the foot of Saltmarket was still in use until the late 18th century. The Tolbooth, or Town House, which was the city chambers, court and prison, sat on the north side of the Trongate, but was demolished in 1921, with only the seven-storey steeple remaining. For over 400 years on High Street, leading up to the Cathedral from Glasgow Cross, sat Glasgow

University, the Old College, in a fine collection of buildings, quadrangles and gardens demolished in the 19th century when the institution moved to Kelvingrove in the west of the city.

Andrew enthuses to Frank about Glasgow's impressive 13th-century cathedral which is considered the finest example of pre-Reformation Gothic in Europe and the only medieval church on the Scottish mainland to survive the Reformation: 'Ah! It's a brave kirk – nane o' yer whigmaleeries and curliewurlies.' He proceeds vividly to relate how it was saved from destruction during the Reformation by the zeal of the crafts guildsmen of the city repelling the iconoclastic reformers. The church was built on an earlier foundation and tomb of the 7th-century St Kentigern or Mungo, whose shrine is in the vaulted lower church. The cathedral was built on two levels on a sloping site by a ravine containing a 'wandering rivulet', the Molendinar Burn, with a rocky hill beyond which later became the site of the Necropolis. After the Reformation there was division into three congregations housed in the nave, choir and lower level (the Laigh or Lower Church) which from 1595 housed the Barony congregation, serving the local parish until 1801 when their dedicated church building was built about a hundred yards south-west of the cathedral. At this time the lower level was part filled with earth and used as a cemetery before eventual restoration and union as a cathedral in 1833.

For his purposes Scott fused the Tron/Laigh Kirk and Barony Kirk. Frank is to be contacted at the Barony Kirk and they are swept along by the crowds heading to the 'ancient and massive pile' of the Cathedral Church. In the congregation of the Barony Kirk he hears the ominous whisper of a voice, presumably that of Rob Roy, from behind a pillar saying: 'You are in danger in this city ... Meet me tonight on the Brigg, at twelve precisely.' Campbell invites Jarvie and Frank 'as far as Drymen or Bucklivie or the Clachan of Aberfoil', some 27 miles north of Glasgow, now reached by the A81 and A811, en route to Rob Roy's lair. For them the road 'had become wild and open as soon as we had left Glasgow a mile or two behind us', a route by heaths and peat bogs. They cross a bridge at the upper reaches of the River Forth (shortly before Aberfoyle) the fords of Frew, around the dividing line between Highlands and Lowlands where the scenery alters abruptly. To the south lies lowland pasture land and to the north and west of Aberfoyle lie the Trossachs, the delightful area of forested glens, rugged mountains and lochs which Scott had celebrated in best-selling poems. Much of the area is now the Queen Elizabeth Forest Park and the steep Duke's Road from Aberfoyle, built in 1875, rises to around 800 feet then drops into the heart of the Trossachs at Loch Achray.

Before the first half of the 19th century Aberfoyle ('the confluence of streams') comprised three primitive agricultural 'toons': on the north bank of the River Forth thatched stone-built cottages described by Scott as 'miserable little bourrocks' straggled west along the road from the ancient humpbacked bridge over the Forth. There was a corn mill and inn and, south of the river, a cluster of thatched cottages around the kirk and manse at Kirkton. The modern village is centred on the north bank of the river, east of the site of the action of the novel. Frank and Jarvie approach the Clachan (hamlet) of Aberfoyle and the inn which is the scene of the famous dramatic episode where the Bailie brandishes in self-defence a red-hot coulter (a plough shaft) which is used as a poker for the fire.

The village's Bailie Nicol Jarvie Hotel is the successor to the original inn which lay about half-a-mile to the west and opposite it a coulter used to hang from a tree, described as Bailie Nicol Jarvie's poker, at the junction of Main Street and the Kirkton Road. In the inn Jarvie is challenged by three highlanders who draw swords and advance menacingly. The bailie, normally a restrained man, reaches for his sword but it is stuck in its sheath. He grabs the poker and brandishes it, setting an attacker's plaid on fire, but honour is satisfied and the poker replaced. Thereafter Jarvie and Frank spend the night in a turf-roofed clay house.

The real Rob Roy was born about 1660 at Glengyle at the head of Loch Katrine, two miles to the north of the B829 at Stronachlachar and accessible only on foot. He inherited the chieftainship of the clan MacGregor, 'the children of the mist', which in 1671 had been granted the land of Craigroystan on the east shore of Loch Lomond. He was a man of substance, a farmer and cattle drover, but, as a Jacobite in the 1715 Rising and hostile to the establishment, events conspired to make him a freebooter, outlawed and persecuted. Meanwhile he was distinguished in personal combat and famous for daring escapes from the law. He twice captured and destroyed the military garrison at Inversnaid on Loch Lomond.

At the foot of Ben Lomond before Inversnaid is 'Rob Roy's prison', a small rock cave by a large crag where he reputedly kept hostages and beyond Inversnaid, a mile-and-a-half further north on the lochside, on a rough wooded shoreline path, now part of the West Highland Way, is Rob Roy's Cave where it is claimed he hid. His generosity to the poor, in the manner of Robin Hood, was legendary. He died peacefully in 1740 at Kirkton in Balquhidder, some 14 miles north and west of Callander, off the A84, having become a farmer and elder statesman at Inverlocharig, to the west along Loch Voil and was buried alongside his wife and two sons in Balquhidder old churchyard, two miles west of Kingshouse, where a plaque reads 'MacGregor Despite Them'.

The novel reflected a developing nostalgia for native peoples and the wild grandeur of their environment as a backward society is gradually absorbed into a larger commercial and political one. Scott bought Rob Roy's musket, sgian dhu (his dirk), sword and sporran and he pictures vividly the man hunted but elusive and resourceful, who thwarts a plot against Francis by appearing at critical moments in the story.

From Aberfoyle the pretty single track B829, which for the MacGregors was a droving or war-bound route, runs west for about 15 miles to Inversnaid, passing along the north shore of the wooded Loch Ard and Loch Chon to reach Stronachlachar on Loch Katrine, beyond which a road continues by Loch Arklet and descends to Inversnaid. Some of the most stirring passages in the novel are associated with the stretch by Loch Ard. The Campbell character of earlier in the novel is now openly the 'celebrated freebooter Rob Roy' and the setting 'that mountainous and desolate territory, which, lying between the lakes of Loch Lomond, Loch Katrine, and Loch Ard, was at this time currently called Rob Roy's, or the MacGregor, country.' The

MacGregor sentinel hill of Craigmore looks down on the eastern end of Loch Ard with Ben Lomond beyond. The pass skirting Loch Ard and Loch Chon is the scene of the fight where the Bailie and Frank, escorted by government redcoat troops under Captain Thornton, are confronted by Rob Roy's redoubtable wife Helen (historically called Mary), feather-bonneted and brandishing a sword, together with her clansmen who rout them. Alongside the Aberfoyle to Inversnaid road is Echo Rock where it is believed the real Rob Roy hid and an echo tricked enemies into thinking they were surrounded. Behind the farm buildings at Ledard Farm, where it is believed Scott stayed and made notes for the novel, a signposted track leads to the fine pool and waterfall where Frank takes his leave of Helen MacGregor.

An attractive track from the car park at Milton, off the B829 on the edge of Aberfoyle, to Kinlochard and the Mill of Chon passes along the southern shore of Loch Ard, where Forestry Commission conifer plantings stretch to the eastern slope of Ben Lomond. The most striking of Rob Roy's caves is situated near this track, across the loch from a bluff called Helen's (Ellen's) Rock, formerly a site of execution and Scott has a character hurled from the summit into the water from this crag.

After the skirmish at Loch Ard Rob Roy says the Bailie and Frank must return by boat 'down to the Ferry o' Balloch on Loch Lomond' for their own safety. They proceed by the edge of Loch Ard for six miles to a hamlet, escorted by MacGregors, including Helen MacGregor and her sons, to the sound of bagpipes. They pass a splendid waterfall with double falls and proceed with Ben Lomond on the right – 'here the predominant monarch of the mountains', then through a pass in the hills to the side of Loch Lomond where there is a garrison. On returning down Loch Lomond Frank muses that he 'could have consented to live and die a lonely hermit in one of the romantic and beautiful islands amongst which our boat glided.' In Glasgow they hear news of the 1715 rebellion from Andrew Fairservice and travel south in haste through Dumfriesshire and neighbouring counties of England.

Scott was first to record the detail of Rob Roy as having particularly long arms so that he could tie his garters below the knee without stooping and giving him an enormous advantage in sword fights, an image reproduced in a statue of him in Stirling. Another statue of Rob Roy, above the Leuchar Burn at Peterculter outside Aberdeen, dates from the 1850s, visible from the bridge upstream on the A93 as it leaves town heading west.

On the beautiful Loch Katrine, romanticised by Scott in *The Lady of the Lake* ('So wondrous wild, the whole might seem/The scenery of a fairy dream') the 19th-century SS *Sir Walter Scott*, now converted from coal to biofuel, plies the loch in summer time, sailing from the east end at Trossachs Pier for eight miles to Stronachlachar on the far south-western shore.

The tourist potential of the area was further enhanced by the horse-drawn visit of Queen Victoria who stayed at nearby Invertrossachs House before heading north into Perthshire. An official Rob Roy Way follows a 79-mile route from Drymen to Pitlochry, although it does not include the key area around Loch Ard.

TOURIST INFORMATION AND VISITOR ATTRACTIONS

Edinburgh and Lothians Tourist Board
    3 Princes Street, Edinburgh EH2 2QP
    Tel: 0845 225 5121
The Scott Monument
    East Princes Street Gardens, Edinburgh EH2 2EJ
    Tel: 0131 529 4068
The Writers' Museum
    Lady Stair's Close, Lawnmarket, Edinburgh EH1 2PA
    Tel: 0131 529 4901
The Edinburgh Book Lovers' Tour
    Tel: 07770 163641
The Scottish Literary Tour Trust
    34 North Castle Street, Edinburgh EH2 3BN
    Tel: 0800 169 7410/0131 226 6665
Scottish Borders Tourist Board
    Shepherds Mill, Whinfield Road, Selkirk TD7 5DT
    Tel: 0870 6080404

Abbotsford House
   Melrose TD6 9BQ
   Tel: [seasonal] 01896 752043
Bowhill House and Country Estate, Selkirk TD7 5ET
   Tel: [seasonal] 01750 22204
Dryburgh Abbey
   St Boswell's TD6 6RQ
   Tel: 0131 668 8081
VisitScotland Hawick iCentre
   Heart of Hawick, Tower Mill, Hawick TD9 OAE
   Tel: 01450 373993
Visit Scotland Jedburgh iCentre
   Murrays Green, Jedburgh TD8 6BE
   Tel: 01835 863170
VisitScotland Kelso iCentre,
   Town House, The Square, Kelso TD5 7HF
   Tel: 01573 221119
VisitScotland Melrose iCentre
   Priorwsood Gardens, Abbey Street, Melrose TD6 9PZ
   Tel: [seasonal] 01896 820178
VisitScotland Peebles iCentre
   23 High Street, Peebles EH45 8AG
   Tel: 01721 728095
VisitScotland Selkirk iCentre
   Halliwell's House, Market Place, Selkirk TD7 4BL
   Tel: 01750 20054
Smailholm Tower
   Sandyknowe Farm, Kelso TD5 7PG
   Tel: [seasonal] 01573 460365
St Ronan's Well Interpretive Centre
   Wells Brae, Innerleithen EH44 6RB
   Tel: [seasonal] 01896 833583
Sir Walter Scott Courtroom
   Market Place, Selkirk TD7 4BT
   Tel: [seasonal] 01750 720761
Sir Walter Scott Way
   Tel: 01896 822079
VisitScotland Glasgow iCentre
   Gallery of Modern Art, Royal Exchange Square, Glasgow G1 3AH
Glasgow Cathedral
   Cathedral Square, Castle Street, Glasgow G4 OQZ
   Tel: 0141 552 6891
VisitScotland Aberfoyle iCentre
   Trossachs Discovery Centre, Main Street, Aberfoyle FK8 3UQ
   Tel: 01877 381221

Balloch Information Centre
  Old Station Building, Balloch G83 8LQ
  Tel: 01389 753533
Breadalbane Folklore Centre
  Killin FK21 8XE
  Tel: 01567 820254
VisitScotland Callander iCentre
  52-4 Main Street, Callander FK17 8BD
  Tel: 01877 330342
VisitScotland Stirling iCentre
  St John Street, Stirling FK8 1EA
  Tel: 01786 475019
Loch Lomond & Trossachs National Park
  Tel: 01389 722600
SS *Sir Walter Scott*
  Trossachs Pier, Loch Katrine, by Callander FK17 8HZ
  Tel: [seasonal] 01877 376315/6

14

Tobias Smollett

TOBIAS GEORGE SMOLLETT (1721-71) was born at Dalquhurn House, a three-storey building, demolished in 1964, in the Vale of Leven on the estates of his grandfather Sir James Smollett of Bonhill which lay on the opposite bank of the River Leven. The birthplace was just south of Place of Bonhill between Main Street (the B857) and the river, between Renton and Alexandria in Dunbartonshire, some 14 miles west of Glasgow. The writer's father was Archibald Smollett, a laird, judge and Member of Parliament and his mother Barbara Cunningham. Smollett was baptised in the parish church of Cardross.

Smollett's father died soon after his birth and the absent father figure became a common theme in his writings. An older brother died in a shipwreck. Schooling was in Dumbarton, in the Grammar School which was at the bottom of Church Street, under John Love, a headmaster who was a celebrated grammarian and Greek and Latin were prominent in the curriculum. Smollett denied that Love was the model for the nasty schoolmaster in *The Adventures of Roderick Random* (1748).

In the 1730s Glasgow was a compact little city of around 16,000 people where Smollett was apprenticed to the noted surgeon-apothecaries Drs William Stirling and John Gordon in 1736, living in a back attic in the merchant city of the Glasgow tobacco barons. His lodgings were in a corner building known as Gibson's Land in Princes Street, off the Saltmarket, between Glasgow Cross and the River Clyde; the property was later knocked down to make way for the Glasgow and Southwestern Railway. He attended the Old College of Glasgow University which stretched north and east from Glasgow Cross and qualified in medicine in 1739. His satires on the leading Glasgow merchants have not survived, but there was ample experience to acquire the physiological detail which was characteristic of Smollett's subsequent writing, although it may be unfair to claim that Potion in *Roderick Random* was based on his old teachers.

In the summer of 1739 Smollett headed for London, then a city of some 70,000 people, the largest in Europe, determined to find a producer for his play *The Regicide*, a tragedy on the assassination of King James I of Scotland, but lack of success and shortage of cash led to him being engaged as a ship's surgeon bound for the West Indies on HMS *Chichester* as war with Spain commenced. After the fiasco of a campaign which provided excellent earthy comic material for the novel *Roderick Random*, showing Smollett's disgust at commanders and the unsanitary conditions and which was to make him one of the foremost novelists of the sea, he settled for a time in Jamaica before returning to surgery and writing in London. He set up as a surgeon in Downing Street, a cul-de-sac between Whitehall and St James's Park, not yet the official residence of the Prime Minister and still tried to combine the occupations of doctor and playwright. In 1745 his patriotic poem on the disaster of Culloden 'Tears of Scotland' made him better known, as did satires and pamphleteering. In 1746 he moved to Chapel Street in Mayfair where his wife, Anne Lassells, a Creole heiress of well-to-do planters, joined him from Jamaica and their only child, Elizabeth, was born in 1748. Smollett was unable to access his wife's family wealth.

With the success of *Roderick Random*, published in January 1748 and with four editions by January 1750, Smollett moved to better lodgings in Beaufort Street between the Strand and the River Thames, nearer to the theatres and pubs of Covent Garden and the booksellers of Fleet Street and St Paul's.

He gained an MD from Aberdeen University in 1750 and soon after the picaresque work *The Adventures of Peregrine Pickle* (1751), a satire on the Grand Tour of Europe was published. He worked closely with fellow Scot Andrew Millar, a printer who by the 1750s had the largest print shop in London in Shoe Lane off Fleet Street. Another close Scottish associate was the printer

Archibald Hamilton who was based in Chancery Lane. Eventually *The Regicide* was published and his play *The Reprisal* performed at Drury Lane, proving successful enough to be revived.

Grub Street hack work continued, but the success of *Roderick Random* and *The Adventures of Peregrine Pickle* and his translation of *Gil Blas* and other Spanish and French writings allowed him to retire from medical practice in 1752-3 and devote himself to writing as journalist, dramatist, historian, pamphleteer and novelist, often satirising malpractice in politics, law, medicine and religion. His works were to influence Charles Dickens who is said to have known Smollett's novels by heart from childhood. He had already published poetry and now translated Cervantes and Voltaire, travelling in France and the Low Countries in 1749 and elsewhere in Europe thereafter.

The Adventures of Ferdinand Count Fathom (1753) followed and in 1755 his *History and Adventures of Don Quixote* was published. In 1756 he co-founded the *Critical Review* which he edited until 1763. His *Complete History of England* (1757-8) was very successful. *The Life and Adventures of Sir Launcelot Greaves* appeared in 1762.

The Adventures of Ferdinand Count Fathom showed Smollett's satirical use of his medical knowledge, with its vivid portrayal of the physical detail of naval life, the Bath assembly rooms and Covent Garden streetlife. A flair for the depiction of brutal life in jails, hospitals, naval and military settings and sport became a hallmark.

Improved earnings had allowed him to move to the three-storey Monmouth House in Lawrence Street in Chelsea from 1750-63. There is a plaque at No 16, at the end of the street, on the left beyond the Cross Keys pub. The street runs down to the Thames and to the west is Chelsea Old Church where Smollett's daughter and mother-in-law are buried and to the east the Physic Garden and Chelsea Hospital and, just beyond, the site of Ranelagh Gardens which he was later to describe vividly. He frequented the White Swan pub on the river bank and nearby on Cheyne Walk was the famous coffee house Don Saltero's at No 18 which closed in the 1860s. In *The Expedition of Humphry*

Clinker (1771) Jery is taken to dine in Chelsea with S_____ (clearly Smollett) and enjoys a meal in the garden. Every Sunday Smollett hosted 'brothers of the quill', fellow toilers in Grub Street, in his house and garden for dinner. Antipathy towards Scots in London meant that Smollett was especially drawn to fellow Scots who tended to congregate in the coffee houses around Charing Cross, like the Golden Ball, on the corner of Cockspur Street, Forrest's, opposite Mews Gate and the British Coffee-House in Cockspur Street.

Disappointed at the reception for *The Adventures ofFerdinand Count Fathom*, Smollett abandoned novels for seven years. He left for Scotland to visit friends and relatives, first his mother, living with his sister Jane and her husband Alexander Telfer in Scotstoun in Peeblesshire, then Alexander 'Jupiter' Carlyle in Musselburgh, followed by old friends in Edinburgh and Glasgow. Smollett's four-volume *Complete History of England*, completed in 14 months, took a great toll on his health.

In 1760 he returned to Scotland again and stayed with Telfer. In the same year his libel of Admiral Knowles in the *Critical Review* led to a fine of £100 and three months in the King's Bench Prison, recently built in St George's Fields, a mile or so south of Westminster on the south bank. Smollett wrote part of *Sir Launcelot Greaves* there, but it proved to be a disappointment – his weakest novel.

In 1762 the death of his only child occurred and so he left Chelsea and in June 1763 set off travelling abroad through France and Italy, publishing after a two-year absence his master-piece of travel literature, *Travels through France and Italy* (1766) which closely observed both the colourful and the repulsive.

On return to Britain he took a house near Golden Square in London. Although he was in poor health, he worked on a fifth volume of his English history and moved to Bath in October 1765, taking rooms in South Parade. He admitted to being a hypochondriac valetudinarian, yet had the substance and inspi-ration to produce the perceptive observation of people, places and social trends in geography, economics and social history that was *Humphry Clinker*. The novel was begun in Scotland, while staying with a sister at Wanlockhead in Dumfriesshire, written in

Italy and told in a series of letters as a family group travel through England and Scotland, dealing with politics, religion and much else, particularly in resorts for gentlefolk. The Scottish section was no doubt based on his long visit, setting out in May 1766, journeying via Harrogate. He saw his mother and widowed sister in Edinburgh as well as old friends both there and in Glasgow, creating a picture both amusing and affectionate.

In Edinburgh he stayed on the second floor of a tenement at the head of St John Street, since renumbered as No 22 St John Street, entered by a pend, an arched passageway, from No 182 Canongate near the foot of the Royal Mile, above which an inscription records his visit. It was 'up four pairs of stairs, in the High Street, the fourth storey being, in this city, reckoned more genteel than the first.' The property is now part of Moray House School of Education. At the time this was an aristocratic quarter (home of the Earls of Dalhousie and Hyndford and Lord Monboddo) and here Smollett wrote part of *Humphry Clinker* which includes numerous scenes around Edinburgh.

With the growth of the New Town, wealthier residents gradually moved from the congestion and filth of the Old Town and Canongate became a neighbourhood noted for its degradation in the 19th century, although St John Street remained desirable. Like his character Bramble, Smollett met the intelligentsia who formed a 'hot-bed of genius' in the emerging Enlightenment in Edinburgh. He left Scotland for the last time in August 1766 and returned to Bath and took rooms in Gay Street.

The epistolary *Humphry Clinker*, considered Smollett's best novel, was not published until 1771, just months before his death and nearly three years after he left Britain for the last time. In the autumn of 1768 he went to Pisa and in the spring of 1770 to a villa called Il Giardino in Antignano on the slopes of Mount Nero, three miles south of Livorno (Leghorn), where he died and is buried in the English cemetery.

STORYTRAIL: *The Expedition of Humphry Clinker*

THE MAIN CHARACTERS
Matthew Bramble, a Welsh squire, travelling with family and
	servants for his health's sake.
Tabitha Bramble, eligible sister to Matthew.
Jeremy Melford, nephew to Matthew.
Lydia Melford, his sister.
Mrs Winifred Jenkins, the Brambles' maid.
Humphry Clinker, resourceful stableman who joins the
	company on their travels.
Lieutenant Obadiah Lismahago, an eccentric Scots soldier.

The novel was innovative in combining elements of a travel
book with social commentary and arose largely out of Smollett's
own tour of Britain in 1766. In epistolary form it records a party
travelling through the Britain of George III. Smollett ensures a
multiplicity of viewpoints: Mr Matthew Bramble is the opinion-
ated, outwardly misanthropic, yet warm-hearted old Welsh
country squire who is the central character; Tabitha, the unchar-
itable, man-seeking sister; Jeremy (Jery) Melford, the energetic
Oxford scholar; Lydia is his romantic and impressionable sister;
Mrs Winifred Jenkins (Win), the Welsh maid, and there is the
colourful Scots lieutenant Obadiah Lismahago. Clinker, the
resourceful ostler, appears later as Bramble's long-lost illegitimate
son. There is charm in the company's reaction to the towns and
countryside they pass through and people met, with fine observation and social satire, at times comic or absurd as the principal
characters strike poses and observe the niceties of English social
life.

　　The departure point for the anti-clockwise trip around
Britain is the fictitious and delightfully described Brambleton
Hall in Monmouthshire, 'within a day's ride of Abergavenny'
according to Win's letter from Bath. The route was by
Gloucester, Clifton/Hot Well, Bath, London, Harrogate, York,
Scarborough, Whitby, Guisborough, Durham, Newcastle-on-
Tyne, Morpeth, Berwick-on-Tweed, Haddington, Edinburgh,
Linlithgow, Glasgow, Hamilton, Paisley, Dumbarton, Inveraray,

the islands of Islay, Jura, Mull and Iona, then by Greenock, Dumfries, Carlisle and Manchester. Chatsworth near Buxton in Derbyshire was on Bramble's intended route although there is no report that they stopped there.

At Hot Well (Hotwells), now Clifton, to the west of Bristol a curative spring was discovered at the foot of St Vincent's Rocks on the bank of the River Avon and a Pump Room and Assembly Rooms were established above. A zigzag path from Clifton led down to the well. A colonnade remains of the building which was destroyed in the 19th century. Lydia Melford describes the 'enchanting variety of moving pictures' as ships passed 'close under the windows'. Here 'The air is so pure. The Downs are so agreeable … ' She goes on to say: 'If we go to Bath, I shall send you my simple remarks upon that famous centre of polite amusement.'

A shrewd observer, Smollett knew Bath well having stayed variously at South Parade, the Bear Inn and Gay Street. The city rapidly expanded in its Palladian style as an elegant spa resort for the fashionable and moneyed classes in the 18th century, its population trebling between 1700 and 1765. By 1757, 23 coaches were arriving from London each week. In Smollett's travelogue Bath is variously observed: 'Thus the number of people and the number of houses continue to increase; and this will ever be the case, till the streams that swell this irresistible torrent of folly and extravagance shall either be exhausted, or turned into other channels, by incidents and events which I do not pretend to foresee.'

The famous Circus of the elder John Wood is considered 'a pretty bauble, contrived for show, and looks like Vespasian's amphitheatre turned outside in.' Bramble notes Bath's urbanisation, noise, confusion, luxury and the effects of colonial exploitation, war profiteering and materialism. He considers it 'the very centre of racket and dissipation' and 'a sink of profligacy and extortion'.

He condemns it for being a place attractive to the sick, hypochondriac and pleasure-loving and those who preyed on them, including gamblers and fortune hunters and the waters of the baths were unhealthy and dirty. Smollett tried to practise medicine in Bath, living in Gay Street in 1767 and supported his fellow Scottish doctor Archibald Cleland who exposed the truth of the health risks of drinking the waters. Bramble realises that unsanitary water is being consumed.

Jery, lodging on a first floor on South Parade, says he is 'near the Bath, and remote from the noise of carriages.' Bramble resides in Milsam Street and admires the architecture. Lydia loves the 'gaiety, good-humour, and diversion'. She is impressed by the Square, Circus, Parades and new rows 'like so many enchanted castles'. They visit the Pump Room, with the King's bath, a huge cistern below, 'where you see the patients up to their necks in hot water', the neighbouring coffee-house and across the river the Spring Garden, with walks and ponds and parterres of flowers, east of the Abbey Church on the east bank of the River Avon and the two Assembly Rooms. Jery visits the Bear Inn in Stall Street, famous for over a century for its luxury and the Three Tuns, the well-known inn in Stall Street in the centre of Bath.

Heading towards London from Bath, the company has an accident on Marlborough Downs as the coach overturns between Chippenham and Marlborough. Then they meet Humphry Clinker when they stop at a castle on Spin (Speen) Hill near Speenhamland in Berkshire. They dine the following day at Salt Hill near Slough in Buckinghamshire.

Bramble lodges in Golden Square in London, near Smollett's own residence in Brewer Street at the time. London sights are vividly pictured, like Sadler's Wells, Ranelagh Gardens and the life of the Thames, yet alongside the fine London scenes there is the image of London as diseased. Bramble complains that 'the Capital has become an overgrown monster which, like a dropsical head, will in time leave the body and extremities without nourishment and support.' He compares the Arcadian purity of Brambleton Hall and the filth of London with its stench and din. He is searing in his criticism of the luxury, corruption, noise, dirt and bustle of London, yet there is accompanying good humour.

Bramble is amazed at the range of streets, squares, palaces and churches, the result of the city's rapid growth. There are gatherings at Carlisle House in Soho Square. Bramble visits the British Museum and Montague House. Win goes to the Tower of

London with her mistress 'to see the crowns and wild beasts'. There is a party at Sadler's Wells and entertainment at a music hall in Islington. Jery describes dining with 'S_____', ie Smollett, at Monmouth House which was demolished in 1834. Jery turns down Longacre, between St Martin's Lane and Drury Lane, where there is a Methodist Church meeting and Clinker is conducting worship.

There is lengthy description of Ranelagh Gardens, to the east of Chelsea Royal Hospital grounds and the site of the annual Chelsea Flower show since 1913. The gardens opened to the public in 1742 for leisure and entertainment, offering patrons alfresco meals, balls, concerts, fireworks, a canal with gondolas and spectacles in the Rotunda. The central bandstand was surrounded by boxes and there was music in the evenings. Mozart performed here in 1764. Bramble and Lydia provide differing views on the entertainments. A small pavilion on the site now tells the story of the gardens as a Georgian pleasure resort with a 'thousand golden lamps that emulate the noon-day sun' where one could take the air and avoid the city's smoke and fog. The site can now be entered from the East Walk and Chelsea Bridge Road passes between Ranelagh Gardens and the Chelsea Barracks.

Vauxhall Gardens, a place of fashionable summer resort patronised by the Prince of Wales and gentry, was laid out on a 12-acre site in 1660 in Lambeth on the south bank of the Thames. The gardens occupied an area bounded by the present Golding Street, Laud Street, Kennington Lane and St Oswald Place and were accessed by a wherry across the river before Westminster Bridge was built in 1750. There were paths through the trees, shrubbery, gravelled walks, vistas, triumphal arches, statues, pseudo-Italian ruins, rotundas, Chinese pavilions, 50 supper boxes decorated by Hogarth and others, concert and music halls and a round bandstand. Lydia considered the walks delightful while Bramble condemns the gardens as baubles.

The Vauxhall St Peter's Heritage Centre, at 310 Kennington Lane, provides the story of the Gardens and Vauxhall area. A large grassy expanse and the Vauxhall City Farm are all that remain of the former gardens. Plans have been mooted to redevelop the site as a modern version of the Pleasure Gardens with exhibition space, performance area, music venue and exhibitions.

The company heads north from London but a horse loses a shoe at Barnet and there is the possibility of highwaymen a mile short of Hatfield, where they dine, then continue to Stevenage. Bramble suffers from jolting in the carriage between Newark and Wetherby until they are safely installed at the New Inn in Harrogate in north Yorkshire, a fashionable health resort since the late 16th century and, like Bath, noted for its combination of 'gaiety and dissipation'. The waters, believed to be health-giving because of the sulphur and iron in the springs, are unflatteringly described.

At York they visit the Castle, Minster and Assembly Room. At Scarborough where they are intent upon sea-bathing, which Smollett, as a doctor, recommended. Bramble is saved from the embarrassment of drowning. Jery describes one of the new-fangled bathing machines as 'extravagant ideas of decency and decorum' and so the party leave the next day. They cross the moors for Whitby, the Tees at Stockton, spend a night at Guisborough and head for Durham. There is an accident with the carriage, but fortunately there is a forge nearby and they are helped by Clinker 'who is a surprising compound of genius and simplicity'. At Durham they meet Lieutenant Obadiah Lismahago (the name recalling Lesmahagow, a village near Lanark), modelled on Captain Robert Stobo, a Scots merchant who emigrated to Virginia and became a professional soldier. From Doncaster as they head northwards towards Berwick they note the insults to Scots inscribed on the windows of inns.

In his treatment of Scotland Smollett is keen to inform ignorant southerners. He was among the first to make fun of things conventionally pertaining to the Scots: whisky, bagpipes and haggis. The tone is amiable and perceptive and Scotland is clearly interpreted as a high point in beauty and civility contrasting with squalor and corruption in England.

Jery says they enter Scotland by 'a frightful moor of sixteen miles' and pass through Dunbar, 'a neat little town, situated on the sea-side.' Bramble speaks of 'fine seats' between the border and Edinburgh. They dine at Haddington (Win conflates

Haddington and Edinburgh as Haddingborough) and then head for Edinburgh which is 'very romantic, from its situation on the declivity of a hill, having a fortified castle at the top, and a royal palace at the bottom.' They note the height of houses of six, seven, eight and even 12 storeys.

The teeming life of Edinburgh Old Town, where all social classes mixed in the tenement buildings around the Royal Mile between the castle and Holyroodhouse in the mid-18th century before the building of the New Town, is vividly described and Smollett, through his mouthpieces, celebrates the intellectual ferment of the Old Town and its distinguished Enlightenment figures like David Hume, Adam Smith and Adam Ferguson for 'Edinburgh is a hot-bed of genius.' Jery comments that the palace of Holyroodhouse 'is a jewel in architecture, thrust into a hollow where it cannot be seen.' Bramble notes that at the Mercat Cross by Parliament Square crowds gathered to hear news, merchants met and executions took place, although the High Street was spoiled by the presence of the Lucken-Booths, the teeming network of market stalls.

There are dancing assemblies and visits to Leith, whose harbour contains over a hundred ships and where the nobility resort to watch horse racing and archery contests and promenade by the sands at Leith and Musselburgh. At the foot of Leith Walk the travellers cross Constitution Street, take second left off Duke Street on to Duncan Place, then right on to Leith Links, the alleged birthplace of golf where in the 15th century an irate King James IV proscribed the sport since it distracted men from archery. Golf on the links attracts 'a multitude of all ranks'. The view of Edinburgh is clearly affectionate despite the enormous sanitation problem.

The company takes in Fife visiting St Andrews and country seats and castles. They pass through Linlithgow with its 'elegant royal palace' which is 'now gone to decay' and Stirling has a 'fine old castle.' They head west to Glasgow with its clean and smart flag-stoned pavements, 'the pride of Scotland' and, says Bramble, 'one of the prettiest towns in Europe' with its venerable cathedral and college stretching down to the Cross. Downstream on the River Clyde is Dumbarton with its castle and from here 'the

West Highlands appear in the form of huge, dusky mountains, piled one over another.' Nearby is Smollett's birthplace and they 'pitched our headquarters at Cameron House, a very neat country-house belonging to Com S ... like a Druid's temple, in a grove of oak, close by the side of Lough-Lomond.' Win Jenkins speaks of Carman Hill, accessed by the Cardross Road which goes west of the B857 from Renton under the A82 road to the West Highlands. Here, above Place of Bonhill, is the site of a vitrified fort, a place superstitiously associated with fairies. At this point Smollett is visiting the scenes of his childhood and his mouthpiece Bramble declares that the country is 'romantic beyond imagination' ... 'All is sublimity, silence, and solitude' and introduces the rhapsodic 'Ode to Leven Water'. Lydia calls Loch Lomond 'one of the most enchanting spots in the whole world.' Bramble prefers Loch Lomond to the Italian lakes and Geneva and the Western Isles are 'one of the most ravishing prospects in the whole world.' Smollett's moving recollection written from Leghorn may be the first literary recognition of the sublimity of the Scottish Highlands.

The company rambles thorough the mountains and glens of Argyll, visiting the adjacent islands of Ila (Islay), Jura, Mull and Icolmkill (Iona), then return from the Cowal peninsula to Greenock. From Glasgow they head to Lanark, Bramble enthusing about the stately homes in the Clyde valley, take in the fine Falls of Clyde, then head south into Nithsdale for Dumfries and the western borders of England, the route roughly of the present M74. Drumlanrig Castle of the Duke of Queensberry, where they spend a night, is 'like a magnificent palace erected by magic, in the midst of a wilderness.' Journeying by Manchester, they make for Chatsworth House in the Peak District. Tabitha is excited about the Devil's Arse, or Peak's Cavern, a large cavern off the A625 near Castleton and Eldon Hole, a massive pot-hole by the A623 at Peak Forest.

TOURIST INFORMATION
AND VISITOR ATTRACTIONS

Balloch Information Centre
    Old Station Building, Balloch G83 8LQ
    Tel: 01389 753533
Cameron House
    Loch Lomond, Alexandria G83 8QZ
    Tel: 0871 222 4681
Edinburgh and Lothians Tourist Board
    3 Princes Street, Edinburgh EH2 2Q,
    Tel: 0845 225 5121
VisitScotland Glasgow iCentre
    Gallery of Modern Art, Royal Exchange Square, Glasgow G1 3AH
Bath TIC
    Abbey Chambers, Abbey Church Yard, Bath BA1 1LY
    Tel: 01225 322442
Harrogate TIC
    Royal Baths, Crescent Road, Harrogate HG1 2RR
    Tel: 01423 537300
City of London Information Centre
    St Paul's Churchyard, London EC4M 8BX
    Tel: 020 7332 3456
The Royal Hospital Chelsea
    London SW3 4SR
    Tel: 020 7881 5200
Vauxhall Pleasure Gardens
    139 Vauxhall Walk, Lambeth, London SE11 5HL
    Tel: 020 7926 9000
Vauxhall St Peter's Heritage Centre
    310 Kennington Lane, Lambeth, London SE11 5HY
    Tel: 020 7735 3403

15

Muriel Spark

DAME MURIEL SPARK (1918-2006) was born in Edinburgh to a Jewish father, Bernard Camberg, an engineer, and Sarah (Cissy) Uezzell, a piano teacher. Muriel was brought up in a first-floor flat at No 160 Bruntsfield Place, part of the A702 which continues south on to Morningside Road. She attended James Gillespie's High School for Girls which was founded in 1803. The school building, now used as student accommodation for Edinburgh University, was at the end of Warrender Park Terrace, with Edwardian-type windows looking over the leafy Bruntsfield Links. Spark had a ten-minute walk to school through avenues of tall trees and the large public common, wearing a maroon blazer and hat with 'JGS' monogrammed on the badge. Her literary abilities were obvious at school and she gained a reputation for being a poet and dreamer. It was popularly said that you can spot a former pupil of Gillespie's from her use of the semicolon.

James Gillespie High School has been comprehensive and coeducational since 1972 and is now housed in a new building situated in nearby Lauderdale Street. In 1996 Spark donated the proceeds from a literature prize she won to install a new suite of rooms bearing her name for the encouragement of arts, especially literature and drama, in the school.

Spark describes her teacher at age 11, Miss Christina Kay, as in certain respects the model for her famous fictional character Jean Brodie. Miss Kay was 'that character in search of an author,' charismatic, with an idiosyncratic, but not subversive, enthusiasm for culture, who took Spark and her friend Frances Niven to theatre, films and concerts. Miss Kay's classroom walls displayed

Renaissance paintings and a newspaper cutting of Mussolini's Fascisti marching in Rome. Spark reckons that Miss Kay would have put Jean Brodie in her place, yet there were similarities. There was a personal drama about lessons and Miss Kay told the class they were the crème de la crème. At Gillespie's a handsome art master Arthur Couling once smashed a saucer, an incident later used in *The Prime of Miss Jean Brodie* (1961). A young American, Charlotte Rule, who taught Spark to read at age three, had the maiden name of Brodie and was a schoolteacher before marriage.

As a child Spark loved Bruntsfield Links across from her home in all seasons. In summer she practised putting with her brother and friends and would go round the course looking for golf balls. From age ten to 16 she spent much of her free time in Morningside Public Library. She loved Robert Louis Stevenson and treasured her copy of *A Child's Garden of Verses*. There were excursions to the Braid Hills, Blackford Hill and pond, a pleasant green space with a panorama of Edinburgh, the Firth of Forth and Fife and to the Pentland hills which were celebrated in Stevenson's poems. His 'hills of home' were hers too. There were seaside excursions to Portobello.

The Heriot Watt College, predecessor of the university of the same name, was in Chambers Street. Here she did a course on business English, with précis writing, typing and shorthand. She taught for a time at a small private day-school, the Hill School, at No 35 Colinton Road in the Merchiston district near her home, teaching English, arithmetic and nature study. Then at age 18 she became secretary to the owner of William Small & Sons, the west-end department store, at No 106 Princes Street. Spark later developed the habit of beginning a novel with its title written on the front of an exercise-book, always bought from James Thin booksellers (now Blackwell's) on South Bridge.

While never returning to live in Edinburgh, Spark uses its topography, history and literary past and an Edinburgh middle-class idiom. Jean Brodie has a double life as a spinster with a freedom from the conventions of the bourgeoisie, including a weekend lover. Spark notes the importance of the conjunction 'niverthelace' (nevertheless) in the Edinburgh mentality of the time.

Of school she said: ' ... in my day Tolerance was decidedly the prevailing religion, always with a puritanical slant.' Her most famous novel was written in just four weeks in 1960 when Spark returned to stay with her parents.

Determined to see the world, in 1937 Spark married an older man, Sydney Oswald Spark, whom she met at a dance at the Overseas Club in Princes Street. His work as a teacher took them to Southern Rhodesia (Zimbabwe). There was a farewell tea with Miss Kay and Frances. There were signs, however, of instability and violence in the husband who did not reveal seeing a psychiatrist before marriage. He was nicknamed 'S.O.S.' and Spark noted the irony in his initials. The early autobiographical novel *Robinson* (1958) has a writer as castaway on a desert island with an unstable man.

Spark became pregnant and gave birth to a son, Samuel (Robin), in 1938. The marriage failed and the child was brought up by her parents; he lived in his grandparents' flat until his death in 2016. She appreciated the enrichment of her experience as a writer from living in South Africa where writing could come first and there was no need to do housework because of domestic help. In 1944 she returned to Edinburgh and then, having divorced, to wartime London and a job in the Political Intelligence section of MI6 as Duty Secretary in Sefton Delmer's Compound at Milton Bryan in Bedfordshire, a village between Milton Keynes and Luton, then a high-security centre for black propaganda. Here she worked on fake radio broadcasts designed to undermine German morale.

After the war Spark worked on the quarterly magazine *Argentor* and was General Secretary of the Poetry Society from 1947-9 and in 1949 editor of *Poetry Review* with offices at No 33 Portman Square (now Earls Court Square). She tried to modernise practices but found that mediocre poets were paying to have poems included. With consequent in-fighting, she was dismissed and founded the rival *Forum*, using the experience in *Loitering with Intent* (1981). She lived at No 82 Lancaster Gate in London for various spells, with a room of her own to the rear at the top of the house which overlooked Kensington Gardens. This property was home to the Helena Club, a hostel, now a hotel, which was the model for the May of Teck Club in *The Girls of Slender Means* (1963), Spark's own favourite of her novels.

In January 1949 she moved to a small room on the ground floor of the pretty Georgian Eras House at No 1 Vicarage Gate on Kensington Church Street. This room with its gas ring and wash-hand basin was largely the setting for *Loitering with Intent*. In the summer of 1950 she moved to a larger furnished fourth-floor room at No 8 Sussex Mansions, part of Old Brompton Road. She was now working part-time at the Falco Press as secretary, experience reflected in *A Far Cry from Kensington* (1988).

In March 1953 she moved to No 1 Queen's Gate Terrace close to St Augustine's Church where she took her first communion shortly afterwards. From August 1955 she lodged at No 13 Baldwin Crescent near Camberwell New Road in south-east London, occupying attic rooms facing the back garden. Here she wrote *The Ballad of Peckham Rye* (1960) the action of which takes place in Camberwell and Peckham. She stayed for 11 years and returned there, even after moving to New York and Rome. On visits to England Spark also stayed at the house of an acquaintance in Pimlico and at his country home, the Queen Anne-style Old Rectory in the village of Terling in Essex.

In May 1954 Spark was received into the Catholic Church in the Jesuit Church in Farm Street after instruction from Father Agius at Ealing Priory. She was baptised at St Bride's Church off Fleet Street and considered becoming a nun. Suffering from nervous exhaustion she moved in October to The Friars, the Carmelite Aylesford Priory near Maidstone in Kent. Here she stayed initially at the guesthouse and then in a cottage in the grounds of nearby Allington Castle, owned by the Carmelites, until August 1955. She was ill while she wrote her first novel here, *The Comforters* (1957), based upon hallucinatory word games which arose from doses of Dexedrine she took as an appetite suppressant.

She won a short-story competition organised by *The Observer* newspaper in 1951 and then turned principally to fiction. *The Go-away Bird* (1958) was a first volume of short stories which reflected her African experiences. After religious conversion themes of good and evil became characteristic of her works. Another popular theme was the combination of the bizarre and the ordinary in human life with the stripping away of human pretension. Subsequent novels included *Memento Mori* (1959), which was adapted for the stage, *The Bachelors* (1960), *The Mandelbaum Gate* (1965), *The Public Image* (1968), *The Driver's Seat* (1970), *Not To Disturb* (1971), *The Abbess of Crewe* (1974), *The Takeover* (1976), *Territorial Rights* (1979), *The Only Problem* (1984), *Symposium* (1990), *Reality and Dreams* (1996), *Aiding and Abetting* (2000) and *The Finishing School* (2004). She also produced literary biographies or editions of Wordsworth, Mary Shelley, Emily Brontë, JH Newman and John Masefield and two children's books.

Spark moved to New York in 1962 and an apartment on the 13th floor of the Beaux Arts Hotel at No 310, East 44th Street. *The Hothouse by the East River* (1973) concerns a couple who meet working on counter intelligence at 'the Compound', a secret location, and later marry and move to America. *The Prime of Miss Jean Brodie* first appeared in *The New Yorker* where she had an office, at West 43rd Street opposite the Algonquin Hotel.

In 1966 Spark moved to Italy where she took up permanent residence. She met the British sculptor Penelope Jardine at a hairdressing salon in Rome in1968 and she became Spark's secretary shortly afterwards. They lived together in Rome and then from 1985 entirely in Jardine's house called San Giovanni, formerly the presbytery of a neighbouring deconsecrated 13th-century church on a hillside at Oliveto, near Civitella di Chiana and Arezzo in Tuscany. Here Spark died and is buried.

Her son Robin became a successful painter in Edinburgh, continued to live in the house of the grandparents who raised him while Spark sought to earn a living in London. A controversy developed between mother and son, having its roots perhaps in the childhood abandonment, but also in a dispute concerning whether both grandparents were in fact Jewish. Robin said he was not interested in his mother's estate which in any case was bequeathed to Jardine. Spark admitted that her son reminded her of her repulsive husband.

Curriculum Vitae, her autobiography, appeared in 1992 and collected plays, short stories and poetry have also appeared. *The Golden Fleece: Essays* appeared in 2014. She became a Dame of the British Empire in 1997. Although a distinguished novelist, Spark thought of herself primarily as a poet. An inscribed slab dedicated to Spark lies outside the Scottish Writers' Museum off Edinburgh's Lawnmarket.

STORYTRAIL: *The Prime of Miss Jean Brodie*

THE MAIN CHARACTERS
Miss Jean Brodie, schoolmistress in an Edinburgh girls' school.
Gordon Lowther, singing master at the school.
Teddy Lloyd, art master at the school, attracted to Jean Brodie.
Miss Mackay, the headmistress.
The Brodie set: Rose Stanley, Monica Douglas, Eunice Gardiner,
    Jenny Gray, Mary Macgregor and Sandy Stranger.
Joyce Emily Hammond, a pupil who is rejected by the Brodie
    set, is inspired to join the Spanish Civil War and is killed.

The girls who are the Brodie set, her 'crème de la crème', fraternise with boys outside the gates of the Marcia Blane School for Girls in 1930's Edinburgh. They are now aged 16, but were in the charismatic Jean Brodie's class since age ten. She appears and reveals that there is another attempt to sack her. Her lessons were unorthodox, some out of doors, subversively referring to her enthusiasms rather than the orthodox curriculum. She declared she was in her 'prime' and her fiancé had been killed in Flanders. The story uses flashback and also flashes forward. We learn that the clumsy Mary Macgregor later dies in a hotel fire. Sandy Stewart, based upon Spark herself and who later becomes a nun, and Jenny talk of sex. Eunice Gardiner later puts flowers on Jean Brodie's grave.

During the first year with Miss Brodie in March 1931 she takes the class on a walk through the Old Town of Edinburgh. 'The wind blew from the icy Forth and the sky was loaded with forthcoming snow' as they set off across the Meadows, 'a gusty expanse of common land', by the Middle Meadow Walk, at the end of which 'It occurred to Sandy ... that the Brodie set was Miss Brodie's fascisti.' They approach the Old Town, 'which none of the girls had properly seen before, because none of their parents was so historically minded as to be moved to conduct their young into the reeking network of slums which the Old Town constituted in those years. The Canongate, The Grassmarket, The Lawnmarket, were names which betokened a misty region of crime and desperation: "Lawnmarket man jailed" '.

They reach the Grassmarket, the castle looming in the gaps between houses where aristocracy once lived. They see obvious destitution from which they are sheltered in their middle-class seclusion. They head up to the High Street where they observe casual domestic violence and Sandy realises 'there were other people's Edinburghs.' There is not enough time for St Giles' Cathedral, says Miss Brodie, the church representing the Calvinist Elect and Sandy is intimidated by it, seeing symbolism in the dark stone. Near the end of the novel 'Fully to savour her position, Sandy would go and stand outside St Giles' Cathedral, or the Tolbooth, and contemplate these emblems of a dark and terrible salvation.'

The group moves on into Chambers Street, three abreast, and Miss Brodie declares that the headmistress wishes to challenge her teaching methods. They reach the end of Lauriston Place and pass the fire station where, with the exception of Sandy, they get a tram to go to tea at Miss Brodie's flat in Church Hill and note the long line of unemployed men. At other times there are visits to Sunday Concerts at the Usher Hall off Lothian Road.

Most of the novel is set in and around Edinburgh and ends in an unnamed convent located somewhere in the country with Sandy meeting a stream of visitors, now a famous author who betrayed Brodie and engineered her removal from the school. Sandy has a conversation with Brodie in the Braid Hills Hotel, a prominent landmark above the Braid Road, off the A702 beyond Morningside and Church Hill, in the autumn of 1945 when Brodie is ill but has heard of Sandy going into a convent. Spark describes them as 'eating sandwiches and drinking tea which Miss Brodie's rations at home would not run to. Miss Brodie sat shrivelled and betrayed in her long-preserved dark musquash coat. She had been retired before her time. She said, "I am past my prime." "It was a good prime," said Sandy. They looked out of the wide windows at the little Braid Burn trickling through the fields and at the hills beyond ... '

Brodie, the repressed spinster rebelling against the conventions of the bourgeoisie, whom Spark described as 'an Edinburgh festival all in herself,' claimed descent from Deacon Brodie the notorious 18th-century figure who was a respectable citizen by day and a burglar by night. The Deacon Brodie Tavern in the Lawnmarket recalls him with an effigy between the bars beneath the stairway. Dual character is a characteristic of the novel and in the end Brodie is a pathetic figure, her vigour and charisma lost, yet earlier: 'It was then that Miss Brodie looked beautiful and fragile, just as dark heavy Edinburgh itself could suddenly be changed into a floating city when the light was a special pearly white and fell upon one of the gracefully fashioned streets.'

On Saturdays the girls visit Gordon Lowther's mock-turreted, secluded house in Cramond, the 18th-century village off the A90 Queensferry Road, west of the city, where pretty white houses rise in tiers above the harbour quay on the east bank of the River Almond which flows into the Firth of Forth. Brodie admits to an affair with Lowther at Cramond.

Sandy Stranger realises that Brodie manipulates lives and so experiences a vicarious life, as do the others in the set. One of Brodie's protégés, Joyce Emily, goes to Spain and dies fighting for Franco while the placid Rose becomes the lover of Teddy Lloyd, the married art teacher whom Brodie herself desired. Sandy realises Brodie wishes to exercise control, like a Calvinist God, over her crème de la crème, the Elect. Sandy does likewise, betraying Brodie to the school authorities, on grounds of her love of fascism.

TOURIST INFORMATION
AND VISITOR ATTRACTIONS

Edinburgh and Lothians Tourist Board
    3 Princes Street, Edinburgh EH2 2QP
    Tel: 0845 225 5121
The Scottish Literary Tour Trust
    34 North Castle Street, Edinburgh EH2 3BN
    Tel: 0800 169 7410/0131 226 6665
The Edinburgh Book Lovers' Tour
    Tel: 07770 163641
City of London Information Centre
    St Paul's Churchyard, London EC4M 8BX
    Tel: 020 7332 3456

16

Robert Louis Stevenson

ROBERT LOUIS STEVENSON (1850-94) was born in Edinburgh, son of Thomas Stevenson, engineer and lighthouse builder and Margaret Balfour, daughter of a Church of Scotland minister. Stevenson was born in a ground-floor bedroom at the back of the house at No 8 Howard Place, part of Inverleith Row, a Georgian terrace on the northern edge of the Edinburgh New Town. In 1853 the family moved to No 1, now No 9, Inverleith Terrace, a larger residence around the corner and in 1857 they left that damp and uncomfortable house for the grand No 17 Heriot Row, overlooking Queen Street Gardens in the Edinburgh New Town and Stevenson's home until 1880. This house is not generally open to the public, but provides accommodation and hospitality.

Alison Cunningham, known as Cummy, a weaver's daughter from Fife, was nurse to the boy who was sickly from childhood and anxiety about his health meant much of his schooling was at home and a room on the top floor was made into a study. A bookcase and chest of drawers in the nursery were supposedly made by the 18th-century cabinetmaker and notorious criminal William Brodie and Cummy told lurid tales about the furniture and other stirring stories. The delightful *A Child's Garden of Verses* (1885) was dedicated to Cummy.

Stevenson's bedroom was on the top floor, seen on the far right when facing the house, while Cummy's bedroom at the back had a view of the Firth of Forth and Fife. From his bedroom window he observed the Leerie, or lamplighter, as each night Cummy carried him to the window where he saw the lights of the houses in Queen Street across the gardens. Outside

No 17 a reproduction globe-shaped lamp, painted black, powered now by electricity rather than gas, recalls the famous 'Lamplighter' poem. The pond in the centre of the gardens opposite, where Stevenson played, he pictured as a sea surrounding an island full of pirates. Cummy took him to play in Princes Street Gardens and wander along the Water of Leith, which flows from the Pentland hills, past his grandfather's manse at Colinton, through Edinburgh to Leith through the mysterious Warriston Cemetery and Royal Botanic Garden near his home. A stationer's shop at the corner of Union Street and Antigua Street at Leith Walk was a favourite of Stevenson because it had a working model of a theatre.

A plaque outside the Baptist Church at Munro Place in Canonmills indicates that Stevenson went to Canonmills School on that site at age seven. He later attended school at Mr Henderson's in India Street and then at the age of almost 11 the prestigious Edinburgh Academy on the north side of Henderson Row. He was fond of the school although he tended to be solitary. Two years later he went to Menton in France with his mother for the sake of her health and in November 1863 spent one term at boarding school at Spring Grove in Isleworth in west London, as his parents were abroad. An aunt lived nearby and two cousins attended the school. Stevenson returned to Edinburgh and the school of Robert Thomson on the northwest side of Frederick Street near his home until 1867.

Stevenson studied engineering and then, from 1870, law at the Old College of the University of Edinburgh between 1867-75. This meant a daily walk uphill to the old quadrangle off South Bridge, but Stevenson was unhappy at university and not an enthusiastic student. He passed his examinations for the Bar in 1875 but never practised. He would skip classes and explore the disreputable Old Town, from Lothian Road to Leith Walk: 'I was the companion of sea-men, chimney-sweeps and thieves; my circle was continually changed by the action of the police magistrate.' Rutherford's Bar at No 8 Drummond Street, across South Bridge from the Old College, known to students as the Pump, was a favourite watering hole, now converted into an Italian restaurant called the Hispaniola with a *Treasure Island* theme and there is a commemorative plaque at the street corner. In Advocate's Close, off the High Street, he founded a secret society with meetings in a pub and engaged in long drinking bouts. He frequented Bannerman's Bar, at No 212 Cowgate, with a plain exterior but having a series of vaulted cellars in a crypt beneath the Royal Mile. It was built in the 1770s as a port cellar and oyster bar and restored as licensed premises in 1980 after having been a dwelling house and bleach workshop. Nearer home there were tiny pubs in Jamaica Street beyond Henderson Row which he frequented and assorted drinking dens on Leith Walk.

After the imposing Georgian streets, squares and crescents of the New Town had been built in the late 18th-century, the middle classes left the Old Town with its medieval closes and wynds beneath its towering tenements or 'lands' and it became a slum area once more. And yet, said Stevenson, 'You look down an alley and see ships tacking for the Baltic.' Greyfriars Cemetery, off George IV Bridge and Candlemaker Row, where the Covenant was signed, was a favourite spot for Stevenson. Here he visualised the activities of Burke and Hare, the body snatchers who stole cadavers to sell for medical experiments. Another favourite spot was Arthur's Seat, the volcanic rock in Holyrood Park, which to him was as exciting 'as the hoariest summit of the Alps'.

There is a Stevenson family grave in the New Calton Burying Ground, just off Waterloo Place at the foot of Calton Hill, beyond the east end of Princes Street, where his parents and grandparents are interred in a walled tomb surrounded by railings. Stevenson is commemorated here and in a simple half column memorial monument erected among birch trees in West Princes Street Gardens on the centenary of his death.

A huge bronze monument to Stevenson is set in a side chapel in the Moray Aisle in the Church of St Giles in the High Street. Beneath an oriel window in the west wall a frieze by Augustus Saint-Gaudens quotes the writer's 'Requiem' concluding:

> Here he lies where he longed to be;
> Home is the sailor, home from the sea;
> And the hunter home from the hill.

The Writers' Museum, in the 17th century Lady Stair's House, through James Close off the High Street, holds one of the most significant Stevenson collections including personal belongings, paintings, photographs and early editions and materials brought back from Samoa where he finally settled. After the house at Howard Place was sold some of its furniture and other mementoes went to this museum. The Museum of Scotland in Chambers Street also has Samoan artefacts with a Stevenson connection.

Stevenson and others are referred to in a literary pub tour, organised by the Scottish Literary Tour Trust, which departs from the Beehive Inn in the Grassmarket. The Edinburgh Book Lover's Tour similarly leaves from the Writers' Museum, near Deacon Brodie's Tavern in the High Street. A Robert Louis Stevenson Day takes place in November, organised by Edinburgh's Napier University since 2011. Edinburgh is the first UNESCO City of Literature.

The young Stevenson took long walks, always carrying a notebook, to the villages of Morningside and Corstorphine which eventually became suburbs. The grave of Alison Cunningham, Stevenson's beloved nurse, is in Morningside Cemetery, near the large war memorial, on Morningside Drive off Morningside Road. She had retired to nearby Balcarres Street and then to No 1 Comiston Place where she died at age 91 in 1913. A posy of wild flowers from the village of Swanston, where the Stevensons had a country retreat, was put on her grave.

Stevenson spent many happy holidays at Colinton manse, home of his maternal grandparents and the birthplace of his mother, then in a rural setting south-west of the city and it inspired some of his poems. He considered the place Arcadian. His grandfather, Revd Dr Lewis Balfour, was Church of Scotland minister there for 37 years. The church and manse can be reached by the B701 Redford Road, Colinton Road and Spylaw Street, then crossing the Water of Leith where the church is situated just beyond the bridge. A plaque explains the Stevenson connection and a poetry trail, opened in 2014, which begins at the Long Steps on Bridge Road, celebrates the link.

The manse is private but can be seen from the churchyard and the great yew tree beside the driveway where Stevenson played on the lower branches is still there. Grandfather Balfour died at Colinton manse when Stevenson was almost 11 and there is a memorial to him at the north end of the churchyard near the church door. A bronze statue by Alan Heriot showing Stevenson as a child with his dog was erected outside the church grounds in 2013.

Further south-west of Edinburgh, in the lee of the Pentland hills, lies the pretty village of Swanston and the cottage which Stevenson's parents rented for fourteen years from 1867. A track just before the village and Swanston Farm leads to the 18th-century cottage which is private, a whitewashed two-storey building facing the Pentland Hills. Stevenson's bedroom was on the first floor. There is a 'St Ives' window, slightly to the rear of the house in the east gable since he made it the home of the heroine of *St Ives* (1897). He spent much of his sickly boyhood at 'secluded Swanston, lapped in a fold of the Pentlands', beyond the smoke of Auld Reekie, a retreat also when he was a student and an Arcadian substitute for Colinton Manse after his grandfather's death.

Stevenson loved the freedom of solitary walks on the edge of Covenanting country, taking paths up into the Pentland Hills where their conventicles took place, stretching to the south-west and providing superb views over the city. Here Stevenson got to know workers on the land and was inspired to write his pamphlet on the Covenanters, *The Pentland Rising* (1866). John Todd, the Swanston shepherd, was a close associate with whom he climbed hills and discovered local lore and vocabulary, hearing tales of drovers sleeping on the hillside, robbery, unjust imprisonment and escape, material Stevenson used in future novels. Sim and Candlish, the drovers in St Ives, recall Todd and there are local farmers in *Weir of Hermiston* (1896).

In his final years, self-exiled in Samoa, Stevenson was to be haunted by memories of Swanston and the Pentlands, craving to look down again on the city:

> From Halkerside, from topmost Allermuir,
> Or steep Caerketton, dreaming.

The Pentland Hills Regional Park contains signed footpaths and cycle tracks and can be accessed variously from Bonaly, Hillend Visitor Centre, Boghall Farm, Flotterstone and Harlaw Visitor Centre.

Stevenson journeyed to and from Swanston along Morningside Road and then climbed up on Braid Road to a former toll point and a path high on the west side of the Braidburn Valley which can still be reached off Greenbank Crescent and Fly Walk. He crossed the Braid Burn at Oxgangs Avenue and took a footpath on the left towards Comiston Farmhouse, continuing into Caiystane Gardens and Oxgangs Road. West along the B701, near the junction of Oxgangs Avenue, a police station occupies the site of the old Oxgangs farmhouse where Stevenson would linger. There is a cedar tree where he loved to sit on the lower branches and composed some poems which appeared in *A Child's Garden of Verses*. He marked his height on a wooden door and signed it, an artefact salvaged during renovation of the farmhouse which appeared as part of a Stevenson exhibition in Oxgangs Primary School. Back east along the B701, past the Hunter's Tryst pub which he frequented, there is a right turn on to Swanston Road where Stevenson proceeded down another little valley, now traversed by the city by-pass, then up the initial slope of the Pentlands, taking in a view which is largely unchanged.

The villages of Cramond and South Queensferry, west of the city off the A90 on the shores of the Firth of Forth, were favourite destinations for jaunts by Stevenson. The 17th-century Cramond Inn, three-quarters of a mile upstream on the River Almond beside Queensferry Road, was a favourite haunt and Cramond Island was another and a possible influence upon the notion of *Treasure Island*. In 1871 during a walk at Cramond he told his father that the engineering life was not for him. He would also tramp out to South Queensferry, off the M90 and A90, where in *Kidnapped* (1886) David Balfour is lured on to the brig *Covenant*. One can still stand on the pier and look out over the firth, in David's time filled with shipping bound for Europe and the Americas. The 350-year-old Hawes Inn, which has abundant local memorabilia, has wonderful views over the river and its crossing points. Stevenson began writing *Kidnapped* here, opposite the old slipway for the ferry across the River Forth to Fife and in the shadow of the Forth Railway Bridge, the building of which had commenced at the time of writing. Stevenson stayed in room No 13, 'a small room, with a bed in it and heated like an oven by a great fire of coal'. A sign above the door of the inn pictures David being assaulted by thuggish sailors. At the end of *Kidnapped* David Balfour is back at South Queensferry to meet the lawyer and claim his rightful inheritance.

Summer holidays for the younger Stevenson were spent at his grandfather's house called Anchor Villa in North Berwick in East Lothian and here he explored the beaches, rocks and caves, lit campfires, fished and imagined pirates, leading to scenes in *Treasure Island* (1883), *The Black Arrow* (1888), *Kidnapped* and *Catriona* (1893). 'The Wreckers' uses the idea of misleading lights to lure ships on to rocks for the sake of plunder. He also visited Scougall Farm, opposite the Bass Rock, which belonged to the Dales who were relatives.

There were some ten family visits to the spa town of Bridge of Allan near Stirling between 1852 and 1875 and Stevenson loved this spot on the edge of the Highlands. At age nine he climbed Dumyat (pronounced 'dumb-eye-at'), off the Sheriffmuir Road, which provides a fine viewpoint at the western end of the Ochil hills, which he was to call the Ochil Mountains in *Kidnapped*. The family first stayed in Kenilworth House, then frequently at Viewforth, and later at Queen's Hotel, Louis Villa and Darnley House in Henderson Street. The Royal Hotel has a plaque (inaccurately) giving the date of their visit. Minewood Cottage where they stayed in 1860 has his initials etched on a window. The only proper memorial in town is a mural on the outside wall of the public toilets.

The Darn Glen which links Bridge of Allan and Dunblane has a small dark cave beside the river which was one of Stevenson's favourite places and a model, it has been argued, for Ben Gunn's cave in *Treasure Island*. Near the confluence of Allan Water and the Forth is an islet, now barely perceptible, where Stevenson played as a boy and he made it a place where David and Alan lie low in *Kidnapped*. It is said that even some of the topography of *Treasure Island* recalls the locality. His White Rock may be a reference to the Ordnance Survey pillar on the summit of Dumyat or simply rocks glinting in sun. In the distance lies Uamh Var or Mhor ('the place of the big cave/cleft'), a hill overlooking Glen Artney on one side and the Braes o' Doune on the other which Stevenson makes the spot where David and Alan spend a night in *Kidnapped*. In the sequel *Catriona* David returns to Balquhidder by way of Allan Water and Uamh Var. The Den above Logie Kirk and under Carlin Crag may have provided settings for the stories 'Thrawn Janet' and 'Tale of Tod Lapraik'.

In 1848 Stevenson spent part of his summer holidays as a student studying harbour works at Anstruther and living at Cunzie House on Crail Road, where there is a plaque, but he considered the experience bleak. In the autumn of 1863 his father took him on a tour of the Fife lighthouses to introduce Stevenson further to the family business. As an engineering student and apprentice Stevenson had to visit works in progress at various locations around the Scottish coast. His father was an eminent engineer in a dynasty of lighthouse and harbour builders and, like his father before him, consulting engineer to the Commissioners of Northern Lights.

Between 1790 and 1840 eight members of the family had designed and constructed 97 manned lighthouses around the Scottish coast, a chain stretching from Bell Rock off Fife to Skerryvore in the Hebrides. Stevenson stayed at No 9 Harbour Terrace, later the Customs and Excise Office, in Pulteneytown, part of Wick, where there is a plaque, for six weeks in the autumn of 1868 while his father's firm constructed a breakwater, destroyed by the sea in 1871. It is said that Ben Gunn in *Treasure Island*, the marooned member of the crew of Flint's ship, whose surname is popular in Caithness, was based upon a local sailor.

In 1869 an inspection trip with his father took him to the Northern Isles, Lewis and Skye, where he observed departing emigrants, a scene he appears to have used in *Kidnapped* as David Balfour sees emigrants leaving Loch Aline. In 1869 Stevenson was on Muckle Flugga and Unst to see work in progress and it has been pointed out that his map of Treasure Island closely resembles Unst. In August 1870 he took a steamer from Glasgow to Oban up the spectacular west coast by Tarbert and Ardrishaig, past the islands of Erraid, Mull, Iona and Staffa to Portree on Skye. From a base on the tidal island of Erraid, where Stevenson spent three weeks, the firm was building the Dhu Heartach (*Dubh Artach*) lighthouse, completed in 1844. The brig *Covenant* which is wrecked on the Torran reef near the Ross of Mull in *Kidnapped*, if sailing a hundred years later, would have been helped by the light on Dubh Artach. The Museum of Scottish Lighthouses is housed in what was Scotland's first lighthouse on Kinnaird Head at Fraserburgh, on the A90 north of Aberdeen. It celebrates the contribution of the Stevensons with interesting artefacts and audio-visual display.

Stevenson travelled abroad, much of it in the interests of his health. He visited Menton in the south of France in 1873 and Barbizon, a bohemian community outside Paris where he was to meet his future wife, the American Fanny Osbourne. Charming travel writings followed, including *An Inland Voyage* (1878) inspired by canoeing on Belgian and French canals and rivers in 1876 and *Travels with a Donkey in the Cevennes* (1879). In 1877 Stevenson went to California on an emigrant ship and lived with Fanny in Monterey, where there is a Stevenson museum, before returning to Edinburgh after their marriage.

In late May 1881 Stevenson and Fanny shared with his parents Kinnaird Cottage, a roadside farmhouse on the A924, a mile-and-a-half north-east of Pitlochry in Perthshire's Vale of Atholl, where he wrote the short stories 'Thrawn Janet', 'The Body Snatchers' and 'The Merry Men' and where there is a plaque on the garden wall. *The Master of Ballantrae* (1889), he said, was conceived 'on the moors between Pitlochry and Strathardle ... in Highland rain.' He caught a cold and was spitting blood and so the doctor recommended moving to the drier Braemar, on the A93 in the Highlands of Royal Deeside (Queen Victoria was in residence at Balmoral at the time) in a cottage at the beginning of the Glenshee road, near the church, still available for rent and now called Treasure Island Cottage.

It still rained and so, to amuse his 12-year-old stepson Lloyd Osborne, Stevenson told ghost stories and painted an imaginary water-colour map of Treasure Island and started his story 'The Sea Cook' with some piratical names like Skeleton Island and Spyglass Hill on the map. He listed some chapters, beginning with a setting on the Devon Coast and introduced characters. Even his father was caught up in the project and contributed the inventory for Billy Bones's chest and the idea of the apple barrel. By the following day three chapters had been written of Stevenson's first full-length narrative. The first 15 chapters were written at Braemar and the novel was finished at Davos in Switzerland. He later said: 'On a chill September morning, by the cheek of a brisk fire, and the rain drumming on the window, I began The Sea Cook, for that was the original title.' A friend called John Silver lived on Chapel Brae in Braemar. It has been noted that there are similarities between *Treasure Island* and a story called 'Billy Bo'swain' which appeared in a London magazine called *Young Folks* which was shown to Stevenson.

In 1884 Stevenson and his wife Fanny went to Bournemouth, the large resort on the south coast of England, set among pine trees, gardens and steep ravines overlooking Poole Bay, in the hope of improving his health. They stayed in rented accommodation and guesthouses at various addresses, including Bonallie Towers, a furnished house in the leafy Brankstone Park area of the town. Stevenson's father was anxious to keep them in Britain and so bought for them the villa Sea View, about a mile from the sea on the Westbourne cliffs, and renamed it Skerryvore, after the lighthouse off the Scottish west coast which was one of the Stevensons' major engineering achievements.

Only a little of the sea could actually be seen from an upper window at Sea View. A ship's bell was placed in the garden of the property, whose previous owner was a retired naval captain and Stevenson had a model of a lighthouse at the front door which he lit every evening. Fanny happily developed the garden, but Stevenson was restless, considering the place respectable but dull. The house was of yellow brick with a blue slate roof and ivy-clad walls and an acre of land sloping steeply southwards to lawns which stopped at the edge of a narrow ravine called Alum

Chine. The shrubbery included laurel and rhododendron mixed with pine and heather. A stream below was somewhat reminiscent of Scotland.

They stayed there from April 1885 to August 1887, dug in, said Stevenson, 'like a weevil in a biscuit' at the top of Alum Chine Road. *Treasure Island* was selling well and he finished *Kidnapped*, which he considered his best story and *A Child's Garden of Verses*, *New Arabian Nights* (1882) and *Prince Otto* (1885). He wrote 30,000 words of *The Strange Tale of Dr Jekyll and Mr Hyde* (1886) in three days at Skerryvore, but Fanny claimed it had 'missed the allegory' and so he burned the manuscript and promptly wrote another. Fame was instant with 40,000 copies sold in six months in Britain.

Skerryvore became a boarding house until the Second World War when it was bombed and later demolished. A memorial garden was opened nearby in 1957 with dwarf walls representing the originals, a model of a lighthouse and plaque.

In 1887 they left for America in continued search for good health and in 1890 settled in Samoa in the South Seas. Here he was seen as a patriarchal figure and given the title Tusitala (Storyteller). He died suddenly at his home in Vailima of a brain haemorrhage on 3 December 1894 while writing the unfinished *Weir of Hermiston* which was published two years later. He was carried by his Samoan friends to Mount Vaea and buried there.

During his brief life he had written hundreds of works, including short stories, articles, poems, essays, pamphlets, some 30 full-length works and over 100 musical compositions.

STORYTRAIL: *Kidnapped*

THE MAIN CHARACTERS
David Balfour, who is deprived of his inheritance on his father's death.
Ebenezer, uncle to David, who seizes the family estate and arranges for David's kidnapping.
Alan Breck Stewart, a Jacobite outlaw who saves David's life.
Colin Campbell, the 'Red Fox', king's agent and scourge of Jacobites.
Robin Oig, son of Rob Roy Macgregor.

In the year 1751 and during the aftermath of the 1745 Jacobite rebellion the 17-year-old David Balfour, deprived of his inheritance and left in poverty on the death of his father, seeks assistance from his rascally uncle Ebenezer who has seized the estate. He arranges for David's kidnapping and shipping on a slave ship to the American Carolinas, leading to an adventurous trip around and across Scotland.

Topography was at the forefront of Stevenson's mind as he wrote the novel. He provided a map, drawn by his relative David Stevenson and publication was held up until it was ready. It is detailed in places and vague elsewhere to suit the novelist's purpose. The map traces the course of the *Covenant* from Queensferry, passing between Orkney and Shetland, Cape Wrath, through the Minch, round Coll and Tiree to the southwest end of Mull where it founders on the south side of Erraid. In the Dedication to Charles Baxter the author explains that the Torran rocks, scene of the shipwreck, 'have crept so near to Erraid' for the sake of the plot. They are actually three miles south of Erraid where Stevenson spent three weeks as a youth. The famous *Kidnapped* journey which follows takes in 200 miles of the Scottish Highlands and Lowlands.

At the beginning of the story the narrator David Balfour leaves the Borders hamlet of Essendean, the real Ashkirk, south of Selkirk, following 'the green drove road running wide through the heather'. On the second day of walking he comes in sight of the Firth of Forth and 'the city of Edinburgh smoking like a kiln' and descends into country 'pleasantly watered and wooded, and the crops, to my eye, wonderfully good.' Balfour describes what he sees: 'Right in the midst of the narrows lies an islet with some ruins; on the south shore they have built a pier for the service of the ferry; and backed against a pretty garden of holly trees and hawthorns, I could see the building they call the Hawes Inn. The town of Queensferry lies further west, and the neighbourhood of the inn looked pretty lovely at that time of day, for the boat had just gone north with passengers.'

He heads towards Barnton, to the west of Edinburgh and in the parish of Cramond finds the sinister House of Shaws, which may be based upon Cammo House or Cramond Tower or House, in Cramond Glebe Road, or perhaps Barnton House, which was demolished at the end of the First World War. Another possibility is Old Glassingall House in Dunblane. At the House of Shaws Ebenezer tries to murder David by sending him up a crumbling staircase to an almost fatal drop at the top.

Ebenezer and Captain Hoseason then plan David's abduction, and he is tricked to board the *Covenant* which promptly leaves port. It sails anti-clockwise round Scotland until it is met by Alan Breck Stewart, a Jacobite outlaw, who climbs aboard near Mull after his ship collides with the *Covenant*. David helps Alan fight off the crew intent on stealing money which he has on him and, when the boat is shipwrecked on the Torran Rocks, David is thrown on to the beach, 'a sand bay surrounded by low hills' and Stewart also survives, unknown to Balfour. This is on the small rocky island of Erraid, which Stevenson had seen at age 15 and now named Balfour's Bay on some maps. The buildings and pier were erected by the Stevensons as a shore station which then became a lighthouse keeper's home. The house in which Stevenson lived for three weeks in 1870 is now known as Stevenson House and used as a storeroom. In the earlier short story 'The Merry Men' he describes a storm on the island, which in that story he calls Aros, 'not properly a part of the Ross, nor ... quite an islet' and it is a place of shipwrecks, breakers and rocks which are vividly described.

David calls Erraid 'nothing but a jumble of granite rocks ... desert-like and lonesome.' Shipping is now alerted to the Torran

Rocks by the Dubh Artach lighthouse which Stevenson, the apprentice engineer, saw being constructed. Balfour spends four miserable days on Erraid with nothing to eat but raw shellfish while the passing fishermen laugh since he does not know he can leave at low tide, as Stevenson himself learned.

David eventually walks across to Mull and catches sight of the 'great, ancient church', the site of St Columba's sixth-century abbey on Iona. He considers Mull to be 'all bog, and briar, and big stone' and walks the island in four days to arrive at Torosay, whose castle Stevenson knew. He probably followed the pilgrim route across Mull below Ben More, alongside Loch Scridain and the present A849, to the entrance of Glen More or through Glen Forrsa by Derrynaculen, beyond Rossal Farm near the head of Loch Scridain, where there is a good view back over the Ross of Mull. A ferry then and now goes to Lochaline from Fishnish, the shortest route between Mull and the mainland, together with the larger modern one to Oban from Craignure. David notes the emigrant ship at the mouth of Loch Aline and then heads through Morvern, conscious of a wilderness of mountains and moor, contrasting the benign southern landscape and hostile Highlands.

Stevenson catches well the atmosphere of a divided nation five years after Culloden for which the landscapes are a symbol. Balfour is the Whiggish Lowlander and Alan Stewart the bold Highland soldier with courage, cunning and understanding of his environment, whose culture and landscape are savage and alien to David. The Kinlochaline Inn at the head of Loch Aline, where there is no longer an inn, David considers vile and from there he probably followed the path of the modern B8043 to Kingairloch, then by a track by Loch Uisge past Kingairloch House to Camas na Croise ('bay of the cross'), beyond the mouth of Loch a' Choire, where he may have stayed a night. The next day he crossed Loch Linnhe by boat to Appin, at the promontory Rudha Bhaid Beithe, although present-day travellers use the Corran ferry, north-west of Ballachulish across Loch Linnhe to Ardgour.

On a wooded promontory off the A828, some two miles south of the A82 at Ballachulish, a short trail leads up the hillside through a Forestry Commission pine forest to a cairn on the spot where the Red Fox (a nickname given by Stevenson) was assassinated, the famous Appin Murder. Colin Campbell, rent collector for the Crown from the forfeited estates of Jacobite chiefs following the defeat at Culloden, on his way to evict tenants, was notoriously shot on 14 May 1752 (1751 in Stevenson's story), but the killer was never found. There is a yew tree on the spot where a gun was found.

Campbell was heading south towards Kentallen from Ballachulish through the Wood of Lettermore (*Leitir Mhor*), where the road rises away from the lochside, when he was ambushed from a vantage point and escape route which are presumed to be above the bank. The historical Allan Breck (Stevenson has only one 'l' in Alan) appeared on the evening of the murder at Ballachulish House, now a hotel. After the murder Allan Breck hid in the Pap of Glencoe at Coire na Ciche. James Stewart of Acharn (Seumas a'Ghlinne), was tried by a kangaroo court and hanged for the murder on the knoll called Cnap a' Chaolais to the south of the Ballachulish Bridge. A plaque can be found up some steps at the end of the bridge, while the execution spot is just to the west over the River Leven. The remains of James Stewart's house can still be seen at Acharn in Duror and the West Highland Museum in Fort William contains a musket found in a hollow tree in the woods of Lettermore.

Although Highlanders had been disarmed after the 1745 rebellion some opponents of the government retained weapons. While the identity of the killer has been a secret, passed on by word of mouth through the family for centuries, it appears it was Donald, son of James Stewart. It is said that he had to be tied to his bed on the day of execution. The gun known as the Black Gun of Misfortune, now in the National Museum in Edinburgh, was kept for years at Dalness in Glen Etive near Glencoe. Stevenson's fascination for the ongoing mystery made him determined to incorporate the incident into his novel and he went to great lengths to achieve topographical accuracy. Stevenson was also keen to picture the nature and dissolution of the Highland clan system after Culloden. Acharn, the 18th-century farmhouse which was the home of James Stewart of the

Glen, is now a bothy. The hotel at Duror has a Kidnapped Bar with framed prints relating to the Appin Murder.

The fine road and picturesque countryside and seaside between Oban and Ballachulish, through Appin, between Loch Creran and the meeting of Loch Leven and Loch Linnhe, are the setting for this key part of the novel. The massif of Ben Vair, with two mountains over 3000ft, forms a semi-circle between Glen Duror and Ballachulish to the north. Balfour, who spoke to the victim just before the fatal shot, witnesses the murder after which Stevenson has David, now reunited with Alan, fleeing dramatically along the hill tops to Duror, up the south side of the River Duror, then by the north side of the River Creran, over Beinn Maol Chaluim and across the River Coe to hide at the Heugh of Coire na Ciche, Corrynakeigh to Stevenson, below the Pap of Glencoe and above Caolasnacoan farm, now a cara-van park overlooking Loch Leven. Exact locations are not always clear, however, and there is writer's licence in the description of ravines and chasms. The two fugitives leap for their lives across the thundering river and a waterfall in Glencoe after a long hot day on top of a rock as redcoat troops bayonet the heather.

The bleak expanse of Rannoch Moor in Perthshire, 50 square miles of peat bog and lochan, lies mostly east of the A82 between Glencoe and Crianlarich, but can especially be appreciated from the West Highland railway which leaves the roadside after Loch Tulla to cross the moor by Rannoch Station and lonely Corrour. Bogs and lochans abound and the railway is supported at certain points merely on bundles of brushwood. The area is well described in *Kidnapped* although the fictional chase by a regi-ment on horseback would have meant considerable difficulty in negotiating the boggy terrain. From Rannoch Station a footpath goes west by a bleak but spectacular route across the moor.

The pair head for Ben Alder, above Loch Ericht in the cen-tral highlands by the present site of Corrour Station and Loch Ossian. They are taken across Loch Ericht by boat at night to Cluny's cage, hide-out of the Jacobite chieftain of Clan Macpherson for nine years. It has long been assumed that Cluny's Cage was on the southern slopes of Ben Alder where there is a Prince Charlie's Cave, reputed refuge of Charles

Edward Stewart, the Young Pretender, after the battle of Culloden in 1746, who crossed the mountains by night with a price on his head. Nevertheless, it has been convincingly argued that the location is too near the tracks not to be spotted by pursuing redcoats and early maps confirm that the cage was on the east side of Loch Ericht. It was mistakenly called a cage in 1861 and Ordnance Survey maps have called it so since the first edition in 1873, conflating it with the cave on the west side and calling it Prince Charlie's Cave. The structure, 'hanging like a wasp's nest in a green hawthorn bush' was of two storeys on the face of the rock, the upper room for eating and sleeping, the lower room for cooking, built on the rooted trunks of holly trees at Craig na-H'iolare ('crag of the eagle'). There may also have been a hide-out on the west side of Alder Bay where a boat would be hidden.

A route to Loch Ericht, from the B8019 and B846 west of Killiecrankie, by the Camusericht Mill Path near Rannoch Lodge climbs over the hillside through Forestry Commission land to Loch Ericht at Cam Chriochan Bridge and then continues along the lochside. At the cage Alan loses money to Cluny Macpherson at cards. Then the pair follow a track by Loch Rannoch, although Stevenson rather quickly skips over this stage, saying the route is by Glens Lyon, Lochay and Dochart to Balquidder (Balquhidder), the map suggesting by Ben More and Stob Binnein and the Braes of Balquhidder above Loch Voil.

The real Rob Roy Macgregor and his son Robin, whom the heroes encounter, are buried in the churchyard at Balquhidder, having lived at the foot of the Kirkton Glen. Stevenson has Alan Breck challenged by Rob Roy's son, Robin Oig, to a duel, until both agree to a contest with bagpipes rather than swords. David is unwell and carried down, probably by the Kirkton Burn and spends a month recovering in Balquhidder. Stevenson had a romantic attachment to the idea that Stevenson was one of the aliases used by the proscribed Macgregors.

Alan and David then head by Strathyre and over Uam Var (Uamh Mor), Kippen and the upper River Forth to Bridge of Allan and an area familiar to Stevenson from family holidays. 'In Allan Water, nearby where it falls into the Forth, we found a little sandy islet, overgrown with burdock, butterbur, and the like low plants, that would just cover us if we lay flat'. They are in sight of the garrisoned Stirling Castle and at dusk head for the bridge. At the old Stirling Bridge, which dates from 1500, now next to the A9 as it crosses the river and for pedestrians and bikes only, the pair try to sneak over in darkness. 'The bridge is close under the castle hill, an old, high, narrow bridge with pinnacles along the parapet', their route to safety, but there is a sentry and they head instead along the north bank of the Forth, past Alloa, Clackmannan and Culross to the hamlet of Limekilns, a fishing village off the A985 and across the water from Queensferry, where they enter the Ship Inn. Negotiation with a servant girl eventually leads to them being taken by boat across to the southern shore not far from Carriden, off the A904 at Bo'ness. Alan hides 'in the fields by the roadside near to Newhalls' until sunset and David visits the lawyer Mr Rankeillor after which, on the road beyond the Hawes Inn, Alan rises from behind a bush to rejoin David.

There is an emotional parting of Alan and David, the romantic Highlander and the Hanoverian Lowlander who shared extreme hardship, danger and near death, on Corstorphine Hill west of Edinburgh city centre, at what is now the Rest and Be Thankful viewpoint, accessible from the Ravelston Dykes Road side of the hill.

Alan is heading for a ship and safety and David has walked 'the long street of Queensferry' where he is back secure among Lowland values and the city where now his due fortune awaits, yet he is as lost in Edinburgh as on Erraid. The moment of leave-taking is commemorated by Alexander Stoddart's bronze figures looking towards the Pentlands outside the Scottish and Newcastle brewery headquarters on Corstorphine Road, the A8, at Ellersly Road and Western Corner, unveiled in 2004 by Sir Sean Connery. It is said that Balfour and Stewart represent two sides of Stevenson's own character, the adventurer and the rationalist, having both passion and a sense of duty.

In Tobacco Dock off The Highway in Wapping in the east end of London and to the rear of the canal is moored *The Sea Lark*, a historic American-built merchant schooner which ceased trading in 1885 and provides its own version of the classic adventure of *Kidnapped*.

TOURIST INFORMATION
AND VISITOR ATTRACTIONS

Edinburgh & Lothians Tourist Board
  3 Princes Street, Edinburgh EH2 2QP
  Tel: 0845 225 5121
The Edinburgh Book Lovers' Tour
  Tel: 07770 163641
The National Museum of Scotland
  Chambers Street, Edinburgh EH1 1JF
  Tel: 0131 123 6789
The Robert Louis Stevenson Experience
  45 Niddry Street, Edinburgh EH1 1LG
  Tel: 0131 557 4700
The Scottish Literary Tour Trust
  34 North Castle Street, Edinburgh EH2 3BN
  Tel: 0800 169 7410/0131 226 6665
The Stevenson House
  17 Heriot Row, Edinburgh EH3 6H
  Tel: 0131 556 1896
The Writers' Museum
  Lady Stair's Close, Lawnmarket, Edinburgh EH1 2PA
  Tel: 0131 529 4901
Pentland Hills Regional Park
  Biggar Road, Edinburgh EH10 7DX
  Tel: 0131 445 5969
North Berwick TIC
  School Road, North Berwick EH39 4JU
  Tel: 01620 89219
The Hawes Inn
  7 Newhalls Road, South Queensferry EH30 9TA
  Tel: 0131 331 1990
VisitScotland Fort William iCentre
  15 High Street, Fort William PH33 6DH
  Tel: 01397 701801
The West Highland Museum
  Cameron Square, Fort William PH33 6AJ
  Tel: 01397 702169
VisitScotland Stirling iCentre
  St John Street, Stirling FK8 1EA
  Tel: 01786 475019
Ballachulish Visitor & Information Centre
  Albert Road, Ballachulish PH49 4JB
  Tel: 01855 811866

Glencoe & North Lorn Folk Museum
    Glencoe PH49 4HS
    Tel: [seasonal] 01855 811664
NTS Visitor Centre
    Glencoe PH49 4HX
    Tel: 01855 811307
VisitScotland Craignure iCentre
    The Pier, Craignure, Isle of Mull PA65 6AY
    Tel: 01680 812377
VisitScotland Oban iCentre
    Columba Buildings, 3 North Pier, Oban PA34 5QD
    Tel: 01631 563122
Inveraray Castle
    Cherrypark, Inveraray PA32 8XE
    Tel: [seasonal] 01499 302203
Fraserburgh TIC
    The Museum of Scottish Lighthouses
    Kinnaird Head, Castle Terrace, Fraserburgh AB43 9DU
    Tel: 01346 518315
Anstruther TIC
    Harbourhead, Anstruther KY10 3AX
    Tel: [seasonal] 01333 311073
VisitScotland Braemar iCentre
    Unit 3, The Mews, Mar Road, Braemar AB35 5YL
    Tel: 01339 741600
Treasure Island Cottage
    Castleton Terrace, Braemar AB35 5YL
    Tel: 01339 741600
Bournemouth TIC
    Pier Approach, Bournemouth BH2 5AA
    Tel: 01202 451734
Bristol Visitor Information Centre
    Anchor Road, Harbourside, Bristol BS1 5DB
    Tel: 0906 7112191
Pete 'the Pirate' Martin
    6 Silverton Court, Knowle, Bristol BS4 1DF
    Tel: 07950 566483

17

Irvine Welsh

IRVINE WELSH (b.1958) was born in a second-floor corner tenement flat at No 2 Wellington Place, Leith, the port of Edinburgh. His father was a docker who became a carpet sales-man, his mother Jean a waitress who still lives on a council estate in Edinburgh. At the age of 18 months the family moved to Muirhouse, a peripheral housing estate west of Leith along the Firth of Forth where he later declared there was no real com-munity. His secondary education was at Ainslie Park School which occupied a building in Pilton Avenue and is now the North Campus of Telford College. As a boy he would play foot-ball between two maisonette blocks in Muirhouse Avenue, num-bers 14 and 50, until nightfall or until beckoned inside by par-ents. In his teens he enjoyed going to the State Cinema in Leith and the Easter Road ground of Hibernian Football Club. His favourite Leith pub became the Boundary Bar at No 379 Leith Walk, now called City Limits, but he ran the gauntlet of pubs on Leith Walk like the Central Bar and Port o' Leith Bar. He found the atmosphere of these Leith settings to be darkly romantic where hard men were characters in a storytelling culture.

He left school at 16, working briefly as a television repairer before going to London where he took various jobs, including those of builder, removal man, waiter, cook and kitchen porter. He also worked with punk rock bands and in the offices of Hackney Council on an unemployment training programme. He lived in a squat, used heroin and ran foul of the law. He was a heroin addict for 18 months, having spent three or four years 'careering towards' it, he admitted. During the 1980s he bought and sold properties during the property boom, including No 79

Amhurst Road, his first house, near Hackney Down station in 1983 and properties in Camden, Thornton Heath and Croydon, eventually owning six flats which he renovated.

Welsh then spent some time in Amsterdam but returned to Edinburgh where he became a training officer in Edinburgh City Council's Housing Department from 1986-94 while studying computing at Heriot-Watt University from 1988-90, graduating with an MBA. From his council office he was able to look down on the Dockers Club in Academy Street near the Foot of the [Leith] Walk, the 'Fit ay the Walk' to locals, and from personal experience, observation and professional contact realised the isolation of a local group of heroin addicts and AIDS sufferers whom he depicted in his writing which revealed the seamier side of life in the sink estates. Edinburgh at the time had the biggest HIV problem in Europe and Leith was a gateway for drugs. Welsh used heroin intermittently while writing.

Trainspotting (1993) was begun on a Greyhound bus between New York and Los Angeles in the summer of 1988 and completed by 1991, but it also drew on journals he had kept since the early 1980s. It developed not so much as a novel but a loose collection of vignettes about several different characters who were the antithesis of the Scotland of mass tourist appeal, their lives affected by cheap heroin and the risk of HIV through needle sharing. From an original print run of 3,000 copies the novel was a runaway success which resulted in Welsh abandoning his day job for full-time writing. He has also since been a partner in a film production company. The best-selling cult novel was successfully dramatised for stage and film.

Subsequent novels include *Marabou Stork Nightmares* (1995), *Filth* (1998), *Glue* (2001), *Porno* (2002), *The Bedroom Secrets of the Master Chefs* (2006), *Crime* (2008), *Skagboys* (2012), a prequel to *Trainspotting* which follows the characters' descent into heroin ('skag') addiction, *The Sex Lives of Siamese Twins* (2014) and *A Decent Ride* (2015). Short story collections include *The Acid House* (1994), *Ecstasy: Three Tales of Chemical Romance* (1996), *If You Liked School, You'll Love Work* (2007) and *Reheated Cabbage* (2009). Plays include *Headstate* (1994), *You'll Have Had Your Hole* (1998) and the co-written *Babylon Heights* (2006). Screenplays include *The Meat Trade* (2009), which has an Edinburgh setting and concerns a psychopath (recalling the Victorian body-snatchers Burke and Hare) who murders for body parts sold on the internet. *Wedding Belles* (2007) was a television drama about four women drug addicts in Edinburgh and *Good Arrows* (2009) a film for television concerning a degenerate darts player returning to the limelight which displays a characteristic preoccupation with the unpleasant. Welsh married his first wife Anne Antsy, a social worker from Croydon, in 1984. In 2005 he married the Irish-American Elizabeth (Beth) Quinn from Chicago, having taught for a semester at Chicago's Columbia College. The filming of *Porno* as a sequel to *Trainspotting* has recently been completed and released as *T2 Trainspotting*.

STORYTRAIL: *Trainspotting*

THE MAIN CHARACTERS
Mark Renton, the main character, heroin user.
Simon 'Sick Boy' Williamson, promiscuous fellow addict.
Francis 'Franco' Begbie, psychopathic violent drug user.
Daniel 'Spud' Murphy, more gentle, heroin user.
Tommy Laurence, sometime heroin user.
Johnny Swan, drug dealer.
Michael Forrester, drug user.

The novel comprises 43 loosely connected parts within seven sections, mainly narrated in the first person and present tense, 21 of them by Mark Renton, providing interior monologue by the characters who are immersed in their subcultures and forming, says Welsh, 'a bunch of voices shouting to be heard.' The action is set around Edinburgh with the exception of Tommy and Mark's trip to Glasgow for an Iggy Pop concert and the latter's trip to London alone.

Leith, a mile-and-a-half to the north down Leith Street and Leith Walk from the east end of Princes Street, has an 800-year history as the commercial port for Edinburgh and was incorporated into the city in 1920. In recent years a policy of restoration has transformed much of Leith following a long period of neg-

lect. Where Leith Walk meets Great Junction Street a bronze statue of Queen Victoria gazes primly down on the site of Leith
Central Station, a gathering place for drunks, addicts and the
homeless in the novel, the title of which refers ironically to their
desultory behaviour, since there had been no passenger trains
since 1952, and total demolition of the station was eventually
carried out in 1989. Now the location is occupied by a Tesco
supermarket (at No 76 Duke Street) and a soft play centre. The
industrial relic in the novel symbolises a disintegrating and
ignored community where violence, hard drug use and alcoholism are normal in the grimmer housing estates.

Alongside the bleak areas of Edinburgh and Leith which
tourists hardly see, the novel provides an occasional contrast in
the instant appeal of Princes Street, the Castle and Royal Mile,
but the novel's publicity annoyed local politicians and tourist
officials. The endemic crime, violence and drug abuse in the
novel have not disappeared with gentrification. There is still relative deprivation for those marooned in high-rise blocks like the
one Sick Boy grew up in, popularly known as the 'banana flats'
block because of its curved shape, on the B900 Cables Wynd
road.

Of the main characters Mark Renton (Rents), Simon
Williamson or Sick Boy (Si, Simon) Spud or Danny Murphy
and Francis Begbie, only Renton moves on at the end, having
stolen money from the gang during a London drug deal before
disappearing to Amsterdam.

The settings of the novel are flats, streets, pubs, clubs, parks,
public buildings, shopping precincts and bus routes.
Unemployment, giro schemes, disreputability, alcoholism, violence, drugs and prostitution are portrayed alongside the work
ethic of respectable Edinburgh. Welsh said the action of the novel
is set between 1982 and 1988, but internal evidence reveals that
the period is actually 1988-91, when Welsh was writing the
book.

The first four sections are set in August at Edinburgh Festival
time. Mark Renton and Sick Boy find getting a taxi difficult
because of 'fat, rich festival cunts too fuckin lazy tae walk a hundred fuckin yards fae one poxy church hall tae another fir thir

fuckin show.' They head to Tollcross and the home of drug dealer Johnny Swan, where drug-using friends and contacts gather,
after which Mark heads back to Leith.

Mark, living in Montgomery Street overlooking Leith Links
near the 'Fit ay the Walk', heads round to the supermarket in
Kirkgate and gets the No 32 bus to Muirhouse where he gets off
at Pennywell Road opposite the shopping centre where the bookmaker has a toilet at the back. The Muirhouse of the novel is a
gloomy drug-ridden housing estate with high unemployment,
one of several post-Second World War estates between Leith and
Cramond, the others being Pilton and Granton where Welsh grew
up. Michael Forrester lives in a five-storey flat here. The area can
be reached by the No 37 or No 32 from Bernard Street in Leith.
The bookmaker's shop in the shopping centre in Pennywell
Road, between Ferry Road (the A902) and West Granton
Road/Muirhouse Parkway, where Renton scrambles to recover
his drugs in the cesspit of a toilet, has been demolished, as are the
'jigsaw' flats off West Granton Road where Tommy died of AIDS.

In the novel the story is told of an aunt, an immigrant from
an island off the west coast of Ireland, who sees 'the castle n
Princes Street, n the High Street' and thinks 'the whole fuckin
place wis like that.' She submits an application to the Housing
Office and ends up in West Granton. 'Instead ay a view ay the
castle, she's goat a view ay the gasworks.' Mark sits on a wall at
the bus stop awaiting a returning No 32 bus.

Returning from London, Renton 'pad[s] it doon fae the
Waverley'. Two fellows are screaming at each other under the
archway in Calton Road by the Post Office depot. He reaches
Leith Street and passes his old Montgomery Street home and on
Albert Street receives a violent threat but it makes him feel at
home. He goes to Tommy Younger's pub and meets Begbie and
they go down the Walk. They are caught short and Renton
explains: 'We go for a pish at the old station at the Fit ay the Walk.'
In the empty shell of Leith Central Station it is impossible to spot
trains, thus the irony of the novel's title and a lack of useful
human contact is symbolised. Begbie takes his frustration out on
'a guy in Duke Street' who happens to be passing.

The newsagent's shop frequented by Renton is at a corner

near the Foot of the Walk where the regular pub haunt of Begbie and company is the classic late-Victorian Central Bar. The gang lie on the Links at the bottom of the running track watching girls' athletics. Later at the Foot of the Walk Renton clocks Franco at 'Queen Sticky-Vicky', the statue, and cuts through Woolworths. His grandmother lives in sheltered housing at the foot of Easter Road, his parents in a flat in Oxgangs.

From the pub at the Foot of the Walk he strolls down Great Junction Street, while members of the Orange Order, through from Glasgow for the annual ceremonial walk, gather. The story of Laura McEwan relates to a pub on a side street between Easter Road and Leith Walk, on a corner 'propping up a tenement', sooty and black. Renton is here in the early morning after a few days' partying with a need for a fix. Robbie's Bar on the corner of Iona Street and Leith Walk is another port of call. As Renton is recovering from severe 'cauld turkey' he goes down Great Junction Street to the Dockers Club with his parents.

On the Bridges, the street which heads south across the Royal Mile from the east end of Princes Street, Renton mocks posh English-speaking tourists who are looking for the Royal Mile. Later he and Begbie visit Deacon Brodie's Tavern at No 435 Lawnmarket, where the Mound and George IV Bridge meet the Royal Mile and there is a gathering there after a nearby court appearance. On another occasion Renton and Begbie meet in a pub in Rose Street, the famous pub-filled back street parallel to Princes Street, but 'only arseholes, wankers and tourists set fit in Rose Street.' From the pub balcony Francis drops a beer glass on a man in a group below. A fight breaks out and continues in the precinct outside.

In Rutherford's, the pub on Drummond Street off South Bridge, now a restaurant named Hispaniola, the barmaid Kelly is teased as, in the presence of Mark, Spud and others, Sick Boy telephones from across the street to the pub in a posh voice looking for 'Mark Hunt' and as she calls out the name the pun is a joke at her expense.

Swan, pretending to be a Falklands' war veteran with only one leg, begs at the Market Street exit of Waverley Station. In the bus station concourse near St Andrew Square Sick Boy begs £10 off a prostitute before he and Renton leave for London towards the end of the novel.

In London, Renton, unable to cadge a bed, heads down Hammersmith Broadway in the direction of Victoria to the Britannia pub. He spends time at an all-night pornographic cinema. Later he is offered a bed in Stoke Newington, off Church Street, before Newington Green. He wonders if he is homosexual when he goes back with Giovanni to the basement flat 'somewhere oafay Church Street' and ponders whether he could be a victim of a mass murderer. He goes to a café down Ridley Road by the market, Stoke Newington High Street and Kingsland Road. There is a party at Dalston.

The climax of the novel has the gang heading by bus from Edinburgh to London's Victoria Bus Station carrying their 'load of smack'. They take a taxi to Finsbury Park and the hotel-cum-brothel of Andreas, a London-Greek associate of Sick Boy. A deal is clinched here for £16,000. Spud and Second Prize head for Soho to celebrate. Sick Boy and Begbie head to the pool room in the Sir George Robey pub at No 240 Seven Sisters Road, a venue especially popular for punk gigs, closed in 2004 and demolished in 2015. Back at the hotel Renton, alone with the money in Begbie's bag, makes an impulse decision. He heads out for a No 253 bus to Hackney and then to Liverpool Street Station. Here he puts £9,000 into his own meagre account at the Abbey National and leaves with the remaining £7,000 and buys a ticket for Amsterdam, heading to Harwich's Parkeston Quay and sails to the Hook of Holland. Spud is the only one he feels guilty about: 'He loved Spud'.

An Irvine Welsh Walk led by Tim Bell, a former prison chaplain who points out 'this gig's nae for bairns', starts and finishes at the Port o' Leith Bar, taking in the Leith Dockers Social Club, the former dole office, the site of the old train station, Sick Boy's tenement flat and the park where he strangles a dog to death. Bell acknowledges the seamy side of life which Welsh immortalised, maintaining that, while the area is transformed, the dark side is still there. A bus trip recalls that of Renton visiting Mikey Forrester and takes in the site of the bookmaker's toilet in Pennywell Road, the Sheriff Court and Deacon Brodie's Tavern.

Mary Moriarty, owner of the Port O' Leith Bar, said in 2005: 'It was horrendous but that period is gone and this [Tim Bell's Trainspotting tour] is like a history tour.'

TOURIST INFORMATION
AND VISITOR ATTRACTIONS

Edinburgh and Lothians Tourist Board
   3 Princes Street, Edinburgh EH2 2QP
   Tel: 0845 225 5121
Central Bar
   7-9 Leith Walk, Edinburgh EH6 8LN
   Tel: 0871 9170007
The Edinburgh Book Lovers' Tour
   Tel: 07770 163641
The Scottish Literary Tour Trust
   34 North Castle Street, Edinburgh EH2 3BN
   Tel: 0800 169 7410/0131 226 6665
Trainspotting Tours
   Tel: 0131 555 2500
City of London Information Centre
   St Paul's Churchyard, London EC4M 8BX
   Tel: 020 7332 3456

Index

Index